CONTEMPORARY'S

PRE-GED

MATHEMATICS

**McGraw-Hill
Contemporary**

Executive Editor: Linda Kwil
Creative Director: Michael E. Kelly
Marketing Manager: Sean Klunder
Production Manager: Genevieve Kelley

Interior Design by Think Design Group LLC

McGraw-Hill/Contemporary
A Division of The **McGraw·Hill** Companies

Send all inquiries to:
McGraw-Hill/Contemporary
1 Prudential Plaza, Suite 400
Chicago, IL 60601

ISBN: 0-07-252760-9

Printed in the United States of America.

3 4 5 6 7 8 9 10 QPD 07 06 05 04 03

Table of Contents

To the Student   vi
Pretest   1
Pretest Answer Key   6
Pretest Evaluation Chart   8

CHAPTER 1   WHOLE NUMBERS   10

Place Value   10
Reading and Writing Whole Numbers   12
Adding Whole Numbers   15
Subtracting Whole Numbers   17
Multiplying Whole Numbers   18
Dividing Whole Numbers   19
Rounding   21
Estimation   23
Whole Numbers Review   26

CHAPTER 2   USING A CALCULATOR   27

Adding Whole Numbers   28
Subtracting Whole Numbers   29
Multiplying Whole Numbers   30
Dividing Whole Numbers   31
Calculator Review   33

CHAPTER 3   PROBLEM SOLVING   34

How to Solve Word Problems   34
Clues in Choosing an Operation   38
Mental Math Strategies   41
Estimation with Word Problems   44
Problem-Solving Strategies   45
Problems with Multiple Steps   50
Using a Number Grid   52
Problem-Solving Review   55

CHAPTER 4 DECIMALS   57

Understanding Decimals   57
Rounding Decimals   62
Adding and Subtracting Decimals   64
Multiplying Decimals   67
Dividing Decimals   70
Using a Number Grid with Decimals   73
Decimals Review   75

CHAPTER 5 FRACTIONS   78

Understanding Fractions   78
Equivalent Fractions   82
Changing Fractions to Decimals   84
Changing Decimals to Fractions   85
Choosing a Common Denominator   86
Comparing and Ordering Fractions   88
Adding and Subtracting Fractions That Have Like Denominators   90
Adding and Subtracting Fractions That Have Unlike Denominators   93
Adding Mixed Numbers   97
Subtracting Mixed Numbers   99
Multiplying Fractions and Mixed Numbers   101
Dividing Fractions and Mixed Numbers   102
Using a Number Grid with Fractions   105
Using a Calculator with Fractions   107
Fractions Review   109

CHAPTER 6 RATIOS AND PROPORTIONS   112

Understanding Ratios   112
Understanding Rates   115
Understanding Proportions   117
Problem Solving with Proportions   121
Ratios and Proportions Review   123

CHAPTER 7 PERCENT   125

Understanding Percent   125
Common Percents, Fractions, and Decimals   129
Percent of a Number   131
Interest Problems   134
Using Proportion with Percent   136
Percent Review   141

CHAPTER 8 WORKING WITH DATA 144

Mean, Median, Mode, and Range 144
Bar Graphs 149
Line Graphs 156
Circle Graphs 164
Probability 173
Favorable Outcomes 177
Working with Data Review 181

CHAPTER 9 BASIC ALGEBRA 187

Exponents and Square Roots 187
Order of Operations 193
Variables and Simple Equations 196
Formulas 200
The Coordinate Plane 204
Basic Algebra Review 208

CHAPTER 10 MEASUREMENT AND GEOMETRY 212

Customary Measures 212
Mixed Units 215
The Metric System 216
Measuring Line Segments 219
Geometric Definitions 222
Perimeter and Circumference 225
Area 229
Volume 233
Problem Solving with Measurement and Geometry 236
Perimeter, Circumference, Area, and Volume Problems 238
Measurement and Geometry Review 242

Posttest 246
Posttest Answer Key 256
Posttest Evaluation Chart 259
Answer Key 260
Glossary 299
Index 302

To the Student

Congratulations on your decision to use *Pre-GED Mathematics* to strengthen your mathematical and problem-solving skills! The skills you develop by using this book will help you in many ways in the classroom, your daily life, and on the job.

Pre-GED Mathematics presents the important math skills that everyone should have mastered. If you have not previously learned the skills presented in this book as well as you would have liked to, now is your chance. Or, if you would like more practice in order to build your confidence, here is your opportunity. Regardless of your background, you can use this book to learn and practice the mathematical and problem-solving skills that are most important.

Here is an overview of what you will find in this book, along with some tips for using the book.

Mathematics Pretest The Mathematics Pretest, found on pages 1–9, will help you decide which skills you need to work on the most. It will give you an overall picture of your current mathematical ability in reference to topics presented in this book. It will direct you to the parts of the book you may want to spend the most time with. Before you start working through the chapters in this book, take the Mathematics Pretest that begins on page 1.

Chapter 1: Whole Numbers By working through Chapter 1, you will review whole numbers and basic computational skills. You will begin to work word problems. You will learn and practice estimation skills after reviewing how to round numbers.

Chapter 2: Using a Calculator In this chapter you will learn how to use the Casio *fx*-260 calculator, the only one allowed with the GED tests. You will use the calculator to solve addition, subtraction, multiplication, and division whole-number problems. In later chapters, you will use the same calculator for decimal, percent, and fraction problems.

Chapter 3: Problem Solving In this chapter you will learn and practice problem-solving strategies, mental math strategies, and estimation strategies. These strategies will help you do much more with numbers than simply calculate. You will also learn how to fill in the number grid used on the GED math test.

Chapter 4: Decimals In this chapter you will learn and practice all the necessary computational skills with decimals. Many word problems involve money and require calculations with decimal numbers, since our monetary system is based on decimals. This chapter will also prepare you well for working with percent, found in Chapter 7.

Chapter 5: Fractions This chapter teaches you to add, subtract, multiply, and divide fractions and mixed numbers. And, as with every other chapter in this book, you will have plenty of practice solving word problems. You will need to know how to do fractions for most other areas of mathematics, including ratios and proportions (Chapter 6) and probability (Chapter 8).

Chapter 6: Ratios and Proportions This chapter presents plenty of problem-solving practice with ratios and proportions. You will also see and use the important relationships among fractions and decimals. By working through this chapter, you will strengthen your skills with decimal numbers and fractions.

Chapter 7: Percent In this chapter you will learn what percent means, as well as how to change decimals or fractions to percents. You will also learn how to use percents in problem solving. You will see the relationships among decimals, fractions, and percents. Included are practice problems for you to use with your calculator.

Chapter 8: Working with Data The ideas presented in this chapter are commonly found in daily life but have not traditionally been emphasized in schools, so some of the ideas may be new to you altogether. This chapter includes concepts, such as mean, median, mode, range, bar graphs, line graphs, circle graphs, and probability. The probability sections will give you another chance to see the relationships among decimals, fractions, and percents.

Chapter 9: Basic Algebra This chapter gives a solid introduction to algebra. You will study exponents, square roots, and order of operations. You will solve equations, use formulas, and graph points on a coordinate plane.

Chapter 10: Measurement and Geometry In this chapter you will learn to use standard metric units of measurement. You will learn the basic definitions of geometry. You will learn how to find perimeter, circumference, area, and volume of basic geometric figures. You will need to understand these ideas completely in order to learn the geometry for GED math.

Pre-GED Practice At the end of each chapter, a review of key concepts is provided. These reviews include many five-item multiple-choice questions that help you prepare for GED-level study.

Mathematics Posttest The Mathematics Posttest, found on pages 246–258, will help you to see how well you have learned the mathematics and problem-solving skills presented in this book. The Mathematics Posttest contains 56 five-item multiple-choice problems.

Answer Key This feature provides answers and steps for solving all the problems. Use the answer key only after you have attempted a problem yourself. If your answer to a problem is incorrect, look at the steps given, and compare them to your own.

Glossary Throughout the book, key terms that are important for you to know are printed in boldface and italic type and are defined in the glossary at the back of the book.

Good luck with your studies! Keep in mind that mathematics and problem-solving skills are worth learning for many reasons.

Mathematics

The Mathematics Pretest that follows is a guide to using this book. You should take the Pretest before you begin working on any of the chapters. The test consists of 64 problems that correspond to the ten chapters in this book.

Read and work each problem as carefully as possible. Check your work. Do not look at the answers until you are finished with the test. If you find that a problem is too difficult, skip it and come back to the problem later. When you have completed the test, check your answers on pages 6–7.

Using the Evaluation Chart on pages 8–9, circle the number of each question that you missed. If you missed many of the problems that correspond to a certain mathematical skill, you will want to pay special attention to that skill as you work through the book.

If you do very well on the Pretest, congratulations! You can strengthen and broaden your skills, as well as gain confidence, by working through this book. More practice doing mathematics and solving problems will only help you.

PRETEST

Directions: Solve each whole-number problem.

1. Write the value of the underlined digit.
   4<u>6</u>3,250

2. Write the value of the underlined digit.
   240.6<u>3</u>8

3. Add: 68,145 + 9,828

4. Subtract: 90,627 – 19,544

5. Multiply: 174 × 28

6. Divide: 8,241 ÷ 3

7. Write as a whole number: three million, two hundred nine thousand, six hundred fifty-one

8. Round to the nearest dollar: $14.49

9. On January 10, 1911, in Rapid City, South Dakota, the temperature dropped from 55°F to 8°F in 15 minutes. How much was this drop in temperature?

Directions: Estimate the answer to each problem.

10. 3,792 × 4.13

11. 20,678 – 4,213

12. How many pounds of hamburger were left after about 287 pounds out of the original 400 pounds were used at the company picnic?

Directions: Solve each decimal problem.

13. Which is greater, 0.06 or 0.5?

14. Round 101.6549 to the nearest hundredth.

15. Add: 3.4 + 16.08 + 9.55

16. Subtract: $20 – $4.69

17. Multiply: $16.50 × 4

18. Divide: 1.246 ÷ 0.2

19. Paula has a twenty-dollar bill, three five-dollar bills, six one-dollar bills, five quarters, eight dimes, and four nickels in her purse. Find the value of the money in Paula's purse.

20. Frozen bread dough is priced at $3.39 for 3 loaves. Find the unit price (the price of one loaf).

21. If approximately 20,000 tickets at $15.70 each were sold for the game, what is a reasonable estimate for the total income from ticket sales?

PRETEST

Directions: Solve each fraction problem.

22. Rewrite 9.125 as a mixed number.

23. Rewrite $\frac{3}{5}$ as a decimal.

24. Which is greater, $\frac{3}{4}$ or $\frac{2}{3}$?

25. Add and reduce to lowest terms: $\frac{7}{8} + \frac{3}{8}$

26. Subtract: $\frac{1}{2} - \frac{1}{3}$

27. Subtract: $3\frac{1}{2} - 1\frac{3}{4}$

28. Multiply and reduce to lowest terms: $2\frac{2}{5} \times \frac{1}{4}$

29. Divide and reduce to lowest terms: $\frac{1}{9} \div \frac{1}{3}$

30. On Tuesday Kristin bought $5\frac{3}{4}$ pounds of apples. On Thursday she bought $2\frac{2}{3}$ pounds of apples. How many pounds of apples did Kristin buy that week?

Directions: Solve each measurement and geometry problem.

31. How many minutes are there in one day?

32. Change 68 centimeters to millimeters.

33. Is the statement true or false? "Parallel lines form right angles."

34. Find the perimeter of the rectangle shown below.

6 m

8 m

35. Find the area of the rectangle shown above.

36. Find the circumference of the circle shown below. (Use π ≈ 3.14.)

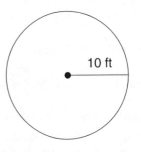

10 ft

37. Find the area of the circle shown above. (Use π ≈ 3.14.)

38. Find the volume of a cube whose side is 9 inches.

39. Change 144 inches to yards.

40. Change 3 gallons to quarts.

41. Jack worked 6 hours and 48 minutes on Tuesday. On Friday he worked 7 hours and 24 minutes. What was the total work time at this part-time job?

Directions: Solve each ratio, proportion, or percent problem.

42. There are 10 women and 15 men at a party. Write the ratio of women to men in lowest terms.

43. Solve the proportion: $\frac{2}{3} = \frac{h}{24}$

44. Change 28% to a decimal and a fraction in lowest terms.

45. Change 0.09 to a percent.

46. Change $\frac{4}{5}$ to a percent.

47. What is 80% of 9,000?

48. What percent of 40 is 8?

49. 25% of what number is 50?

50. At the window factory there are 5 males for every 2 female workers. If there are 270 male employees, how many females work there?

Directions: Solve problems 51–53 using the table below.

HIGH TEMPERATURES FOR A WEEK

Day	Fahrenheit Temperature
Sunday	72°
Monday	80°
Tuesday	83°
Wednesday	78°
Thursday	70°
Friday	74°
Saturday	75°

51. Find the mean (average) high temperature for the week.

52. Find the median high temperature for the week.

53. Find the range of high temperatures for the week.

54. Refer to the bar graph below. How many medals did Canada win in the 1994 Winter Olympics?

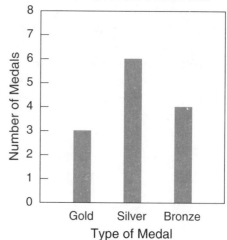

MEDALS WON BY CANADA, 1994 WINTER OLYMPICS

PRETEST

55. Refer to the line graph below. In what year were the revenues from wireless technology almost six billion dollars?

REVENUES FROM WIRELESS TECHNOLOGY
(in billions)

56. Refer to the circle graph below. What percent of the popular vote did Clinton *not* get in the 1992 presidential election?

1992 PRESIDENTIAL ELECTION RESULTS OF THE POPULAR VOTE

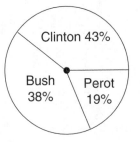

57. When you roll two dice, what is the probability of getting doubles?

Directions: Solve each algebra problem.

58. Find the value of $\sqrt{81}$.

59. Find the value of $8 + 4 \times 62 - (3 + 7)$.

60. Solve: $x + 9 = 21$

61. Solve: $a - 8 = 12$

62. Solve: $4n = 120$

63. Solve: $\frac{y}{7} = 5$

64. If you invest $5,000 for a year and earn $400 interest, what is the annual interest rate? (Use the formula $i = prt$.)

Answers are on page 6.

PRETEST

Answer Key

1. **6 ten-thousands or 60,000**

2. **3 hundredths or $\frac{3}{100}$**

3. **77,973;**
   $$\begin{array}{r} 68,145 \\ +\ 9,828 \\ \hline 77,973 \end{array}$$

4. **71,083;**
   $$\begin{array}{r} 90,627 \\ -\ 19,544 \\ \hline 71,083 \end{array}$$

5. **4,872;**
   $$\begin{array}{r} 174 \\ \times\ 28 \\ \hline 1392 \\ 348 \\ \hline 4,872 \end{array}$$

6. **2,747;**
   $$\begin{array}{r} 2,747 \\ 3\overline{)8,241} \\ 6 \\ \hline 22 \\ 21 \\ \hline 14 \\ 12 \\ \hline 21 \\ 21 \\ \hline 0 \end{array}$$

7. **3,209,651**

8. **$14**

9. **47°F;** $55 - 8 = 47$

10. **16,000;** $4,000 \times 4$

11. **17,000;** $21,000 - 4,000$

12. **100 pounds;** $400 - 300$

13. **0.5**

14. **101.65**

15. **29.03;**
    $$\begin{array}{r} 3.4 \\ 16.08 \\ +\ 9.55 \\ \hline 29.03 \end{array}$$

16. **$15.31;**
    $$\begin{array}{r} \$20.00 \\ -\ 4.69 \\ \hline \$15.31 \end{array}$$

17. **$66;**
    $$\begin{array}{r} \$16.50 \\ \times\ 4 \\ \hline \$66.00 \end{array}$$

18. **6.23;**
    $$0.2\overline{)1.246}\quad 6.23$$

19. **$43.25;** $20 + 3(5) + 6(1) + 5(.25) + 8(.10) + 4(.05) = 20 + 15 + 6 + 1.25 + .80 + .20 = 43.25$

20. **$1.13;** $\$3.39 \div 3 = \$1.13$

21. **$320,000;** $20,000 \times \$16$

22. **$9\frac{1}{8}$;** $9\frac{125}{1000} = 9\frac{1}{8}$

23. **0.6;** $3.0 \div 5 = 0.6$

24. **$\frac{3}{4}$;** $\frac{3}{4} = \frac{9}{12}$; $\frac{2}{3} = \frac{8}{12}$; $\frac{9}{12} > \frac{8}{12}$

25. **$1\frac{1}{4}$;** $\frac{7}{8} + \frac{3}{8} = \frac{10}{8} = 1\frac{2}{8} = 1\frac{1}{4}$

26. **$\frac{1}{6}$;** $\frac{1}{2} - \frac{1}{3} = \frac{3}{6} - \frac{2}{6} = \frac{1}{6}$

27. **$1\frac{3}{4}$;** $3\frac{1}{2} - 1\frac{3}{4} = 3\frac{2}{4} - 1\frac{3}{4} = 2\frac{6}{4} - 1\frac{3}{4} = 1\frac{3}{4}$

28. **$\frac{3}{5}$;** $2\frac{2}{5} \times \frac{1}{4} = \frac{12}{5} \times \frac{1}{4} = \frac{12}{20} = \frac{3}{5}$

29. **$\frac{1}{3}$;** $\frac{1}{9} \div \frac{1}{3} = \frac{1}{9} \times \frac{3}{1} = \frac{3}{9} = \frac{1}{3}$

30. **$8\frac{5}{12}$ pounds;** $5\frac{3}{4} + 2\frac{2}{3} = 5\frac{9}{12} + 2\frac{8}{12} = 7\frac{17}{12} = 8\frac{5}{12}$

31. **1,440 minutes;** 1 day × 24 hours/day × 60 minutes/hour = 1,440 minutes

PRETEST

32. **680 millimeters;** 68 cm × 10 = 680 mm

33. **False;** Parallel lines do not intersect, while perpendicular lines form right angles.

34. **28 m;** Perimeter = 8 + 6 + 8 + 6 = 28

35. **48 m², or 48 square meters;** Area = 8 × 6 = 48

36. **62.8 ft;** Circumference = $\pi \times 2 \times 10 \approx$ 3.14 × 2 × 10 = 62.8

37. **314 ft², or 314 square feet;** Area = $\pi \times 10 \times 10 \approx 3.14 \times 10 \times 10 = 314$

38. **729 in.³, or 729 cubic inches;** Volume = 9 × 9 × 9 = 729

39. **4 yards;** 144 ÷ 36

40. **12 quarts;** 3 × 4

41. **14 hours 12 minutes;**
$$\begin{array}{r} 6 \text{ hr } 48 \text{ min} \\ \underline{7 \text{ hr } 24 \text{ min}} \\ 13 \text{ hr } 72 \text{ min} = \\ 14 \text{ hr } 12 \text{ min} \end{array}$$

42. **2 to 3, or 2 : 3, or $\frac{2}{3}$;** $\frac{\text{women}}{\text{men}} = \frac{10}{15} = \frac{2}{3}$

43. **16;** 2 × 24 ÷ 3 = 16

44. **0.28, $\frac{7}{25}$;** 28% = 0.28 = $\frac{28}{100} = \frac{7}{25}$

45. **9%**

46. **80%;** $\frac{4}{5} = \frac{4 \times 20}{5 \times 20} = \frac{80}{100} = 80\%$

47. **7,200;** 0.8 × 9,000 = 7,200

48. **20%;** $\frac{8}{40} = \frac{h}{100}$; 8 × 100 ÷ 40 = 20

49. **200;** $\frac{50}{h} = \frac{25}{100}$; 50 × 100 ÷ 25 = 200

50. **108 females;** $\frac{2}{5} = \frac{x}{270}$
2 × 270 = 5x

540 ÷ 5 = 108

51. **76°F;** 72 + 80 + 83 + 78 + 70 + 74 + 75 = 532; 532 ÷ 7 = 76

52. **75°F;** in order: 70, 72, 74, 75, 78, 80, 83

53. **13°F;** 83 − 70 = 13

54. **13 medals;** gold medals + silver medals + bronze medals = 3 + 6 + 4 = 13 medals

55. **1991**

56. **57%;** 38% + 19% = 57%

57. **$\frac{1}{6}$;** $\frac{\text{favorable outcomes}}{\text{possible outcomes}} = \frac{6}{36} = \frac{1}{6}$

58. **9;** 9 × 9 = 81, so $\sqrt{81} = 9$

59. **246;**
$$\begin{aligned} 8 + 4 \times 62 - (3 + 7) &= \\ 8 + 4 \times 62 - 10 &= \\ 8 + 248 - 10 &= 246 \end{aligned}$$

60. **x = 12;** x + 9 + 21; x + 9 − 9 = 21 − 9; x = 12

61. **a = 20;** a − 8 = 12; a − 8 + 8 = 12 − 8; a = 20

62. **n = 30;** 4n = 120; $\frac{4n}{4} = \frac{120}{4}$; n = 30

63. **y = 35;** $\frac{y}{7} = 5$; $\frac{y}{7} \times 7 = 5 \times 7$; y = 35

64. **8%;** i = prt; 400 = 5,000 × r × 1;

$r = \frac{400}{5000} = 0.08 = 8\%$

Evaluation Chart

On the following chart, circle the number of any problem you got wrong. After each problem you will see the name of the section (or sections) where you can find the skills you need to solve the problem.

Problem	Section	Starting Page
1, 2	Place Value	10
3, 4, 5, 6	The Basic Operations	15
7	Writing Whole Numbers	12
9	Problem-Solving Strategies	45
10, 11, 12	Estimation with Whole Numbers	23
13	Comparing Decimals	57
14	Rounding Decimals	62
15, 16	Adding and Subtracting Decimals	64
17	Multiplying Decimals	67
18	Dividing Decimals	70
19, 20	Solving Problems Involving Decimals	62
8, 21	Estimation with Decimals	61
22	Changing Fractions to Mixed Numbers	85
23	Changing Fractions to Decimals	84
24	Comparing and Ordering Fractions	88
25	Adding Fractions (Like Denominators)	90
26	Subtracting Fractions (Unlike Denominators)	93
27	Subtracting Mixed Numbers	99
28	Multiplying Fractions and Mixed Numbers	101
29	Dividing Fractions and Mixed Numbers	102
30	Fraction Word Problems	96
31	Customary Units	212
32	Metric Units	216
39, 40, 41	Changing Units	213
33	Geometric Definitions	219
34, 36	Perimeter and Circumference	225
35, 37	Area	229
38	Volume	233

PRETEST

Problem	Section	Starting Page
42	Ratios	112
43	Solving Proportions	121
44, 45, 46	Common Percents, Fractions, and Decimals	129
47	Percent of a Number	131
48, 49	Percent Problems and Proportions	136
50	Proportion Word Problems	136
51, 52, 53	Mean, Median, Mode, and Range	144
54	Bar Graphs	149
55	Line Graphs	156
56	Circle Graphs	164
57	Probability	173
58	Exponents and Square Roots	187
59	Arithmetic Expressions	193
60, 61, 62, 63	Variables and Simple Equations	196
64	Formulas and Problem Solving	200

Chapter 1

Whole Numbers

Place Value

The **number system** used today is based on the **digits** 0 through 9 arranged in a particular pattern. The numbers beginning with 0, 1, 2, 3, and so on are the set of **whole numbers.**

The value, or amount, of a digit depends on its position in that number.

WHOLE NUMBER CHART

9 , 8 7 6 , 5 4 3 , 2 1 0

billions | hundred millions | ten millions | millions | hundred thousands | ten thousands | thousands | hundreds | tens | ones

millions period   thousands period

Starting from the ones position, commas are inserted to separate the numbers into groups of three, or **periods.**

Example 1   Find the value of the 2 in the number 23,476.

STEP 1   Write the digit and insert zeros for each position to the right of the number.

23,476 → 20,000

STEP 2   Determine the value of the 2. Use the chart, if necessary. The 2 is in the ten thousands position. The value of the 2 is 20,000.

Example 2   Find the value of the 3 in 23,476.

STEP 1   Think of 2**3**,476 as a 3 followed by three zeros, or 3,000.

STEP 2   The 3 is in the thousands position. The value of the 3 is 3,000.

<u>Example 3</u>   What is the value of each digit in the number 98,015?

STEP 1   The 9 is in the ten thousands place. Its value is **9 ten thousands,** which is written 90,000.

STEP 2   The 8 is in the thousands place. The value of the 8 is **8 thousands,** or 8,000.

STEP 3   The 0 is in the hundreds place. Therefore, no hundreds are in the number 98,015.

STEP 4   The 1 is in the tens place. Its value is **1 ten** or 10.

STEP 5   The 5 is in the ones place. Its value is **5 ones** or 5.

Now review Examples 1–3 looking for a general method to find the value of a digit within a number. A summary is written in the box below.

PLACE VALUE SUMMARY

1) Write the digit and insert zeros for each position to the right of the number.

2) Determine the value of the new number by referring to the whole number chart or its position in terms of the periods.

EXERCISE 1

Directions: Write the value of each underlined digit. The first one is done for you.

1. 3<u>7</u>8   <u>7 tens or 70</u>

2. 1,42<u>9</u>,871,552 _____

3. 9,26<u>5</u>   _____

4. 697,<u>0</u>38   _____

5. 7,3<u>0</u>0,561,892 _____

6. 2,<u>8</u>76,913   _____

7. 2<u>1</u>,350   _____

8. <u>6</u>94,720,581   _____

9. 4,8<u>2</u>9,156   _____

10. <u>5</u>,829,003,524 _____

11. <u>4</u>,002   _____

12. 34,87<u>1</u>   _____

13. 9<u>9</u>0,980   _____

14. <u>6</u>00   _____

15. <u>6</u>0   _____

16. <u>6</u>   _____

Answers are on page 260.

Reading and Writing Whole Numbers

To read a whole number, you combine the values of its digits.

Example 1   Read the number 28,304.

STEP 1   Think of what periods are involved in 28,304.

Of the 2 and 8 are part of the thousands period. The 3, 0, and 4 (the last three digits) are treated separately and are not considered to be a group.

STEP 2   The number 28,304 means 28 **thousands,** 3 **hundreds,** 0 **tens,** and 4 **ones.**

STEP 3   Read the number 28,304 as "twenty-eight thousand, three hundred four."

To write a number, imagine positions and periods from the whole number chart. Remember the following points:

- Numbers from 21 to 99 are written with a hyphen between the tens and ones value. For example, 67 is written as *sixty-seven* and 83,000 is written as *eighty-three thousand.*

- The word *and* is not read or written as part of a whole number. For example, 5,728 is read as *five thousand, seven hundred twenty-eight.*

- A comma is placed after each period except for the last three digits.

Example 2   Write *six million, two hundred ninety-one thousand, fifty* as a whole number.

STEP 1   *Six million* becomes 6,000,000.
Two hundred ninety-one thousand becomes 291,000.
Fifty becomes 50.

STEP 2   Combine the whole number parts.

6,000,000 + 291,000 + 50 = 6,291,050

TIP
Remember that zeros hold a position and should not be ignored. Write a zero for each position that is not expressed in words.

Now review Examples 1 and 2. A method for reading or writing whole numbers is given below.

READING AND WRITING WHOLE NUMBERS SUMMARY

To read whole numbers:

1) Concentrate on each period and the position of all digits.

2) Write whole numbers by thinking of the whole number chart.

3) Insert zeros as needed.

EXERCISE 2

Directions: Fill in the blanks with the correct digits.

1. 97 has _____ tens and _____ ones.

2. 8,502 has _____ thousands, _____ hundreds, _____ tens, and _____ ones.

3. 364 has _____ hundreds, _____ tens, and _____ ones.

4. 316,008 has _____ hundred thousands, _____ ten thousands, _____ thousands, _____ hundreds, _____ tens, and _____ ones.

5. 4,870,921 has _____ millions, _____ hundred thousands, _____ ten thousands, _____ thousands, _____ hundreds, _____ tens, and _____ ones.

6. 7,915,243,600 has _____ billions, _____ hundred millions, _____ ten millions, _____ millions, _____ hundred thousands, _____ ten thousands, _____ thousands, _____ hundreds, _____ tens, and _____ ones.

Directions: Write each of the following number phrases in symbols.

7. Two hundred fourteen _____

8. Sixty-nine thousand, four hundred thirty-six

    _____

9. Nine million, one hundred ninety thousand, six hundred forty-seven _____

10. Four billion, eight hundred nine million, one hundred ninety thousand, two _____

11. Seventy million, nine hundred thirty-three thousand, eighty-eight

    _____

Directions: Write the value of each digit for each number.

12. 532,907 _____

_____

_____

_____

13. 4,605,873 _____

_____

_____

_____

14. 39,901 _____

_____

_____

_____

Answers are on page 260.

EXERCISE 3

Directions: In each box write the sum of the row and column number.

1.

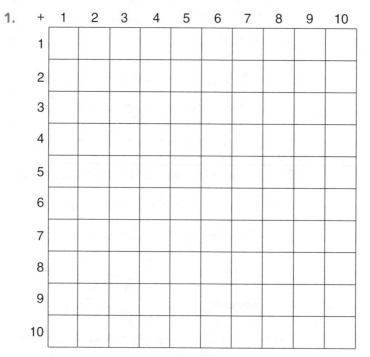

Directions: In each box write the product of the row and column number.

Answers are on page 260.

Adding Whole Numbers

The answer to an addition problem is called the **sum** or total.

Example 1	32 + 47

STEP 1	Line up the digits with ones under ones, tens under tens, and so on.	$\begin{array}{r} 32 \\ + 47 \\ \hline 79 \end{array}$
STEP 2	Add each column.	

Example 2	248 + 36 + 1,982

STEP 1	Line up the digits.	$\begin{array}{r} {\scriptstyle 1\;11} \\ 248 \\ 36 \\ + 1,982 \\ \hline 2,266 \end{array}$
STEP 2	Add each column and carry the digit on the left of each sum to the next column.	

EXERCISE 4

Directions: Solve each problem.

1. 6 + 38

2. 24 + 27

3. 46 + 9

4. 37 + 86

5. 329 + 477

6. 8,645 + 289

7. 7,564
   + 8,562

8. 7,008
   + 9,647

9.   348
      7,493
   +   975

10.   964
     1,673
   +   386

11. Jared delivered 327 newspapers on Tuesday, 489 on Wednesday, 387 on Thursday, and 628 on Saturday. How many papers did he deliver this week?

12. The specialty shop sold 2,498 T-shirts on Saturday and 3,565 on Sunday. How many T-shirts were sold that weekend?

13. During the week, Brad drove these distances: 456 miles, 482 miles, 449 miles, 479 miles, and 468 miles. How many miles did he put on the company truck during the week?

14. In 1999 Story City collected $794,856 in property tax. In 2000 the collection was $675,928. In 2001 it was $738,996. How much was collected in the three-year period?

Answers are on page 261.

Subtracting Whole Numbers

The answer to a subtraction problem is called the **difference.**

Example   Find the difference between 145 and 739.

STEP 1   Put the larger number, 739, on top. Line up the digits with units under units, tens under tens, and so on. Start subtracting with the units. $9 - 5 = 4$

$$\begin{array}{r} {}^{6}\cancel{7}{}^{1}39 \\ -\ 145 \\ \hline 594 \end{array}$$

STEP 2   Regroup to subtract the hundreds column.

EXERCISE 5

Directions: Solve each problem.

1. $62 - 39$

2. $700 - 468$

3. $80 - 41$

4. $2,374 - 1,687$

5. $4,005 - 2,748$

6. $63,225 - 8,949$

7. $90,000 - 48,904$

8. $37,402 - 29,876$

9. $10,500 - 8,643$

10. $267,093 - 188,475$

11. Ahmed's gross pay for the week is $525. If his deductions are $138, what is his net pay?

12. Last week there were 54,067 fans at the game. This week there were 48,978. How many more attended last week?

13. Adam bought a car for $8,750. Two years later it had depreciated $1,900. How much is his car worth now?

14. Last year the food company sold 937,642 packages of carrots. This year 1,000,000 were sold. How many more packages of carrots were sold this year?

Answers are on page 261.

Multiplying Whole Numbers

The answer to a multiplication problem is called the **product.** An × or a dot ·
can be used to show multiplication.

Here are two ways to write 3 times 9 equals 27.

$3 \times 9 = 27$ $3 \cdot 9 = 27$

Example 736×45

STEP 1   Put the number with more digits on top.
Multiply each digit in 736 by 5 in 45 to
find the first partial product.

736
× 45
3680 partial product

STEP 2   Multiply each digit in 736 by the 4 in 45.
Start the second partial product under the 8.

2944 partial product

STEP 3   Add the partial products.

33,120

EXERCISE 6

Directions: Solve each problem.

1. 17×4

2. 38×18

3. 46×9

4. 96×37

5. 390×4

6. 48×207

7. 63×311

8. 100×482

9. 394×29

10. $1,467 \times 35$

11. Bob sells tools. If the average price per tool is $15 and he sold
36 tools, how much money did he collect that day?

12. If Rafael pays $75 monthly for health insurance, how much does he
pay in two years?

13. The ticket office sold 64,750 tickets to the playoff game. If the
cost is $27 per ticket, how much money did the ticket sales
generate?

14. José is doing some landscaping. The perennial he wants to use
costs $18. If he buys 15 plants, how much will this cost?

Answers are on page 261.

Dividing Whole Numbers

The answer to a division problem is called the **quotient.** There are several ways to show division.

$$24 \div 8 \qquad 8\overline{)24} \qquad 24/8 \qquad \frac{24}{8}$$

Example 1 $372 \div 6$

STEP 1   Since you can not divide 6 into 3, you start this problem by dividing 6 into 37, the first two digits of 372.

STEP 2   Continue to multiply, subtract, and bring down the next number. Divide 6 into 12.

STEP 3   Multiply and subtract.

$$\begin{array}{r} 62 \\ 6\overline{)372} \\ -36 \\ \hline 12 \\ -12 \\ \hline 0 \end{array}$$

Example 2 $4\overline{)2374}$

STEP 1   Divide 4 into 23.

STEP 2   Multiply, subtract, and bring down the next number.

STEP 3   Divide 4 into 37.

STEP 4   Multiply, subtract, and bring down the next number.

STEP 5   Divide 4 into 14.

STEP 6   Multiply and subtract. There are no more numbers to bring down. 2 is the remainder.

$$\begin{array}{r} 593 \text{ r}2 \\ 4\overline{)2374} \\ -20 \\ \hline 37 \\ -36 \\ \hline 14 \\ -12 \\ \hline 2 \end{array}$$

EXERCISE 7

Directions: Solve each problem.

1. 41 ÷ 3

2. 186 ÷ 6

3. 200 ÷ 10

4. 480 ÷ 15

5. 248 ÷ 16

6. 409 ÷ 12

7. 3,246 ÷ 16

8. 984 ÷ 9

9. 1,200 ÷ 6

10. 625 ÷ 39

11. During the year, Juanita spent $480 for electricity. How much should she budget monthly for electricity?

12. Harold had 4,866 stamps in his stamp collection equally divided into six stamp books. How many stamps are in each of his six stamp books?

13. The high school swim team generated $432 in ticket sales. If the tickets are $3 each, how many tickets were purchased?

14. Find the quotient of 47,962 divided by 21.

Answers are on page 261.

EXERCISE 8

Directions: Add, subtract, multiply, or divide.

1. 16,394
   + 8,067

2. 803
   × 95

3. 6)1,926

4. 803,497
   − 197,868

5. 3,042
   × 15

6. 24)840

7. 86,942
   1,738
   + 54

8. 69,304
   − 17,290

9. 346
   × 13

10. 7)4,995

11. 95,403
    − 6,771

12. 456,208
    121,113
    + 55,158

13. 598
    + 769
	16. 39,907
	    − 17,488
		19. 83,592
		    290,033
		    + 7,366
			22. 123,123
			    − 87,654

14. 795
    × 13
	17. 5,739
	    × 20
		20. 283,006
		    − 79,658
			23. 15,778 ÷ 7

15. 9)73,584	18. 25)$82.75	21. 357
		    42
		    + 5,028
			24. 305
			    × 17

Answers are on page 261.

Rounding

For some problems, an exact answer is not necessary. An **estimate** (an approximate or "about" answer) will be sufficient. It is also wise to estimate an answer first, solve the problem, and then check your solution by comparing the estimate to the exact answer.

One of the most common estimation strategies is **rounding.** Think of a number as being part of a hilly number line like the one below.

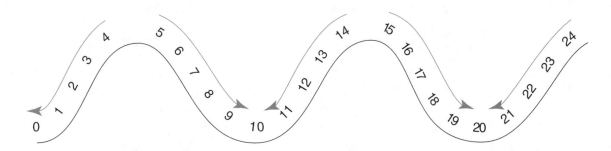

The numbers have a tendency to roll forward or backward to the closest valley. Numbers ending in 0, 1, 2, 3, and 4 will roll back to the nearest 0. Numbers ending in 5, 6, 7, 8, or 9 will roll ahead to the nearest 0.

<u>Example</u>   Round each number to the nearest ten or nearest hundred: 53 and 227.

To the nearest ten, 53 rounds backward to 50.

To the nearest hundred, 53 rounds forward to 100.

To the nearest ten, 227 rounds forward to 230.

To the nearest hundred, 227 rounds backward to 200.

EXERCISE 9

Directions: Round to the nearest 100.

1. 623	6. 2,540
2. 897	7. 3,111
3. 126	8. 8,673
4. 573	9. 3,887
5. 1,296	10. 419

Directions: Round to the nearest 10.

11. 41	16. 286
12. 83	17. 716
13. 67	18. 301
14. 38	19. 409
15. 142	20. 281

Directions: Round to the nearest 1,000.

21. 4,279	26. 26,401
22. 3,640	27. 47,509
23. 1,190	28. 8,742
24. 2,475	29. 9,313
25. 17,536	30. 65,656

Answers are on page 262.

EXERCISE 10

Directions: Write each of the following amounts using a dollar sign and decimal point. Then round each amount to the nearest dollar.

1. Four dollars and fifteen cents   _____

2. Twenty-eight dollars and sixty cents   _____

3. Thirteen dollars and ninety-five cents   _____

4. Two dollars and a quarter   _____

5. A ten-dollar bill and eight nickels   _____

6. A five-dollar bill, six one-dollar bills, four dimes, three nickels, and twelve pennies   _____

7. Two twenty-dollar bills, three five-dollar bills, five quarters, a dime, and twelve pennies   _____

Answers are on page 262.

Estimation

Estimation can often save you time when an exact answer is not needed or when you want to check whether an exact answer is reasonable.

We have already used the strategy of **rounding.** Another estimation strategy involves using the far-left digits or **front-end digits.**

Example 1   Estimate the sum of 259, 673, and 110.

STEP 1   Rewrite each number using its front-end digit followed by zeros to replace the other numbers.

$259 \rightarrow 200$ $673 \rightarrow 600$ $110 \rightarrow 100$

STEP 2   Perform the appropriate operation. (In this case, add.)

$$
\begin{array}{ccc}
259 & & 200 \\
673 & \text{becomes} & 600 \\
+\,110 & & +\,100 \\
\hline
 & & 900
\end{array}
$$

Answer: The sum of 259, 673, and 110 is **about** 900.

TIP

When you add, make sure that you line up the numbers correctly. Sometimes you will be able to apply a mental math strategy during your estimation process.

Sometimes numbers that are close to the original numbers are used instead of the numbers to make the solution easier or quicker to achieve. As with the mental math strategy, these numbers are called **compatible numbers.**

Example 2   Estimate the quotient of 1,239 divided by 37.

STEP 1   Change 1,239 and 37 to numbers that are easier to divide.

$$1,239 \rightarrow 1,200 \qquad 37 \rightarrow 40$$

STEP 2   Divide using the new numbers.

$$\begin{array}{r} 30 \\ 40\overline{)1,200} \\ \underline{120} \\ 00 \end{array}$$

Answer: 1,239 divided by 37 is about 30.

STEP 3   Check the estimate.

Multiply 30 and 40 (mentally if possible). The product 1,200 is close to 1,239, so the estimate is reasonable.

TIP

Remember that estimates are only approximations. Often there are several different ways to estimate an answer, and these estimates may or may not be the same.

EXERCISE 11

Directions: Estimate each answer using one of the estimation strategies. Then list the strategy you used (rounding, front-end digits, or compatible numbers).

1. Estimate the sum of 87 and 31. _____

    Strategy used: _____

2. Estimate the difference of 485 and 211. _____

    Strategy used: _____

3. Estimate the product of 1,986 and 421. _____

   Strategy used: _____

4. Estimate the sum of 56 and 71. _____

   Strategy used: _____

5. Estimate the sum of 278, 318, and 594. _____

   Strategy used: _____

6. Estimate the quotient of 1,475 and 319. _____

   Strategy used: _____

Directions: Estimate each answer using each of the estimation strategies.

7. 98×57

   | rounding: _____ | front-end digits: _____ | compatible numbers: _____ |

8. $2,783 + 907 + 1,346$

   | rounding: _____ | front-end digits: _____ | compatible numbers: _____ |

9. 587 divided by 24

   | rounding: _____ | front-end digits: _____ | compatible numbers: _____ |

10. $4,864 - 2,173$

    | rounding: _____ | front-end digits: _____ | compatible numbers: _____ |

Answers are on page 262.

Whole Numbers Review

Directions: Write the value of each underlined digit.

1. <u>2</u>75 _____

2. 1,79<u>6</u> _____

3. 28,4<u>0</u>2 _____

4. 7<u>8</u>9,040 _____

5. <u>6</u>,748 _____

6. <u>4</u>,869,302 _____

Directions: Solve each problem by estimating. Show your work. Then solve the problems using the actual numbers. Compare your best estimate with the actual answer.

7. $\begin{array}{r} 297 \\ + 112 \\ \hline \end{array}$

8. $\begin{array}{r} 6,928 \\ - 3,014 \\ \hline \end{array}$

9. $\begin{array}{r} 2,165 \\ \times 498 \\ \hline \end{array}$

10. $31\overline{)11,935}$

11. $318 + 21 + 594$

12. $12,878 - 9,142$

Directions: Write each of the following number phrases in symbols.

13. Nineteen hundred fifty-six

14. Eight hundred thousand, three hundred forty-three

15. One million, four hundred three thousand, one

16. Twenty-three thousand, two hundred fifteen

Directions: Solve each word problem.

17. There were 6,347 more people at the final game than the first football game of the season. If 58,473 attended the final game, how many attended the first game?

18. Luis bought 18 baseball hats for his little league team. The hats cost $4 each. How much did he spend?

Directions: Estimate the answer for each problem.

19. Estimate the quotient of 7,859 and 38.

20. Estimate the product of 423 and 79.

Answers are on page 262.

Chapter 2

Using a Calculator

The GED Mathematics Test permits the use of a calculator on half of the mathematics test. The Casio *fx*-260 solar is the only calculator permitted with the test.

The calculator directions throughout this book refer specifically to the Casio *fx*-260. Other calculators may not work the same way.

To turn the calculator on, press the **ON** key at the upper right or the red **AC** key. A small "DEG" will appear at the top center of the display, and "0." will appear at the right of the display.

To perform any arithmetic operation, first press **AC** (all clear) to clear the display. Then enter the numbers and operating signs. Then press **=** (the equals sign) key when you are finished.

Adding Whole Numbers on a Calculator

Follow these examples to add whole numbers on your calculator.

Example 1   Use a calculator to find the sum of 8 + 6.

Press **AC**

Press **8** **+** **6** **=**

The display should read [14.].

Example 2   Use the calculator to find the total of 36,479 + 2,999 + 80,467.

Press **AC**

The display should read [119945.].

EXERCISE 1

Directions: Use your calculator to solve these problems.

1. 16 + 8

2. 27 + 36

3. 4 + 29

4. 346 + 82

5. 947 + 586

6. 23 + 146 + 197

7. 2,641 + 8,397

8. 297 + 4,374

9. 23,472 + 6,050 + 98,642

10. 247,962 + 89,775

11. 3,847 + 29 + 46,999

12. 66,666 + 50,505

13. 100,000 + 3,847

14. 2,739 + 96,248 + 397

15. 872 + 9,463 + 248

16. Kristin read 228 pages on Monday, 47 pages on Tuesday, and 86 pages on Friday. How many pages of her history book did she read in those 3 days?

17. A trucker had a load of 26,700 pounds. He added 476 pounds of merchandise. How much is his total load?

18. The Gardenas family had these expenses in March: rent $350, food $275, utilities $150, insurance $87, medical $49, and entertainment $51. How much were their family expenses in March?

19. In four games the Bulldogs scored 72, 85, 69, and 91 points. What was the total numbers of points scored during the four games?

20. There were 36,487 fans on Tuesday for the football game, 51,344 on Saturday, and 48,999 on the following Thursday. How many total people saw these games?

Answers are on page 263.

Subtracting Whole Numbers on a Calculator

Follow this example to subtract whole numbers on your calculator.

Example   Use a calculator to find the difference of 14 – 6.

Press [AC]

Press [1] [4] [–] [6] [=]

The display should read [8.].

EXERCISE 2

Directions: Use a calculator to solve these problems.

1. 11 – 5

2. 9 – 2

3. 29 – 16

4. 37 – 28

5. 426 – 103

6. 347 – 268

7. 3,742 – 39

8. 876 – 499

9. 27,364 – 14,982

10. 40,000 – 26,475

11. 9,641 – 3,897

12. 14,176 – 4,000

13. 765,908 – 673,233

14. 48,907 – 30,040

15. 5,960 – 4,837

16. Juan had $48 to go grocery shopping. If his groceries cost $37, how much did he have left?

17. The inventory at the warehouse had 4,800 tool belts in stock. After shipping 987 tool belts, how many were left?

18. On opening day, there were 69,457 fans at the game. At the second game there were 59,877 fans. How many more fans attended the opening game?

19. Before Taffy's shift started, there was $250 in the cash drawer. At the end of her shift, there was $806. How much money had Taffy added to the cash drawer?

20. Lake City collected $961,487 in property tax last year. This year the amount is $1,147,028. How much more revenue in property tax was collected this year?

Answers are on page 263.

Multiplying Whole Numbers on a Calculator

Follow these examples to multiply whole numbers on your calculator.

Example 1   Use a calculator to find the product of 6 × 4.

Press AC.
Press 6 × 4 =.
The display should read ⎿   24.⏌.

Example 2   Use a calculator to find the product of 36 × 129.

Press AC.
Press 3 6 × 1 2 9 =.
The display should read ⎿   4644.⏌.

EXERCISE 3

Directions: Use your calculator to solve these problems.

1. 9×3
2. 46×2
3. 8×31
4. 57×64
5. 86×10

6. 100×31
7. 426×25
8. 587×83
9. 261×260
10. 407×30

11. 908×602
12. $4{,}738 \times 84$
13. $26 \times 97{,}462$
14. $301 \times 4{,}006$
15. $287 \times 9{,}999$

16. How many eggs are in 18 dozen?

17. Ned wants to buy 6 new windows for his house at $183 each. How much will the new windows cost him?

18. Robert gets paid monthly. If he pays $97 a month for health insurance, how much does he pay in one year?

19. The average property tax bill in Mountainside is $1,482 per house. If there are 928 houses, how much property tax will be collected?

20. If 21,475 teenagers paid $23 per ticket for a concert, how much money was collected in ticket sales?

Answers are on page 263.

Dividing Whole Numbers on a Calculator

Follow these examples to divide whole numbers on a calculator.

Example 1 Use a calculator to find the quotient of $5\overline{)735}$.

Press [AC].
Press [7] [3] [5] [÷] [5] [=].
The display should read [147.].

Example 2 Use a calculator to find the quotient of $45{,}762 \div 87$.

Press [AC].
Press [4] [5] [7] [6] [2] [÷] [8] [7] [=].
The display should read [526.].

EXERCISE 4

Directions: Use a calculator to solve these problems.

1. 81 ÷ 3

2. 324 ÷ 4

3. 1,058 ÷ 23

4. 3,315 ÷ 39

5. 250 ÷ 50

6. $45\overline{)720}$

7. $89\overline{)12,727}$

8. $3\overline{)11,088}$

9. $75\overline{)6,000}$

10. $933\overline{)41,985}$

11. $4,256\overline{)161,728}$

12. $6,000\overline{)348,000}$

13. $632\overline{)1,608,440}$

14. $96\overline{)57,504}$

15. $398\overline{)3,124,698}$

16. There were only four trucks available to deliver 7,960 pounds of produce. How much produce should be loaded on each truck?

17. Jess wants to pay off a $600 debt in one year. How much will he pay monthly?

18. The town collected $75,000 for parking fines. If the average parking fine is $25, how many tickets were issued?

19. The company profits of $49,840 are to be divided equally among the 56 employees. How much will each receive?

20. Eighteen trophies were awarded during the local soccer tournament. If the bill for the trophies was $270, how much did each trophy cost?

Answers are on page 263.

Calculator Review

Directions: Use your calculator to solve each problem.

1. $16 + 17$

2. $23 - 9$

3. 48×3

4. $96 \div 4$

5. $86 + 923$

6. $407 - 388$

7. 289×97

8. $12,000 \div 40$

9. $2,894 + 19,073$

10. $4,872 - 3,990$

11. 850×381

12. $58,590 \div 62$

13. $387 + 4,296 + 38$

14. $10,000 - 4,675$

15. $1,411 \times 3,879$

16. $2,295,370 \div 5,962$

Directions: Use your calculator to solve each problem. Choose the correct answer.

17. In the month of June, it rained on 18 days. How many days did it not rain?

   (1) 12
   (2) 13
   (3) 18
   (4) 30
   (5) 31

18. Which of the following represents the largest amount?

   (1) $486 - 99$
   (2) 33×17
   (3) $965 \div 5$
   (4) $5,038 - 4,765$
   (5) $2,460 \div 3$

19. How many 18-inch strips can be cut from a 10-yard piece of cord?
   (**Hint:** 1 yard = 36 inches)

   (1) 10
   (2) 18
   (3) 20
   (4) 30
   (5) 360

20. Which represents the smallest number?

   (1) 56×13
   (2) $425 \div 25$
   (3) $9 + 29$
   (4) $826 - 749$
   (5) 38×4

Answers are on page 264.

Problem Solving

How to Solve Word Problems

Problem solving is an important part of your study of mathematics and everyday life.

The following five-step approach will help you solve problems of all types and will help you organize your thinking.

- **STEP 1** After reading (and rereading) the problem carefully, decide what the problem asks you to find. In other words, **understand the question.**

- **STEP 2 Decide what information is needed** to solve the problem. Also determine what information is irrelevant to the question.

- **STEP 3 Choose the most appropriate operation** or operations (addition, subtraction, multiplication, or division) to solve the problem.

- **STEP 4 Solve the problem.** Make sure your solution answers the question asked.

- **STEP 5 Check your answer** by reading the question again to see if your answer makes sense.

<u>Example 1</u> Paul works from 4 P.M. to 7 P.M. Monday through Friday. How many hours does he work each week?

STEP 1 Reread the problem to understand the question.

The problem asks you to find the number of hours Paul works each week.

STEP 2 Decide what information is needed.

You know that Paul works three hours (from 4 P.M. to 7 P.M.) five days a week (Monday through Friday). You want to determine how many hours he works each week.

STEP 3 Choose the most appropriate operation.

You want to multiply the number of hours worked each day (3 hours) by the number of days worked each week (5 days).

STEP 4   Solve the problem.

3 hours per day × 5 days per week = 15 hours per week

STEP 5   Check your answer.

If Paul works three hours for five days a week, he works fifteen hours each week. The answer makes sense.

TIP

Sometimes more information is given than you need to solve the problem asked. Be careful to ignore unnecessary information.

Other times information is not provided directly in the problem. Necessary information could be found in a related list, chart, or drawing.

<u>Example 2</u>   Marcella bought shampoo for $3.19, hair rinse for $2.38, and a brush for $1.99. She gave the clerk a ten-dollar bill. How much did the items cost altogether?

STEP 1   Understand the question.

The problem asks you to find the total cost of three items.

STEP 2   Find the necessary information.

You must know the cost of the three items: $3.19, $2.38, and $1.99.

STEP 3   Choose an arithmetic operation.

Decide whether you should add, subtract, multiply, or divide. Since you are finding a total, you must add.

STEP 4   Solve the problem.
$$\begin{array}{r} \$3.19 \\ 2.38 \\ +\ 1.99 \\ \hline \$7.56 \end{array}$$

STEP 5   Check your answer.

If you rounded the prices to the nearest dollar, the sum would be $7 ($3 + $2 + $2) so an answer of $7.56 seems reasonable.

EXERCISE 1

Directions: For each problem below, circle the letter of each phrase that best describes what you are asked to find. Solve each problem, showing your work.

1. The Bodemer family watches about 25 hours of television each week. About how many hours of television do they watch per month?
   a. hours of television per day
   b. hours of television per week
   c. hours of television per month

2. Sixteen men and fourteen women were enrolled in Mr. Judd's class. If two students dropped the course, how many students finished the class?
   a. men in the class
   b. women in the class
   c. men and women finishing the class

3. When Julio receives his paycheck, $156.82 has been deducted for federal income tax, $78.14 for state income tax, and $10.83 for city income tax. How much tax is deducted each paycheck?
   a. city and state taxes
   b. federal, state, and city taxes
   c. federal and state taxes

4. In June, Mary Jane paid $438 for rent, $98.52 for electricity, $152.75 for her car payment, $25 for cable television, and $64.39 for phone calls. If she cancels her cable, estimate her monthly expenses.
   a. rent, electricity, car, cable, and telephone expenses
   b. rent, electricity, and telephone expenses
   c. rent, electricity, car, and telephone expenses

Directions: Underline the numbers that are used to solve each problem. Then solve each problem.

5. George directly supervises three women and four men out of the 25 women and 32 men in his department. How many people does George directly supervise?

6. Nadia estimated that 350 people would attend the family reunion. She expected each person to use three napkins. Only 287 people actually attended the reunion. How many napkins did Nadia buy?

7. One Saturday Mrs. Wu stopped at her bank to get $200. Then she spent $52.49 at the grocery store, $23.50 at the dry cleaners, and $15 for gasoline. How much money did she spend that day?

8. When Helen calls her sister, she must remember that the time in California is two hours earlier than her time in Illinois. If she calls her brother in Georgia, the time is an hour later. If it is 6 P.M. in Georgia, what time is it in California?

Directions: Use the five-step problem-solving method. Underline the necessary or key information, list the operation you will use, and then solve each problem.

9. Karen pays $425 a month for rent. How much rent does she pay in a year?

10. At a garage sale, Mark sold twelve albums for $1.25 each and a turntable for $10. How much money did he receive from his albums?

11. On October 1, 1992, the gas tax in Alaska was 8 cents per gallon. In Rhode Island, the gas tax was 26 cents per gallon. How much more tax would you pay per gallon to drive in Rhode Island than Alaska?

12. According to the National Association of Realtors, in 1983 a median-priced home was worth $70,300. By 1993, the median price had risen $35,800. What was the value of a median-priced home in 1993?

13. In 1992, the gross average weekly earnings for an employee of an iron and steel foundry was $525.46. If the employee worked 43 hours, find the hourly wage.

14. In 1900, over five million women were in the civilian workforce. By 1990, the number of female employees was over 11 times the 1900 figure. Estimate the number of female employees in 1990.

Answers are on page 264.

Clues in Choosing an Operation

Many times the hardest part about solving a problem is deciding whether to add, subtract, multiply, or divide.

One way to determine which operation will be used is to focus on key words. Noticing these words will often provide a clue to determining the appropriate operation. Some key words or phrases are listed below.

Addition	Subtraction	Multiplication	Division
sum	difference	product	quotient
total	more . . . than	times	split
altogether	less than	twice (× 2)	divided by
combined	minus	when finding several of a given amount	when given amount of many and finding one
increased by	decreased by		
when combining different amounts	farther than	when given part and finding the whole	when sharing, cutting, or splitting
	when comparing one amount to another		

Compare the relevant numbers in the problem to your solution to determine if you chose the correct operation.

Remember that adding the same number repeatedly is the same as multiplication, and subtracting the same number repeatedly is the same as division.

Example 1   David rode his bicycle for 17 miles on Saturday. On Sunday he rode it 25 more miles. How many miles did David ride altogether?

STEP 1   Reread the problem to understand the question.

The problem asks you to find the number of miles David rode his bicycle on Saturday and Sunday combined.

STEP 2   Decide what information is needed.

You need to find the total number of miles David biked that weekend.

STEP 3   Choose the most appropriate operation.

The key word *altogether* gives you the clue that you should probably add 17 and 25.

STEP 4   Solve the problem.

$17 + 25 = 42$

Answer: David rode a total of 42 miles this weekend.

STEP 5   Check your answer.

To check an addition problem, you could subtract one of the numbers in the problem from the answer. In this case, if you subtract 25 from 42, the answer is 17 (the other number in the problem). The answer checks.

Example 2   Lucinda ran 9 miles on Saturday. On Sunday she ran 26 more miles. How many more miles did Lucinda run on Sunday than on Saturday?

STEP 1   Reread the problem to understand the question.

The problem asks you to compare the number of miles Lucinda ran on Saturday and Sunday.

STEP 2   Decide what information is needed.

You need to find how many more miles Lucinda ran on Sunday than she ran on Saturday.

STEP 3   Choose the most appropriate operation.

The key phrase *more than* tells you that you should subtract.

STEP 4   Solve the problem.

$26 - 9 = 17$

Answer: Lucinda ran 17 more miles on Sunday than she ran on Saturday.

STEP 5   Check your answer.

To check a subtraction problem, you could add one of the numbers in the problem and the answer. In this case, if you add 9 and 17, the answer is 26 (the other number in the problem). The answer checks.

EXERCISE 2

Directions: Underline the key word, phrase, or idea in each problem. Then solve each problem. Show your work.

1. In May, Jackie's rent is increasing $30. If she pays $415 now, how much will her new rent cost a month?

2. Carmella's car weighs 2,975 pounds. When her trailer is empty, it weighs 475 pounds. What is the combined weight of the car and trailer?

3. Guillaume and three of his friends went out to eat. The check came to $26.56. If they split the check equally, how much does each person pay?

4. Abdul usually averages fifteen service calls a day. Marty can make twice as many. How many service calls does Marty average?

5. Garbage service in the town of Kankakee costs $156 a year. What is the monthly charge for garbage collection?

6. Hector borrowed $1,500 in student loans. He has managed to pay back $985. How much does he have left to pay?

7. If unleaded gasoline is advertised for $1.39 per gallon, how much would 12 gallons cost?

8. How many pieces 8 inches long can be cut from a 96-inch board?

9. In 1992, the Chicago O'Hare Airport, the world's busiest airport that year, flew 64,441,087 passengers. The Dallas/Ft. Worth Airport, ranking second that year, flew 51,943,567 passengers. How many more passengers flew out of Chicago O'Hare than Dallas/Ft. Worth?

10. As of 1993, the highest recorded temperature in June was 127° Fahrenheit (F) on June 15, 1896, at Fort Mojave, Arizona. The lowest recorded temperature in June was 2°F on June 13, 1907, in Tamarack, California. Find the difference between the highest and lowest June temperatures.

Answers are on page 264.

Mental Math Strategies

Sometimes problems are so simple or easy to solve that a solution can be determined without using paper or pencil or other materials such as a calculator. When you find an answer without writing any numbers, you are applying certain **mental math strategies.** Knowing and practicing these strategies will save you time when you need it such as when taking a test having a time limit.

A strategy that you probably already know involves shortcuts for adding or multiplying when zeros are involved. For example, to multiply 48 and 100, first write 48. Since 100 *ends in two zeros,* insert two zeros after the 48.

Think: "$48 \times 1\underline{00} = 4,8\underline{00}$."

Another example would be to add 5,000, 14,000, and 6,000 by thinking "5 + 14 + 6 = 25 and then insert three zeros."

Example 1   Multiply 60 and 200.

You can do this mentally by multiplying 6 and 2 and then inserting **3 zeros** (**1** zero in 60 + **2** zeros in 200).

$$60 \times 200 = 12{,}000$$

$$6 \times 2 \ = 12$$

Another strategy is known as **breaking apart numbers.** You apply this strategy when it is easier to think of a number as the sum of two numbers. For example, to add 73 + 25, mentally think of 73 as 70 + 3 and 25 as 20 + 5. Then you may be able to add 70 + 20 and 3 + 5 to get an answer of 98.

Example 2   Jolene bought three cans of fruit juice. If each can cost 58 cents, how much did she spend?

STEP 1   Choose an appropriate operation.

Since you are finding the price of several items when one is given, you will multiply.

STEP 2   Apply the mental math strategy of breaking apart numbers.

Think: "58 = 50 + 8 so 50 × 3 = 150 and 8 × 3 = 24. 150 + 24 = 174."

STEP 3   Write or state your answer to the problem.

174 cents is more commonly referred to as $1.74.
Jolene spent $1.74 for three cans of juice.

Another mental math strategy is called finding **compatible numbers.** These numbers can be grouped together to form a number that may be easier to use such as 10, 30, 100, 400, and 1,000.

Example 3   Jose has 59 baseball cards, Roseanne has 82 cards, and Aram has 41 cards. How many cards do the three friends have altogether?

STEP 1   Choose an operation.

You want to add 59, 82, and 41.

STEP 2   Apply a mental math strategy.

You notice that $59 + 41 = 100$ so think "$59 + 82 + 41 = 100 + 82 = 182$."

STEP 3   Write or state your answer to the problem.

The three friends have 182 baseball cards altogether.

The last most common strategy is referred to as **substitution** (or **compensation**). To apply this strategy, you change one number so it is easier to perform the necessary operation and then change the other number by its opposite. (The opposite of addition is subtraction and vice versa. The opposite of multiplication is division and vice versa.) For example,

$$57 + 34 = (57 + 3) + (34 - 3) = 60 + 31 = 91.$$

Example 4   Miguel drove 101 miles to the airport. Connie only had to drive 28 miles. How much farther did Miguel drive than Connie?

STEP 1   Choose an appropriate operation.

The key words *farther than* indicate that you will subtract.

STEP 2   Apply the mental math strategy of compensation.

Think: "$101 - 28 = 101 - \mathbf{1} - 28 + \mathbf{1} = 100 - 28 + \mathbf{1} = 72 + 1 = 73$."

STEP 3   Write or state your answer to the problem.

Miguel drove 73 miles farther than Connie.

STEP 4   Check your answer. Since subtraction and addition are opposite, the answer + 28 should equal 101.

Add $28 + 73$ mentally. Think: "$20 + 8 + 70 + 3 = 90 + 11 = 101$." The answer checks.

After you have practiced the different mental math strategies, they should help you save time by allowing you to take shortcuts whenever possible. But remember that you still must know your basic addition and multiplication facts to achieve the correct solution.

EXERCISE 3

Directions: Apply one of the mental math strategies and write the answer.

1. $27 + 52$

2. 19×10

3. 60×90

4. $7 + 36 + 3$

5. $7 \times 5 \times 20$

6. $99 + 53$

7. $102 + 14$

8. $43 + 28$

9. $99 - 37$

10. $1,000 \times 32$

11. $16 + 42 + 34$

12. $500 \times 8,000$

13. 800×300

14. $13 + 5 + 15 + 7$

15. $399 - 12$

16. $37 + 99$

17. Mrs. O'Rourke is the guidance counselor for 28 adults, Mr. Martinez assists 32 adults, and Ms. Wolfe advises 41 adults. How many adults are being assisted by these guidance counselors?

18. Using the numbers in problem 17, how many more adults does Ms. Wolfe advise than Mr. Martinez?

Answers are on page 265.

Estimation with Word Problems

Often you do not need an exact answer and just want to check for a reasonable answer. Rounding is a good strategy to use to find an estimate or reasonable answer to a problem.

Example   Tito wants to find out how much he spends monthly on utilities. About how much total does he spend if he paid $34 for water, $68 for electricity, and $52 for gas?

STEP 1   Determine what operation is to be used. *Total* usually means to add.

STEP 2   Rounding each number to the nearest ten seems reasonable.

STEP 3   Add the numbers. $30 + 70 + 50 = 150$
$150 per month is a reasonable estimate.

EXERCISE 4

Directions: Estimate the answer for each problem below. Name the strategy you used and show your work.

1. During a drive to collect money for a charity, Juan turned in $695. He collected $315 by himself; the rest of this money he collected with Marsha. Marsha turned in $478 (the money she collected by herself). About how much did they collect together?

2. A pet store received a shipment of 105 cartons of dog food. Each carton contained 48 cans. About how many cans of dog food did the pet store receive?

3. The average cheetah can run 70 miles per hour. The average man can run about 28 miles per hour (for a short period of time). On the average, how much faster is the cheetah than man?

4. The Washington Monument is over 403 feet taller than the Statue of Liberty, which is 152 feet high. How tall is the Washington Monument?

5. There are 58 pieces of candy in a bag. Josie bought 5 bags. How many pieces of candy does she have?

6. Estella earns $9.25 per hour. How much will she earn for working 30 hours?

7. The Jones family drove 312 miles in 5 hours and 10 minutes. About how many miles per hour were they driving?

8. The Peters family paid $238 for 40 hours of day care last week. About how much per hour does the day care cost?

9. The soccer team was selling calendars for a fundraiser. They sold 186 the first week, 298 the second week, and 415 the third week. About how many calendars did they sell in three weeks?

10. Joe bought a car for $5,725. Two years later, the value of the car was only $3,390. About how much did the car depreciate?

Answers are on page 265.

Problem-Solving Strategies

The mental math and estimation strategies you have learned are types of problem-solving strategies. These and others you will learn will help you become more successful when you solve problems (both when you are studying mathematics and in your everyday life).

Sometimes to solve a problem you may have drawn a sketch or diagram to help you understand what is being asked. When you do this, you are using the problem-solving strategy called **drawing a picture.** Many people find this strategy the easiest to remember and use.

Example 1   Matthew had driven 12 miles toward his girlfriend's house when he remembered that he had left his concert tickets at home. He went back home and, after a quick phone call to explain why he was late, drove the 25 miles back to her house. How many miles had he added to his odometer when he finally arrived at her house?

STEP 1   Understand the question.

You want to figure out how many miles Matthew drove to get to his girlfriend's house.

STEP 2   Find the necessary information.

If you just write the two numbers that are in the problem (12 and 25), you will probably get the wrong answer. If you draw a picture, you should be able to see that you really have three numbers involved: 12, 12, and 25.

STEP 3   Choose an arithmetic operation.

By looking at the picture plus noticing the key word *added*, you should see that you want to add 12, 12, and 25.

STEP 4   Solve the problem. (Make sure you answer the question asked.)

One way to add the numbers (but not the only way) is to think **12 + 12** + 25 = 24 + 25 = 49.

Answer: Matthew added 49 miles to the odometer driving to his girlfriend's house.

STEP 5   Check your answer.

Add the numbers again, or find an estimate and compare it to your answer. One possible estimate is to think that Matthew was about half way to his girlfriend's house when he had to turn around. Traveling halfway to her house and then returning is about the same as traveling to her house (25 miles). Then Matthew went straight to her house (another 25 miles), so 25 miles + 25 miles = 50 miles. Your answer, 49 miles, is close to your estimate, 50 miles. Your answer is reasonable.

TIP

You do not have to be an artist to practice this strategy. If you know what you are drawing and why, this method can be very useful!

Another very popular problem-solving strategy is called **guess and check.** You are probably using this method quite often but perhaps did not know that it was an acceptable way to solve problems!

Example 2   Which two 2-digit numbers made from the digits 1, 2, 3, 4, and 5 give the largest sum when added together? No single digit may be used more than once.

STEP 1   Understand the question.

You want to find out which two 2-digit numbers give the largest sum when added together.

STEP 2   Find the necessary information.

You can only use the digits 1, 2, 3, 4, and 5. No digit may be used more than once.

STEP 3   Choose an arithmetic operation.

Since you are finding a sum, you should add the digits 1, 2, 3, 4, and 5.

STEP 4   Solve the problem.

First guess: Second guess:

54 + 32 = 86   53 + 42 = 95

Answer: 53 + 42 = 95

STEP 5   Check your answer.

Test your first guess. Ask yourself: Test again. Ask yourself: Is 95 a
Is 86 a reasonable sum? No,   reasonable sum? Yes, 5 and 4
adding 5 and 3 in the tens place   are the largest digits that can
gives 80. If you change 3 to 4 and   appear in the tens column. The
then add 5 and 4 in the tens place,   numbers 2 and 3 are the largest
you get 90; 90 is greater than 80.   digits that can appear in the
                                               ones column. Therefore,
                                               choosing 53 and 42 or 52 and
                                               43 is correct.

Using information from a table is the name of another valuable problem-solving strategy. When a chart, drawing, table, or map is part of a problem, it probably includes some information necessary to solve the problem. After reading the problem carefully, it usually pays to study the table and interpret or sort out what is useful information.

<u>Example 3</u>   Kieron passed the sign shown at the right. He decided to change the oil in his car, rotate his tires, and have his car washed and waxed. How much did he spend on his car?

Special Weekend Rates	
Oil & Filter Change	$12.95
Rotation of Tires	$ 6.95
Car Lubricated	$ 8.75
Wash & Wax	$19.95

STEP 1   Understand the question.

You want to determine the total amount of money Kieron spent on his car.

STEP 2   Find the necessary information.

By looking at the chart, you know that it costs $12.95 for an oil and filter change, $6.95 to rotate tires, and $19.95 to wash and wax a car. (You also know that you do *not* need to use the $8.75 amount.)

STEP 3   Choose an arithmetic operation.

Since you are finding a total, you should add the three prices:
$12.95, $6.95, and $19.95.

STEP 4   Solve the problem.

$$\begin{array}{r} \$12.95 \\ \$\ 6.95 \\ +\ \$19.95 \\ \hline \$39.85 \end{array}$$

Answer: Kieron spent $39.85 on his car.

STEP 5   Check your answer.

One way to check the answer is to round the prices to the nearest dollar and add. The estimate is $13 + $7 + $20, or $20 + $20 = $40. Since $40 is very close to the answer of $39.85, your answer is reasonable.

TIP
It is wise to use estimation either before or after you have found an exact answer to determine if your answer is reasonable.

EXERCISE 5

Directions: Select a strategy to solve each problem. Show your work and state the strategy you used.

1. Five people are in a room. If everyone shakes hands with everyone else once, how many handshakes will there be in all?

2. Which two 3-digit numbers made from the digits 1, 2, 3, 4, 5, and 6 give the largest sum when added together? No single digit may be used more than once.

3. Nadia is driving from Pittsburgh to St. Louis. If she wants to save time, which route should she take?

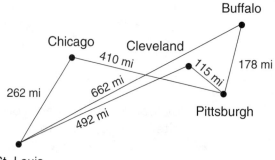

4. Three turtles are in a race. Turtle A was 2 feet behind Turtle B. Turtle C was 4 feet ahead of Turtle A. Turtle B was 6 feet from the starting line. Which turtle was ahead?

5. Which 3-digit and 1-digit number made with the digits 3, 4, 5, and 6 give the largest product when multiplied together? No single digit may be used more than once.

6. Honda was the biggest seller between 1989 and 1992. In what year were the largest number of cars of that make sold?

TOP SELLING PASSENGER CARS IN THE U.S.

Year	Make	Number Sold
1989	Honda Accord	362,707
1990	Honda Accord	417,179
1991	Honda Accord	399,297
1992	Ford Taurus	409,751

7. Which 3-digit and 2-digit numbers made with the digits 1, 2, 3, 4, and 5 give the largest product when multiplied together? No single digit may be used more than once.

8. Five basketball players are in a circle. Each player throws the basketball to every other player once. How many times is the ball thrown?

9. Which two 2-digit numbers made from the digits 5, 6, 7, and 8 give the largest sum when added together? No single digit may be used more than once.

10. Wanda had to hike 20 miles. She walked half the distance the first day. She walked half of the remaining distance the second day. How far did she have to walk the third day to finish the trip?

11. Give the windchill factor for the following.

WINDCHILL FACTOR

wind speed (mph)	Temperature in degrees Fahrenheit					
	15	10	5	0	–5	–10
5	12	7	0	–5	–10	–15
10	–3	–9	–15	–22	–27	–31
15	–11	–18	–25	–31	–38	–45

a. Wind speed is 5 mph, temperature is 5 degrees.

b. Wind speed is 15 mph, temperature is 0 degrees.

c. Wind speed is 10 mph, temperature is –10 degrees.

d. Wind speed is 15 mph, temperature is 15 degrees.

Answers are on page 265.

Problems with Multiple Steps

At times you have to choose more than one operation to solve a problem. To simplify this type of problem, you can first write a **solution sentence.** This sentence is written by identifying phrases and numbers to state the solution in a simple manner. Once a solution sentence is identified, you can determine what information is missing.

Example   Last month Louise bought 5 compact discs (CDs) for $19.95 each and 3 cassettes for $9.99 each. How much did she spend altogether on music?

STEP 1   Write a solution sentence.

Summarize what you know into short phrases.
total cost of music = cost of CDs plus cost of cassettes

STEP 2   Substitute known values and symbols for the phrases.

Known values:
cost of CDs → 5 CDs for $19.95 → 5 × $19.95
cost of cassettes → 3 cassettes for $9.99 → 3 × $9.99

total cost of music = (**5** × **$19.95**) + (**3** × **$9.99**)

STEP 3   Complete the appropriate operations.

First operation: multiply to find the cost of each type of music.
total cost of music = (**$99.75**) + (**$29.97**)

Second operation: add the two costs.
total cost of music = ($99.75) + ($29.97) = $129.72

EXERCISE 6

Directions: Write a solution sentence for each problem. Then solve the problem.

1. Alfredo bought 5 pounds of potatoes at $0.75 per pound and 3 pounds of bananas at $0.45 per pound. How much did he spend altogether?

2. Maria purchased 3 cans of vegetables at $0.89 per can. How much change should she get from a $10 bill?

3. Wong bought 4 adult tickets to a pop concert at $25 per ticket and three child tickets at $10.50 per ticket. How much did he spend altogether for the tickets?

4. Barb spent $11.25 at one store, $15.50 at another store, and $10.75 at a third store. If she has $35 in her checking account, will she have enough money to cover her purchases?

5. Hal deposited $80 in his checking account. He then wrote checks for $5.35, $35.60, $20, $10, and $15. Did he deposit enough money to cover these five checks?

6. Shirley bought 2 tires for her car at $95 each and 6 spark plugs at $1.25 each. How much did she spend altogether?

7. Rosario is buying a 1996 Viper that costs $28,500. The auto dealer will give him $1,900 on a trade-in, and Rosario plans to put $1,200 in cash down. How much will he have to finance?

8. Magda plans to fly to Washington, D.C. Kiwi Airlines is offering fares at $89 one way, and ATA is offering fares at $188 round trip. Which is the better buy?

9. Valencia rented three movies with a 3-for-$6.50 coupon. She rented a fourth one for two nights only at $3.25. How much should she get back if she pays with $20?

10. Bobby Ray pumped nine gallons of gas at $1.27 per gallon. Will he have enough to pay for the gas if he has $12.00 in his wallet?

Answers are on page 266.

Using a Number Grid

A few problems on the GED Math test will ask you to mark your answers on a **number grid.** Each grid has five blanks across the top to write your answer on. Below each blank is a column of numbers and symbols where you color your answer on the circles.

Example Find the quotient of 5,513 divided by 37. Then round your answer to the nearest ten and mark the rounded quotient on the number grid.

STEP 1 Divide 5513 by 37.

$$\begin{array}{r} 149 \rightarrow 150 \\ 37\overline{)5513} \\ \underline{37} \\ 181 \\ \underline{148} \\ 333 \\ \underline{333} \end{array}$$

STEP 2 Round 149 to the nearest ten.
The answer is 150.

To answer the question on a number grid, write the correct answer in the blank boxes at the top of each column. Use a separate column for each digit. Then fill in one circle below each column that corresponds to the digit that you wrote on top.

Below are three correctly filled in grids with the answer 150. The first answer starts at the left side of the grid. The second answer is centered. And the third answer uses the right side of the grid.

Correct Answers

Be careful when you fill in a number grid. Below are two incorrectly filled in grids for the last example. On the first grid, the circles were not filled in. On the second grid, all the circles were filled in the first column.

Incorrect Answers

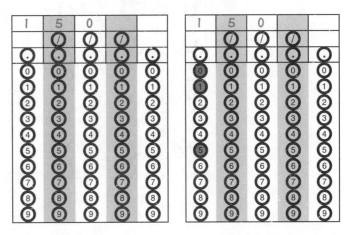

EXERCISE 7

Directions: Mark each answer on the corresponding number grid.

1. 87 + 2,486

3. 23,500 ÷ 50

2. 2,479 − 1,886

4. 235 ÷ 5

5. 48×31

6. 56×243

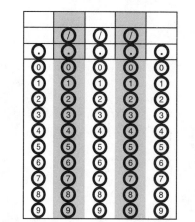

7. Round the quotient of $2{,}473 \div 130$ to the nearest ten.

8. Round the product of 62 and 39 to the nearest hundred.

Answers are on page 266.

Problem-Solving Review

Directions: Write the value of each underlined digit.

1. 3,<u>8</u>67

2. 4<u>2</u>,941

3. 164,80<u>5</u>

4. <u>4</u>87,923

Directions: Write each number phrase in symbols.

5. Nine hundred forty-three

6. Eighteen thousand, seventy-six

7. Three thousand four hundred eighty

8. Two million four hundred thirty-seven thousand

Directions: Round to the nearest 100.

9. 6,795

10. 341

Directions: Round to the nearest 10.

11. 437

12. 23,961

Directions: Solve each problem by estimating. Then solve the problems using the actual numbers.

13. $4,869 + 23,271$

14. $3,189 \times 296$

15. $13,847 \div 42$

16. $21,904 - 16,129$

Directions: Estimate the answer for each word problem. Put each estimated answer on the number grid.

17. Dora bought 12 CDs for $11.89 each. About how much did she spend for the CDs?

18. Warren County collected $23,470 in delinquent taxes in 1999 and $31,067 in 2000. About how much more was collected in 2000?

19. At West High School, there are 380 freshmen, 407 sophomores, 298 juniors, and 321 seniors. About how many students attend West High?

20. At the food pantry there are 389 cans of food to divide among 19 family boxes. About how many cans of food should be put in each box?

Answers are on page 268.

Chapter 4

Decimals

Understanding Decimals

The U.S. monetary system is based on the **decimal system.** Decimals are based on a whole being split into ten equal parts one or more times.

Let's start by thinking of dollars as whole numbers and cents as one type of decimal. When we think about values less than 1, think about money values less than a dollar.

1 dollar = 10 dimes = 100 pennies, so 1 dime = 1 tenth of a dollar

and 1 penny = 1 hundredth of a dollar.

Since our money system is based on decimals, you should notice a similarity.

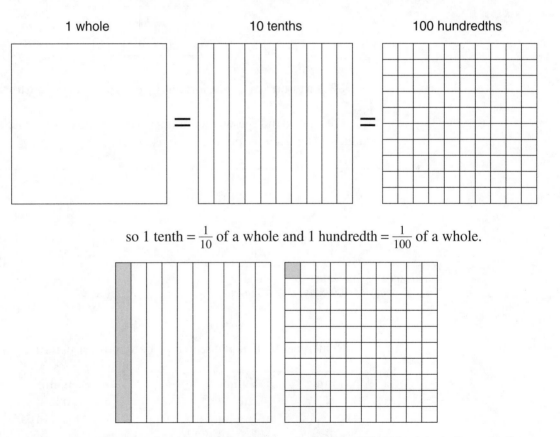

so 1 tenth = $\frac{1}{10}$ of a whole and 1 hundredth = $\frac{1}{100}$ of a whole.

You can describe more precise values by splitting the whole into smaller and smaller parts. Decimals are wholes split into ten parts or multiples of ten parts (100, 1000, 10,000, and so on).

Using money as an example, a quarter is written as 25 cents or $0.25, so 25 **hundredths** written in the form of a decimal is 0.25.

57

Example 1   Write the decimals shown.

7 parts **out of** a whole split into **10** parts = 7 **tenths** = **0.7**

38 parts **out of** a whole split into **100** parts = 38 **hundredths** = **0.38**

We can extend the whole number place value chart to include decimal values. (The decimal point is read as *and.*)

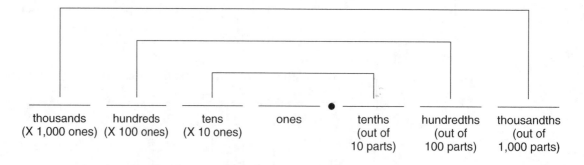

| thousands (X 1,000 ones) | hundreds (X 100 ones) | tens (X 10 ones) | ones | tenths (out of 10 parts) | hundredths (out of 100 parts) | thousandths (out of 1,000 parts) |

Remember that each decimal place stands for part of a whole.

Example	Value	Meaning
0.1	1 tenth	1 out of 10 parts
0.01	1 hundredth	1 out of 100 parts
0.001	1 thousandth	1 out of 1,000 parts
0.0001	1 ten-thousandth	1 out of 10,000 parts
0.00001	1 hundred-thousandth	1 out of 100,000 parts
0.000001	1 millionth	1 out of 1,000,000 parts

Example 2   Use words to express the value of the decimal shown.

2.73 is read *two and seventy-three hundredths.*

To compare two or more values, first compare the whole number digits (the digits to the left of the decimal point) and ignore the decimal digits (to the right). Order the whole number digits. If two or more have the same whole number digits, compare the decimal digits.

Example 3   Which has a greater value: 0.4 or 0.38?

STEP 1   Determine the more precise decimal place.

0.4 has a place value of tenths.
0.38 has a place value of hundredths.
Hundredths is more precise than tenths.

STEP 2   Insert zeros to the right of the decimals as needed so the decimals are written to the same place value.

$$0.4 \qquad = \qquad 0.40$$
4 tenths is the same as 40 hundredths.

STEP 3   Compare the decimals. Which is the larger of the two?

40 hundredths *is greater than* **38** hundredths.
Another way to express this is 0.40 > 0.38 or 0.4 > 0.38.

SUMMARY FOR COMPARING DECIMALS

To compare two or more decimals:

1) Determine the most precise decimal place.

2) Insert zeros to the right of the decimals as needed so the decimals are written to the same place value.

3) Rewrite the decimals using > or < (symbols for *greater than* or *less than*).

EXERCISE 1

Directions: Write the decimals shown or described.

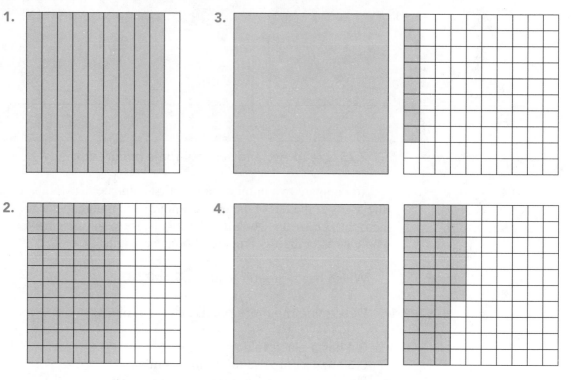

5. 4 out of 10 parts

6. 39 out of 100 parts

7. 821 out of 1,000 parts

8. 5 out of 100 parts

9. 7 out of 1,000 parts

10. 6 wholes and 48 out of 1,000 parts

11. 9 wholes and 81 out of 100 parts

12. 23 wholes and 105 out of 1,000 parts

Directions: Use words to express the value of each decimal.

13. 4.07 _____

14. 15.38 _____

15. 0.169 _____

16. 7.205 _____

17. 9.1 _____

18. 12.86 _____

Directions: Compare each pair of decimals. Write an expression using > or < when comparing.

19. 0.5 ___ 0.8   28. 3.2 ___ 4

20. 0.47 ___ 0.39   29. 0.99 ___ 0.954

21. 4.7 ___ 4.82   30. 8.09 ___ 8.9

22. 5.5 ___ 5.05   31. 6.50 ___ 6.57

23. .001 ___ .010   32. 1.33 ___ 1.303

24. 7.75 ___ .075   33. 9.08 ___ 9.9

25. 3.101 ___ 3.1   34. .03 ___ .25

26. 0.25 ___ 0.257   35. 99.9 ___ 0.999

27. 1.9 ___ 1.999   36. .503 ___ 0.5

Answers are on page 269.

EXERCISE 2

Directions: Write each of the following amounts using a dollar sign and a decimal point. Then round each amount to the nearest dollar.

1. Nine dollars and forty-two cents   _____

2. Nineteen dollars and three quarters   _____

3. Forty-three dollars and five dimes   _____

4. Five quarters, a dime, and six pennies   _____

5. Two ten-dollar bills and eight dimes   _____

Answers are on page 269.

Rounding Decimals

Decimals are rounded just as whole numbers are; however, when an amount of money is rounded, the value is usually rounded up to the next nearest cent.

Example 1   Round 1.537 to the nearest whole number; round 1.537 to the nearest tenth; round 1.537 to the nearest hundredth.

   STEP 1   Identify the place-value digit to be rounded.

Nearest one	Nearest tenth	Nearest hundredth
1.537	1.537	1.537
↑	↑	↑
Digit to be rounded	Digit to be rounded	Digit to be rounded

   STEP 2   Look at the digit immediately to the right of the value to be rounded. If this digit is 5 or greater, round *up* to the next higher digit. If this digit is less than 5, round *down*. The digits to the right of the rounded digit become 0 (if they are part of the whole number) or are eliminated (if they are part of the decimal).

Nearest one	Nearest tenth	Nearest hundredth
1.537	1.537	1.537
↑	↑	↑
Round 1 up to 2.	The 5 stays as a 5.	Round 3 up to 4.
1.537 rounds up to 2.	1.537 rounds down to 1.5.	1.537 rounds up to 1.54.

Example 2   While Eric was waiting in line at the store, he computed the sales tax on the items he bought. His calculator displayed the figure 2.0830. How much tax did he pay?

   STEP 1   Look at the first digit to the right of the hundredths place. If it is greater than zero, round the decimal to the next higher hundredth (or cent).

   STEP 2   Write the calculator display as dollars and cents.

$$2.0830 \rightarrow \$2.09$$

SUMMARY FOR ROUNDING DECIMALS

To round decimal values:

1) For money, round up to the nearest cent.

2) For other decimals, round as you would whole numbers.

Example 3   The ad shown at the right appeared in a local newspaper. What is the unit price of the markers?

3 markers / $4

The price of one item is its **unit price.** To find the unit price of an item, divide the total price by the number of items. In this case, divide $4 by 3. Since $4 is the same as 400 cents, divide 400 by 3. $400 \div 3 = 133$ r1. If the store sells one marker, the price is rounded up to 134 cents, or $1.34.

EXERCISE 3

Directions: Round each decimal.

		Nearest whole	Nearest tenth	Nearest hundredth
1.	5.892	a. _____	b. _____	c. _____
2.	20.492	a. _____	b. _____	c. _____
3.	1.038	a. _____	b. _____	c. _____
4.	6.705	a. _____	b. _____	c. _____

Directions: Round the following amounts to the nearest cent.

5. $1.333

6. 28.7¢

7. $68.5409

8. $0.815

9. $3.739

10. 53.19¢

Directions: Find the unit price for each situation.

11. 5 notebook folders for $1

12. 6 pencils for 49 cents

13. 3 kiwis for $1

14. 3 packs of film for $9.49

15. 12-pack spring water for $8.99

16. a dozen doughnuts for $2.52

Answers are on page 269.

EXERCISE 4

Directions: Solve each problem.

1. One inch equals 2.54 centimeters. What is this length to the nearest tenth of a centimeter?

2. A $\frac{3}{8}$-inch drill bit has a diameter of 0.375 inch. What is the diameter to the nearest hundredth of an inch? What is its diameter to the nearest tenth of an inch?

3. A 12-can pack of soft drinks is on sale for $3.99. What is the price of each soft drink when you buy 12 of them?

4. Ten packs of gum usually cost $1.39 but are on sale for 99 cents. How much does a person save on each pack by buying the gum on sale? How much is saved altogether by buying ten packs of gum on sale?

Answers are on page 269.

Adding and Subtracting Decimals

Add or subtract decimals the same way you add or subtract whole numbers. Look at the following example.

Example 1   Add three quarters and six dimes.

STEP 1   Change each amount of money to cents.

3 quarters → 3 × 25 cents → 75 cents or $0.75
6 dimes → 6 × 10 cents → 60 cents or $0.60

STEP 2   Add the cents.

$$
\begin{array}{r}
75 \text{ cents} \\
+ \ 60 \text{ cents} \\
\hline
135 \text{ cents}
\end{array}
\quad \text{or} \quad
\begin{array}{r}
\$0.75 \\
+ \ \$0.60 \\
\hline
\$1.35
\end{array}
$$

Example 2   Add 3.4, 17.062, and 0.85.

STEP 1   Write the numbers vertically, aligning the decimal points and each place value.

tens	ones	tenths	hundredths	thousandths
	3	4		
1	7	0	6	2
	0	8	5	

STEP 2   Starting at the right, add as you do whole numbers. (Insert zeros to help you align places if necessary.)

$$
\begin{array}{r}
3.4\mathbf{00} \\
17.062 \\
0.85\mathbf{0} \\
\hline
21.312
\end{array}
$$

Move the decimal point straight down.

TIP

When adding or subtracting decimals, write the numbers vertically, align the decimal points, and insert any necessary zeros.

Example 3   Subtract 3.87 from 10.

STEP 1   Write the subtraction problem.

$$\begin{array}{r} 10 \\ -\ 3.87 \end{array}$$ Remember to align digits.

STEP 2   Insert a decimal point and zeros if necessary after a whole number. Subtract.

$$\begin{array}{r} 10.00 \\ -\ 3.87 \end{array} \rightarrow \begin{array}{r} 9.90 \\ -\ 3.87 \\ \hline 6.13 \end{array}$$ Think of 10 ones as 9 ones, 9 tenths, and 10 hundredths.

SUMMARY FOR ADDING OR SUBTRACTING DECIMALS

To add or subtract decimals:

1) Line up the decimal points and all digits. If a number does not have a decimal point, add one at the far right. Add zeros to make subtraction (or addition) easier.

2) Add or subtract as with whole numbers.

3) Bring down the decimal point in the final answer.

EXERCISE 5

Directions: Add the following amounts of money.

1. Three dimes and six nickels

2. Two quarters and nine nickels

3. Eight dimes and one quarter

4. Three quarters, two dimes, and seven nickels

Directions: Add the following decimals.

5. 0.3
   + 0.6

8. 17.35
   + 50.927

11. 6.8
    14.23
   + 20.079

14. 885.61
     37.0
   + 101.2

6. $0.23
   + $0.68

9. 0.18
    8.921
   + 0.58

12. 54.499
     8.67
   + 39.6

15. 5.8
   + 0.5

7. 1.09
   + 0.735

10. 15.7
     7.682
   + 3.09

13. 9.05
     .63
   + .01

16. $0.75
     $1.33
   + $ .06

Directions: Subtract the following decimals.

17. 9.7
   − 2.1

19. 3.985
   − 0.007

21. 42
   − 36.498

23. $27
   − $ 5.72

18. 42.16
   − 9.7

20. $8.10
   − $0.73

22. 9.8
   − 1.032

24. 500.7
   − 138.459

Answers are on page 269.

EXERCISE 6

Directions: Solve each problem.

1. In 1992, the unemployment rate for single men 16 years of age was 13.1 percent. If the unemployment rate for single women was 2.4 percent lower, what was that rate?

2. The number of motor vehicle registrations in Texas in 1992 was 8.655 million for automobiles, 4.057 million for trucks and buses, and 0.19 million for motorcycles. Find the total number of registrations.

3. Regular unleaded gas is selling for $1.269 per gallon. What is the price to the nearest cent per gallon?

4. Colleen's share of the bill for dinner was $12.93. She left a $2 tip. She spent $6.75 to watch a movie. How much did she spend?

Directions: Use your calculator to solve these problems.

5. 31.2 – 16.426

6. 136.486 + 93.947

7. 2,487.93 – 346.873

8. 34.876 + 30.94 + 824.73

9. Tasha's checking account has $148.26 currently. If she adds her weekly wage of $286.37, her tax refund of $156.82, and a check for $37.99 from a friend, what is the new balance in her checking account?

10. How much change from a $50 bill would Jorge have after purchasing gas for $29.36?

11. Sam paid the following bills: $39.75 for gas, $42.31 for electricity, $11.98 for water, and $26.73 for phone service. How much did he pay for these four bills?

12. The grain company had 428.65 tons of corn available for sale. During one week, 386.74 tons were sold. How many tons were still at the grain company?

Answers are on page 269.

Multiplying Decimals

Multiply decimals the same way you multiply whole numbers. You must be careful to put the decimal point in the correct place in the product. To do this, add the number of decimal places in each number being multiplied. Starting at the far right of the product, count that number of decimal places to the left, and insert the decimal point. Look at the following examples.

Example 1   Find the value of 15 quarters by multiplying.

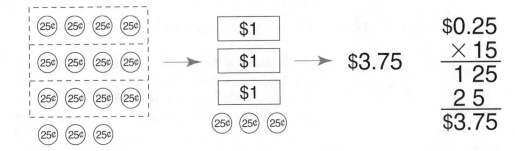

$$\begin{array}{r} \$0.25 \\ \times\, 15 \\ \hline 1\,25 \\ 2\,5 \\ \hline \$3.75 \end{array}$$

Example 2   Multiply 2.3 and 1.2.

STEP 1   Count the number of decimal places in the original numbers.

2.3 has **1** number to the right of the decimal place.
1.2 has **1** number to the right of the decimal place.
The product should have **2** (1 + 1) decimal places.

STEP 2   Multiply as whole numbers.

STEP 3   Start at the far right of the
product. Move 2 places to the
left. Insert the decimal point
between the 2 and the 7.

$$
\begin{array}{r}
2.3 \\
\times\, 1.2 \\
\hline
4\,6 \\
2\,3 \\
\hline
2.76
\end{array}
$$

STEP 4   Check your answer by estimating the product.

2.3 is about 2. 1.2 is about 1. The product of 2.3 and 1.2 should be
slightly greater than 2, so 2.76 seems reasonable. The answer
checks.

Example 3   Multiply 3.7 and 0.15. (0.15 can be written simply as .15.)

STEP 1   Count the number of decimal places in the original problem.

3.7 has **1** decimal place (1 number to the right of the decimal point).
0.15 has **2** decimal places (2 numbers to the right of the decimal
point). The final product will have **3** (1 + 2) decimal places.

STEP 2   Write the problem and multiply
as with whole numbers.

STEP 3   Starting at the far right (since 555
could be written as 555.), move the
point **3** places (from Step 1) to the
left.

$$
\begin{array}{r}
3.7 \\
\times\, .15 \\
\hline
185 \\
37 \\
\hline
555
\end{array}
$$

$3.7 \times .15 = .555$ or 0.555

STEP 4   Check by estimating the product.

3.7 is about 4. Since multiplication
is repeated addition, add .15 four
times. Since .60 is close to .555 (the
product), the answer checks out.

$$
\begin{array}{r}
.15 \\
.15 \\
.15 \\
+\, .15 \\
\hline
.60
\end{array}
$$

SUMMARY FOR MULTIPLYING DECIMALS

To multiply decimals:

1) Count the total number of decimal places in the original problem.

2) Multiply as with whole numbers.

3) Starting at the far right of the product, count the required number of places to the left, and insert the decimal point.

EXERCISE 7

Directions: Find the value of the following amounts.

1. 23 dimes

2. 40 quarters

3. 350 pennies

4. 75 nickels

5. 18 nickels

6. 11 half dollars

7. 11 dimes

8. 8 half dollars

Directions: Find each product.

9. $.5 \times .3$

10. 1.4×1.2

11. 1.5×2.1

12. 3×6.8

13. $.9 \times 1.5$

14. 3×8.72

15. $.25 \times 1.3$

16. 6.9×1.05

17. $4.7 \times .31$

18. $5.37 \times .22$

19. $\$4.35 \times 9$

20. $.985 \times 2.1$

Directions: Use your calculator to solve each problem.

21. 3.8726×4.98

22. 479.38×6.493

23. $98.76 \times .463$

24. Chen wanted to buy 2.5 pounds of ground meat. If the cost is $2.39 per pound, how much will he pay for 2.5 pounds?

25. Jana wants to purchase new towels. If the towels cost $5.39 each, how much will she pay for 6 new towels?

26. The average annual snowfall in Jackson, Mississippi, is 1.2 inches. Madison, Wisconsin, averages 34 times this amount. First estimate its average annual snowfall. Then find the exact average based on this information.

27. In 1973, leaded regular gasoline averaged 38.8 cents per gallon. In 1990, unleaded regular gasoline sold for 3 times this price. What was the 1990 average gasoline price?

Answers are on page 270.

Dividing Decimals

Divide decimals the same way you divide whole numbers. When the divisor is a decimal, however, move the decimal point to the right, writing the divisor as a whole number. Next, move the decimal point in the dividend the same number of places as in the divisor. Put a decimal point in the quotient directly above the dividend's decimal point and divide. Look at the following example.

Example 1   Divide 17.5 by 1.25.

STEP 1   Move the decimal point in the divisor in order to make it a whole number. In this case, move the decimal point **2 places to the right.**

STEP 2   At the same time, move the decimal point in the dividend the same number of places as in Step 1. Insert zeros if necessary.

$$1.25\overline{)17.50}$$

STEP 3   Insert a decimal point in the quotient directly above the "final" decimal point position of the dividend.

$$\begin{array}{r} 14. \\ 125\overline{)1750.} \\ \underline{125} \\ 500 \\ \underline{500} \\ 0 \end{array}$$

STEP 4   Divide as with whole numbers.

STEP 5   Check your answer by multiplying the quotient (answer) by the original divisor. This product should be the original dividend.

$$\begin{array}{r} 14 \leftarrow \text{quotient} \\ \times\ 1.25 \leftarrow \text{divisor} \\ \hline 17.50 \leftarrow \text{dividend} \end{array}$$

Example 2   Yumi and two of her friends earned $22.95 one Saturday washing cars. If they split the money equally, how much did each one receive?

STEP 1   Divide the dollars equally. Each friend receives $7 with $1 plus the original 95 cents left over.

STEP 2 The $1.95 left over can be changed into 19 dimes and 1 nickel. Now divide 19 by 3. Each friend receives 6 dimes, or 60 cents with 1 dime and the nickel left over.

```
        $ 7.6        ← (6 dimes)
    3)$22.95
      21
      195
      18
      15   ($ .15 left)
```

STEP 3 If we change the dime and nickel to 15 pennies, we can now divide by 3. Each friend receives 5 pennies (plus the 7 dollars and 6 dimes they received earlier). Each friend receives $7.65.

```
        $ 7.65       ← (5 pennies)
    3)$22.95
      21
      19
      18
      15
      15
       0   (0 cents left)
```

STEP 4 Check your answer by finding an estimate using compatible numbers.

Since $24 divided by 3 is $8, the three friends should each receive about $8. The quotient, $7.65, rounded to the nearest dollar is $8 (your estimate), so your answer is reasonable.

SUMMARY FOR DIVIDING DECIMALS

To divide decimals:

1) If the divisor is a decimal, move the decimal point to the right to rewrite the divisor as a whole number.

2) Move the decimal point in the dividend the same number of places as the divisor's decimal point was moved. Add zeros as needed.

3) Insert a decimal point in the quotient directly above the new decimal point in the dividend.

4) Divide as with whole numbers.

EXERCISE 8

Directions: Divide.

1. $3\overline{)4.8}$ 5. $1.6\overline{)4.8}$ 9. $8\overline{).72}$ 13. $57.5 \div 2.5$

2. $.3\overline{)48}$ 6. $1.6\overline{)48}$ 10. $.07\overline{)49}$ 14. $9.72 \div 1.2$

3. $.3\overline{).48}$ 7. $.7\overline{)42}$ 11. $.3\overline{)1.47}$ 15. $315 \div 4.5$

4. $.3\overline{)4.8}$ 8. $.9\overline{)5.4}$ 12. $.3\overline{)1.44}$ 16. $84.8 \div .53$

Directions: Use your calculator to solve each problem.

17. The average annual precipitation in Fargo, North Dakota is 19.59 inches. However, there is only precipitation about 100 days out of the year. For these days of precipitation, find the average amount of precipitation.

18. In 1993, the third-class, single-piece cost to mail a 14-ounce letter or package was $1.67. About how much was this cost per ounce?

19. The machinist's blueprint showed that a key should be 2.136 inches long. What is this length to the nearest tenth of an inch? What is this length to the nearest hundredth of an inch?

20. Jennifer can either buy 3 audio tapes for $4.99 or 7 tapes for $5.99. Which is the better buy? Why?

21. According to the U.S. Bureau of the Census, Phoenix, Arizona had increased its 1980 population of 789,704 by 193,699 people by 1990. How many people lived in this city in 1990?

22. The Moffat Railroad in the Rocky Mountains of Colorado is 6.2 miles long. If the Seikan Railroad is 26.9 miles longer, how long is this Japanese railroad?

Answers are on page 270.

Using a Number Grid with Decimals

Sometimes you will have to place your decimal answer on a number grid.

Example   36.3 + 8.9

Step 1   Line up the decimal points.

Step 2   Add the digits.

$$\begin{array}{r} 36.3 \\ + 8.9 \\ \hline 45.2 \end{array}$$

To write the answer on a grid, write the numbers in the blank boxes at the top of each column. Put the decimal point in a box by itself. Fill in one circle below each box. Fill in the decimal point circle below the decimal point.

EXERCISE 9

Directions: Solve each problem and put your answer on the number grid.

1. 26.35 + 8.8

2. 146.7 – 89.9

3. 48 − 39.7

6. 12.3 × 8.1

4. 6.7 + 9

7. 200 ÷ .8

5. 4.2 × 3

8. 1.44 ÷ 1.6

Answers are on page 270.

Decimals Review

Directions: For questions 1–10, answer each question. Show your work at the right.

1. What digit is in the ten-thousandths place in the number 45,832.09617?

2. Which has the greatest value: 0.9, 0.89, or 0.859?

3. What is the value of five ten-dollar bills, seven one-dollar bills, six quarters, and nine nickels?

4. Round 97.635 to
   a) the nearest one
   b) the nearest tenth
   c) the nearest hundredth

5. Determine the unit price of 10 items that are on sale for $38.92.

6. Find the sum of 53.9, 8.25, and .294.

7. Find the difference between 45 and 9.82.

8. What is the product of 3.45 and .9?

9. What is .75 divided by 1.5?

10. What is the quotient of 75 divided by .15?

Directions: Questions 11–26 include whole numbers as well as decimals. Choose the correct answer to each problem. Remember the problem-solving skills you have learned.

11. A baseball player had a .328 batting average at the end of the first month. At the end of the second month, the batting average was .382. How had the batting average changed?

   (1) decreased by .54
   (2) decreased by .066
   (3) increased by .054
   (4) increased by .54
   (5) increased by .066

12. The rates for parking a car at the airport are given below. How much would it cost to park the car for six hours?

   Airport Parking Rates
   Hourly rate: $1.75
   Daily rate: $16
   Weekly rate: $100

   (1) $16
   (2) $96
   (3) $ 2.67
   (4) $16.67
   (5) $10.50

13. Enrique uses pieces of solid wire to make jewelry. He wants to cut a piece of wire 23.2 centimeters long into 8 equal parts. How many centimeters long would each part be?

   (1) 31.2
   (2) 2.9
   (3) 15.2
   (4) 3.9
   (5) Not enough information is given.

14. If you want to check your answer to problem 13 by estimating, how could you find a reasonable estimate?

   (1) Multiply 3 cm by 8.
   (2) Divide 24 cm by 8.
   (3) Divide 23.2 cm by 10.
   (4) all of the above
   (5) none of the above

15. Enrique has another piece of wire that is 127.4 centimeters long. If he cuts off a piece of wire that is 32.8 centimeters, how many centimeters long is the piece that is left?

   (1) 105.4
   (2) 160.21
   (3) 9.46
   (4) 95.4
   (5) none of the above

16. Karen drove 385 miles on 20 gallons of gas. How many miles per gallon did she average?

   (1) about 20
   (2) 19.25
   (3) 17.7
   (4) 1 and 2 are both acceptable answers.
   (5) 1 and 3 are both acceptable answers.

17. Karen's friend Richard averages 28.5 miles per gallon. How many miles can he drive using 17.4 gallons?

   (1) 11.1
   (2) 45.9
   (3) 285
   (4) 495.9
   (5) none of the above

18. Use the drawing to find the length, in inches, of bolt C.

(1) .246
(2) .356
(3) .754
(4) 1.754
(5) .535

Directions: Use your calculator to solve these problems.

19. 16.27 + 9.386

20. 4,276.3 – 2,947.86

21. 327.55 × 4.36

22. 96 ÷ .48

23. Eva spent $16.49 on a T-shirt and $32.99 on a pair of slacks. How much change will she receive from a hundred dollar bill?

24. If Max bought a pound of fruit for $1.29, how much would he pay for 1.34 pounds?

Directions: Solve each problem and write the answer on the number grid.

25. If Kyle bought 12 gallons of gas for $19.20, how much is the gas per gallon?

26. Cable television costs $38.95 per month. How much will the Avia family spend for cable TV during a 2-month period?

Answers are on page 272.

Chapter 5

Fractions

Understanding Fractions

Decimals involve any number of parts out of a whole made up of 10, 100, 1000, or so on. Fractions are another way of showing parts of a whole. A fraction is made up of two numbers. For example, the fraction $\frac{3}{4}$ has a **numerator** of 3 and a **denominator** of 4. The numerator indicates the number of parts. The denominator refers to the number of parts in the whole.

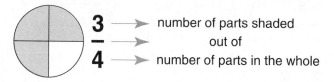

$$\frac{3}{4}$$ → number of parts shaded
→ out of
→ number of parts in the whole

Decimals can be written as fractions. For example, 0.7 means 7 tenths or 7 parts out of 10 parts, so $0.7 = \frac{7}{10}$. This is expressed in the diagram at the right.

The whole number 1 can be expressed as any number divided by itself, such as $\frac{12}{12}$, $\frac{9}{9}$, $\frac{16}{16}$, or $\frac{100}{100}$.

Values between two whole numbers are **mixed numbers,** or the combination of a whole number and a fraction. For example, $2\frac{3}{5}$ is the same as $1 + 1 + \frac{3}{5}$ or $\frac{5}{5} + \frac{5}{5} + \frac{3}{5}$. From the diagram shown, we see that $2\frac{3}{5}$ is the same as $\frac{13}{5}$.

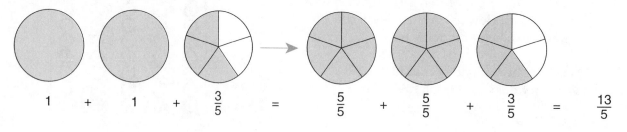

$$1 \quad + \quad 1 \quad + \quad \frac{3}{5} \quad = \quad \frac{5}{5} \quad + \quad \frac{5}{5} \quad + \quad \frac{3}{5} \quad = \quad \frac{13}{5}$$

A fraction with a numerator equal to or greater than its denominator is an **improper fraction.**

Example 1   Rewrite $\frac{23}{6}$ as a whole or mixed number.

STEP 1   First divide the numerator by the denominator.

$$\text{denominator} \rightarrow 6\overline{)23} \leftarrow \text{numerator}$$
$$\begin{array}{r} 3\,r5 \\ \underline{18} \\ 5 \end{array}$$

STEP 2   Make the amount left over a fraction by writing the remainder as the numerator and the divisor as the denominator.

$$\frac{23}{6} \rightarrow 3\,r5 \rightarrow 3\frac{5}{6}$$

STEP 3   Check the answer. One way to check it is to draw a diagram of 3 wholes divided into sixths with an additional 5 sixths. Then add the total number of sixths.

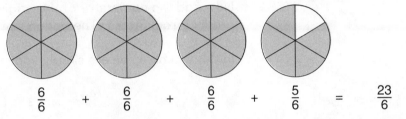

$$\frac{6}{6} \quad + \quad \frac{6}{6} \quad + \quad \frac{6}{6} \quad + \quad \frac{5}{6} \quad = \quad \frac{23}{6}$$

Another way to check the answer is to multiply the whole number by the denominator of the mixed number answer and then add the numerator. This number should be the same as the numerator of the original improper fraction.

$$3\frac{5}{6} \rightarrow \frac{3 \times 6 + 5}{6} \rightarrow \frac{23}{6}$$

SUMMARY FOR CHANGING IMPROPER FRACTIONS TO WHOLE OR MIXED NUMBERS

To change an improper fraction to a whole or mixed number:

1) Divide the numerator of the improper fraction (the dividend) by its denominator (the divisor).

2) If the quotient has a remainder, the improper fraction is rewritten as a mixed number with the remainder becoming the numerator and the divisor becoming the denominator.

Example 2   Rewrite $4\frac{1}{3}$ as an improper fraction.

STEP 1   Multiply the whole number by the denominator.

In this case we multiply 4 by 3 because 4 wholes (or ones) are split into thirds.

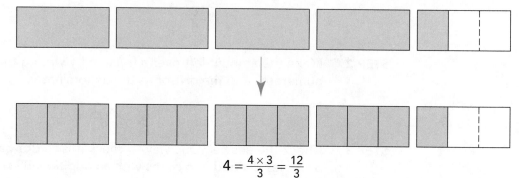

$$4 = \frac{4 \times 3}{3} = \frac{12}{3}$$

STEP 2   Now add the numerator of the original mixed number to the product from Step 1. The denominator stays the same.

In this example, we are simply adding 1 third to 12 thirds.

$$4\frac{1}{3} = \frac{12}{3} + \frac{1}{3} = \frac{13}{3}$$

**SUMMARY FOR CHANGING MIXED NUMBERS
TO IMPROPER FRACTIONS**

To change a mixed number to an improper fraction:

1) Multiply the whole number by the denominator.

2) Add the numerator. This result becomes the numerator of the improper fraction. The denominator is the same as that of the mixed number.

EXERCISE 1

Directions: Rewrite each improper fraction as a whole or mixed number.

1. $\frac{15}{3}$ 4. $\frac{33}{5}$ 7. $\frac{85}{9}$

2. $\frac{21}{4}$ 5. $\frac{41}{6}$ 8. $\frac{99}{8}$

3. $\frac{17}{3}$ 6. $\frac{38}{7}$ 9. $\frac{56}{6}$

Directions: Rewrite each mixed number as an improper fraction.

10. $3\frac{5}{8}$ 13. $4\frac{3}{4}$ 16. $10\frac{11}{12}$

11. $6\frac{2}{3}$ 14. $7\frac{5}{6}$ 17. $9\frac{1}{10}$

12. $4\frac{1}{8}$ 15. $9\frac{3}{5}$ 18. $12\frac{4}{7}$

Directions: Solve each problem.

19. At Anthony's Pizza by the Slice, pizzas are cut into eight slices. If five pizzas are taken out of the oven and then sliced, how many slices are ready to be sold?

20. Sari has $\frac{17}{2}$ yards of material. Does she have more or less than 8 yards of cloth?

21. Jane wants to double a recipe that calls for $1\frac{1}{3}$ cups of flour. How much flour will she need?

22. Pi is the ratio of the circumference of a circle to the diameter. Pi is expressed as $\frac{22}{7}$. If expressed as a mixed number, what would Pi be?

23. Riley cut a board 8 feet long into three equal pieces. How long was each piece?

24. It took Pam 100 minutes to drive to the nearest shopping center. Change the time to hours. (1 hour = 60 minutes)

Answers are on page 272.

Equivalent Fractions

Equivalent fractions are fractions that have the same value. Any fraction multiplied by some form of 1 will yield an equivalent fraction. Look at the illustration below.

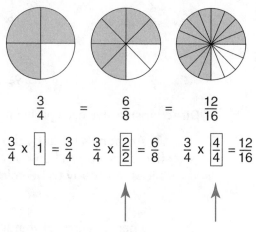

$$\frac{3}{4} \quad = \quad \frac{6}{8} \quad = \quad \frac{12}{16}$$

$$\frac{3}{4} \times \boxed{1} = \frac{3}{4} \qquad \frac{3}{4} \times \boxed{\frac{2}{2}} = \frac{6}{8} \qquad \frac{3}{4} \times \boxed{\frac{4}{4}} = \frac{12}{16}$$

Same as 1   Same as 1

Example 1   Name several fractions equivalent to $\frac{4}{5}$.

Multiply $\frac{4}{5}$ by different forms of 1.

$$\frac{4}{5} \times \frac{4}{4} = \frac{16}{20} \qquad \frac{4}{5} \times \frac{20}{20} = \frac{80}{100} \qquad \frac{4}{5} \times \frac{50}{50} = \frac{200}{250}$$

$$\frac{4}{5} = \frac{16}{20} = \frac{80}{100} = \frac{200}{250}$$

At times we want to identify a specific equivalent fraction.

Example 2   What fraction having a denominator of 12 is equivalent to $\frac{21}{36}$?

Multiply or divide by a form of 1. Think: "36 divided by what number is 12?" Since $36 \div 3 = 12$, we can divide both the numerator and the denominator by 3 ($\frac{3}{3} = 1$).

$$\frac{21}{36} = \frac{?}{12}$$

$$\frac{21 \div 3}{36 \div 3} = \frac{7}{12}$$

A fraction is **in lowest terms** if the numerator and denominator cannot be divided evenly (remainder of zero) by any whole number other than 1. Since fractions can be written as many equivalent fractions, writing a fraction in lowest terms makes comparing answers easier.

Example 3   Rewrite $\frac{20}{24}$ as a fraction in lowest terms.

Divide the numerator and denominator by a number or numbers until it can no longer be divided.

$$\frac{20}{24} = \frac{20 \div 2}{24 \div 2} = \frac{10 \div 2}{12 \div 2} = \frac{5}{6} \text{ or}$$

$$\frac{20}{24} = \frac{20 \div 4}{24 \div 4} = \frac{5}{6}$$

> **TIP**
>
> When rewriting a fraction in lowest terms, try to identify the greatest number by which both the numerator and denominator are evenly divisible.

EXERCISE 2

Directions: Write three equivalent fractions for each given fraction.

1. $\frac{3}{8} =$ _____ = _____ = _____

2. $\frac{1}{6} =$ _____ = _____ = _____

3. $\frac{7}{10} =$ _____ = _____ = _____

4. $\frac{11}{12} =$ _____ = _____ = _____

Directions: Write the missing numerator for each equation.

5. $\frac{15}{25} = \frac{}{5}$

6. $\frac{20}{60} = \frac{}{3}$

7. $\frac{28}{32} = \frac{}{8}$

8. $\frac{23}{25} = \frac{}{100}$

9. $\frac{9}{10} = \frac{}{30}$

10. $\frac{16}{28} = \frac{}{7}$

11. $\frac{96}{100} = \frac{}{50}$

12. $\frac{88}{96} = \frac{}{24}$

13. $\frac{45}{80} = \frac{}{16}$

Answers are on page 272.

Changing Fractions to Decimals

Often a fraction has to be changed to a decimal or a decimal to a fraction.

Example 1 Write $\frac{5}{8}$ as a decimal.

To change $\frac{5}{8}$ to a decimal, divide the numerator by the denominator. Add a decimal point and zeros as needed.

$$\begin{array}{r} 0.625 \\ 8\overline{)5.000} \\ \underline{4\,8} \\ 20 \\ \underline{16} \\ 40 \\ \underline{40} \\ 0 \end{array}$$

$\frac{5}{8} = 0.625$ or $.625$

SUMMARY FOR CHANGING FRACTIONS TO DECIMALS

To change a fraction to a decimal:

1) Divide the numerator of the fraction by its denominator.

2) Insert a decimal point after the numerator, and add additional zeros if necessary. If the fraction is improper, the decimal will be 1 (when the numerator is equal to the denominator) or greater than 1 (when the numerator is greater than the denominator).

Sometimes no matter how many zeros you add in the dividend, the answer either does not end or repeats one or more digits (called a **repeating decimal**).

Example 2 Rewrite $\frac{7}{9}$ as a decimal.

$$\begin{array}{r} 0.777 \\ 9\overline{)7.000} \\ \underline{6\,3} \\ 70 \\ \underline{63} \\ 70 \\ \underline{63} \\ 7 \end{array}$$

Divide the numerator by the denominator. Since the numbers keep repeating, round the answer to a certain place (usually rounding to the nearest hundredth is adequate). Remember that this means you must divide to the thousandths place.

$\frac{7}{9} = 0.777 \ldots$ (symbol for continues in this pattern) $\rightarrow 0.78$

EXERCISE 3

Directions: Rewrite each fraction as a decimal.

1. $\frac{3}{12}$ 4. $\frac{12}{16}$ 7. $\frac{4}{32}$ 10. $\frac{8}{11}$

2. $\frac{7}{8}$ 5. $\frac{33}{50}$ 8. $\frac{17}{40}$ 11. $\frac{7}{15}$

3. $\frac{22}{8}$ 6. $\frac{1}{8}$ 9. $\frac{3}{8}$ 12. $\frac{4}{5}$

Answers are on page 273.

Changing Decimals to Fractions

Sometimes a decimal has to be changed to a fraction.

Example 1 Write .6 as a fraction in lowest terms.

To change .6 to a fraction, write the decimal as a fraction with a denominator which is a multiple of 10. (10, 100, 1000, . . .) $\frac{6}{10}$

You can also write the decimal as you would read it out loud: $\frac{6}{10}$

Then reduce $\frac{6}{10}$ to lowest terms.

$\frac{6 \div 2}{10 \div 2} = \frac{3}{5}$

$.6 = \frac{3}{5}$

Example 2 Write 1.76 as a mixed number in lowest terms.

$$1.76 = 1\frac{76}{100} = \frac{176 \div 4}{100 \div 4} = 1\frac{19}{25}$$

SUMMARY FOR CHANGING FRACTIONS TO DECIMALS

To change a decimal to a fraction or mixed number:

1) Write the decimal as a fraction (or mixed number) with a denominator having a multiple of 10.

2) Write the fraction in lowest terms.

EXERCISE 4

Directions: Rewrite each decimal as a fraction or mixed number.

1. .35	4. 2.4	7. 1.78	10. 7.0125
2. .068	5. 6.52	8. 9.045	11. 4.920
3. 0.75	6. 5.47	9. 1.925	12. 8.5

Answers are on page 273.

Choosing a Common Denominator

Before adding or subtracting fractions or mixed numbers, first find a common denominator. Usually the least or lowest common denominator is used.

Example   Find equivalent fractions for $\frac{2}{3}$ and $\frac{3}{4}$ using a common denominator.

STEP 1   Identify the given denominators.

The denominators for $\frac{2}{3}$ and $\frac{3}{4}$ are 3 (or thirds) and 4 (or fourths).

STEP 2   Determine a common denominator by listing some multiples of each denominator.

Multiples of 3: **3** (3×1), **6** (3×2), **9** (3×3), **<u>12</u>** (3×4)
15 (3×5), **18** (3×6), **21** (3×7), **<u>24</u>** (3×8)
Multiples of 4: **4** (4×1), **8** (4×2), **<u>12</u>** (4×3), **16** (4×4)
20 (4×5), **<u>24</u>** (4×6), **28** (4×7), **32** (4×8)

STEP 3   Write equivalent fractions using any of the common denominators (12, 24, 36, and so on).

$$\frac{2}{3} = \frac{?}{12} \rightarrow \frac{2 \times 4}{3 \times 4} = \frac{8}{12}$$

$$\frac{3}{4} = \frac{?}{12} \rightarrow \frac{3 \times 3}{4 \times 3} = \frac{9}{12}$$

SUMMARY FOR CHOOSING A COMMON DENOMINATOR

To determine a common denominator of two or more fractions:

1) Write multiples of each denominator, and identify one or more common multiples.

2) Write equivalent fractions using one of the common multiples.

EXERCISE 5

Directions: List multiples for each set of numbers. Then identify two common multiples.

1. Multiples of 6: _____

   Multiples of 5: _____

   Common multiples: _____

2. Multiples of 8: _____

   Multiples of 12: _____

   Common multiples: _____

3. Multiples of 9: _____

   Multiples of 36: _____

   Common multiples: _____

4. Multiples of 7: _____

   Multiples of 21: _____

   Common multiples: _____

Directions: Write equivalent fractions using a common denominator of each set of fractions.

5. $\frac{1}{2} = \frac{}{8}$

   $\frac{3}{8} = \frac{}{8}$

6. $\frac{4}{5} = \frac{}{15}$

   $\frac{1}{3} = \frac{}{15}$

7. $\frac{7}{9} = \frac{}{36}$

   $\frac{3}{12} = \frac{}{36}$

8. $\frac{1}{2} = \frac{}{6}$

   $\frac{2}{3} = \frac{}{6}$

9. $\frac{5}{6} = -$

   $\frac{11}{30} = -$

10. $\frac{7}{10} = -$

    $\frac{19}{45} = -$

11. $\frac{8}{15} = -$

    $\frac{13}{18} = -$

12. $\frac{5}{9} = -$

    $\frac{3}{10} = -$

13. $\frac{15}{16} = -$

    $\frac{21}{40} = -$

14. $\frac{13}{20} = -$

    $\frac{19}{45} = -$

15. $\frac{17}{25} = -$

    $\frac{5}{8} = -$

16. $\frac{1}{15} = -$

    $\frac{1}{20} = -$

Answers are on page 273.

Comparing and Ordering Fractions

We often want or need to compare fractions. When we have more than two fractions involved, we usually list the fractions in order from least to greatest or greatest to least.

The marks of a ruler or yardstick indicate fractions ordered from left (least) to right (greatest) as shown below.

A number line can be used to help compare or order fractions.

The fractions $1\frac{2}{5}$ and $\frac{9}{5}$ can be compared easily. Since $1\frac{2}{5}$ (or $\frac{7}{5}$) is to the left of $\frac{9}{5}$, $1\frac{2}{5}$ is *less than* $\frac{9}{5}$. This can be written as $1\frac{2}{5} < \frac{9}{5}$.

To compare $\frac{7}{10}$ and $\frac{3}{5}$, a number line showing fifths and tenths must be drawn.

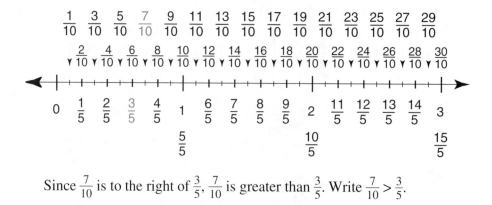

Since $\frac{7}{10}$ is to the right of $\frac{3}{5}$, $\frac{7}{10}$ is greater than $\frac{3}{5}$. Write $\frac{7}{10} > \frac{3}{5}$.

Example 1   Compare $1\frac{6}{10}$ and $1\frac{4}{5}$.

Draw a number line with both fifths and tenths or draw two diagrams.

$1\frac{6}{10}$

$\frac{1}{10}$ $\frac{3}{10}$ $\frac{5}{10}$ $\frac{7}{10}$ $\frac{9}{10}$ $1\frac{1}{10}$ $1\frac{3}{10}$ $1\frac{5}{10}$ $1\frac{7}{10}$ $1\frac{9}{10}$ $2\frac{1}{10}$ $2\frac{3}{10}$ $2\frac{5}{10}$ $2\frac{7}{10}$ $2\frac{9}{10}$

0 $\frac{1}{5}$ $\frac{2}{5}$ $\frac{3}{5}$ $\frac{4}{5}$ 1 $1\frac{1}{5}$ $1\frac{2}{5}$ $1\frac{3}{5}$ $1\frac{4}{5}$ 2 $2\frac{1}{5}$ $2\frac{2}{5}$ $2\frac{3}{5}$ $2\frac{4}{5}$ 3

Since $1\frac{4}{5}$ is greater than $1\frac{6}{10}$, or $1\frac{4}{5}$ is to the right of $1\frac{6}{10}$, write $1\frac{4}{5} > 1\frac{6}{10}$.

Example 2   Compare $\frac{5}{6}$ and $\frac{7}{8}$.

STEP 1   Identify a common denominator for the two fractions. The denominators of $\frac{5}{6}$ and $\frac{7}{8}$ are 6 and 8. List the multiples of 6 and 8 until a **common multiple** is identified.

Multiples of 6: **6** (6×1), **12** (6×2), **18** (6×3), **24** (6×4)

Multiples of 8: **8** (8×1), **16** (8×2), **24** (8×3)

STEP 2   Rewrite $\frac{5}{6}$ and $\frac{7}{8}$ as fractions having denominators of 24 (the common multiple).

$$\frac{5}{6} = \frac{?}{24} \rightarrow \frac{5 \times 4}{6 \times 4} = \frac{20}{24}$$

$$\frac{7}{8} = \frac{?}{24} \rightarrow \frac{7 \times 3}{8 \times 3} = \frac{21}{24}$$

STEP 3   Compare the numerators.

Since $20 < 21$, $\frac{20}{24} < \frac{21}{24}$ and $\frac{5}{6} < \frac{7}{8}$.

EXERCISE 6

Directions: Compare each pair of mixed numbers or fractions using a ruler or a number line. Write a statement using > or <.

1. $\frac{1}{4}$ ____ $\frac{3}{16}$

2. $\frac{5}{8}$ ____ $\frac{11}{16}$

3. $\frac{3}{4}$ ____ $\frac{13}{16}$

4. $1\frac{1}{4}$ ____ $1\frac{1}{8}$

5. $1\frac{4}{5}$ ____ $\frac{8}{5}$

6. $\frac{16}{10}$ ____ $\frac{6}{5}$

Directions: Compare each pair of fractions using common denominators. Then write a statement using > or <.

7. $\frac{3}{8}$ —— $\frac{3}{5}$

8. $\frac{1}{4}$ —— $\frac{1}{6}$

9. $\frac{5}{12}$ —— $\frac{1}{3}$

10. $\frac{13}{16}$ —— $\frac{7}{8}$

11. $\frac{7}{10}$ —— $\frac{7}{9}$

12. $\frac{9}{10}$ —— $\frac{1}{12}$

Answers are on page 273.

Adding and Subtracting Fractions That Have Like Denominators

When adding or subtracting fractions, look to see if the denominators are the same (**like denominators**) or different (**unlike denominators**).

<u>Example 1</u>   Add $\frac{5}{12}$ and $\frac{7}{12}$.

STEP 1   Look at the denominators. If they are the same (12), the sum will have this denominator (12).

$$\frac{5}{12} + \frac{7}{12} = \frac{\square}{12}$$

STEP 2   Think: "How many twelfths result from combining the parts?"
12 *twelfths*

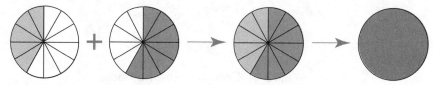

STEP 3   Write the sum as a fraction.

$$\frac{5}{12} + \frac{7}{12} = \frac{12}{12}$$

STEP 4   Simplify the answer. (Reduce to lowest terms or change to a whole or mixed number.)

$$\frac{12}{12} = \mathbf{1}, \text{ so } \frac{5}{12} + \frac{7}{12} = \frac{12}{12} = 1$$

TIP

When adding or subtracting fractions that have like denominators, the denominators remain the same. However, if the answer can be simplified (reduced to lowest terms), the final denominator will change.

Example 2 Subtract $\frac{1}{10}$ from $\frac{7}{10}$.

STEP 1 Look at the denominators. The denominators are the same (10), so the difference will have the same denominator (10).

$$\frac{7}{10} - \frac{1}{10} = \frac{\square}{10}$$

STEP 2 Think: "How many tenths result from removing 1 tenth from 7 tenths?" *6 tenths*

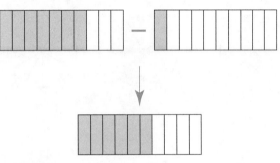

STEP 3 Write the difference as a fraction.

$$\frac{7}{10} - \frac{1}{10} = \frac{6}{10}$$

STEP 4 Simplify the answer $(\frac{6}{10})$.

$$\frac{6 \div 2}{10 \div 2} = \frac{3}{5}, \text{ so } \frac{7}{10} - \frac{1}{10} = \frac{6}{10} = \frac{3}{5}$$

Now review Examples 1 and 2 looking for a general method to add or subtract fractions with like denominators.

SUMMARY FOR ADDING OR SUBTRACTING FRACTIONS THAT HAVE LIKE DENOMINATORS

To add or subtract fractions with like denominators:

1) Add or subtract the numerators. (The denominators will be the same as the original ones.)

2) If necessary, write the answer in lowest terms.

3) Change any improper fractions to whole or mixed numbers.

EXERCISE 7

Directions: Write the addition or subtraction problem illustrated by each diagram. Then find the sum or difference. Be sure every answer is written in lowest terms.

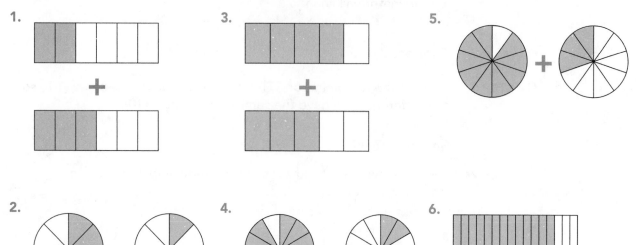

1.

3.

5.

2.

4.

6.

Directions: Find the sum or difference. Reduce every answer to lowest terms.

7. $\dfrac{5}{12} + \dfrac{3}{12}$

8. $\dfrac{7}{8}$
$-\dfrac{1}{8}$

9. $\dfrac{9}{16}$
$-\dfrac{3}{16}$

10. $\dfrac{9}{10} - \dfrac{3}{10}$

11. $\dfrac{7}{16} + \dfrac{3}{16}$

12. $\dfrac{7}{18}$
$-\dfrac{1}{18}$

13. $\dfrac{5}{8} + \dfrac{7}{8}$

14. $\dfrac{11}{20}$
$+\dfrac{9}{20}$

15. $\dfrac{14}{15} - \dfrac{11}{15}$

16. $\dfrac{11}{12} + \dfrac{5}{12}$

17. $\dfrac{23}{25} - \dfrac{18}{25}$

18. $\dfrac{33}{50}$
$-\dfrac{18}{50}$

19. $\dfrac{8}{9}$
$+\dfrac{7}{9}$

20. $\dfrac{31}{36} - \dfrac{5}{36}$

21. $\dfrac{43}{100}$
$+\dfrac{87}{100}$

Answers are on page 273.

Adding and Subtracting
Fractions That Have Unlike Denominators

When adding or subtracting fractions with denominators that are not the same, first find equivalent fractions with common denominators. Then add or subtract the fractions.

Example 1   Add $\frac{7}{12}$ and $\frac{2}{3}$.

STEP 1   Look at the denominators. They are different (12 and 3). Find a common denominator of these two numbers. *12*

$$\frac{7}{12} = \frac{\square}{12}$$
$$+\frac{2}{3} = \frac{\square}{12}$$

STEP 2   Find an equivalent fraction for $\frac{2}{3}$ using a denominator of 12.

$$\frac{2}{3} = \frac{\square}{12} \qquad \text{Think: } 3 \times ? = 12$$

$$\frac{2}{3} \times \frac{4}{4} = \frac{8}{12} \qquad \text{Multiply by } \frac{4}{4} \text{ or } 1.$$

STEP 3   Add using twelfths.

$$\frac{7}{12} = \frac{7}{12} \qquad \text{Add the new numerators.}$$

$$+\frac{2}{3} = \frac{8}{12}$$

$$\frac{15}{12} \qquad \text{The new denominator is 12.}$$

STEP 4   Reduce the answer to lowest terms.

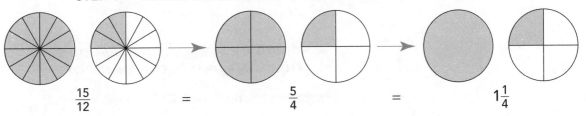

$$\frac{15}{12} \qquad\qquad = \qquad\qquad \frac{5}{4} \qquad\qquad = \qquad\qquad 1\frac{1}{4}$$

<u>Example 2</u>   Subtract $\frac{1}{5}$ from $\frac{3}{4}$.

STEP 1   Look at the denominators. They are different (5 and 4). One common denominator is 20, since $5 \times 4 = 20$ and $4 \times 5 = 20$.

$$\frac{3}{4} = \frac{\square}{20}$$
$$-\frac{1}{5} = \frac{\square}{20}$$

STEP 2   Find equivalent fractions for $\frac{1}{5}$ and $\frac{3}{4}$ with 20 as the denominators.

$\frac{3}{4} = \frac{\square}{20}$ Think: $4 \times ? = 20$ $\frac{1}{5} = \frac{\square}{20}$ Think: $5 \times ? = 20$

$\frac{3}{4} \times \frac{5}{5} = \frac{15}{20}$ Multiply by $\frac{5}{5}$ or 1. $\frac{1}{5} \times \frac{4}{4} = \frac{4}{20}$ Multiply by $\frac{4}{4}$ or 1.

$\frac{3}{4} = \frac{15}{20}$ $\frac{1}{5} = \frac{4}{20}$

STEP 3   Subtract using twentieths.

$$\frac{3}{4} = \frac{15}{20}$$ Subtract the new numerators.

$$-\frac{1}{5} = \frac{4}{20}$$

$$\frac{11}{20}$$ The new denominator is 20.

STEP 4   The answer is already in lowest terms.

TIP
To find a common denominator when adding or subtracting fractions with unlike denominators, multiply the original denominators by each other. Remember to simplify or reduce the answer to lowest terms.

ADDING OR SUBTRACTING FRACTIONS THAT HAVE UNLIKE DENOMINATORS

To add or subtract fractions with unlike denominators:

1) Find a common denominator.

2) Add or subtract the new numerators. The common denominator will be the denominator.

3) If necessary, write the answer in lowest terms.

4) Change any improper fractions to whole or mixed numbers.

EXERCISE 8

Directions: Write the addition or subtraction problem illustrated by each diagram. Then find the sum or difference. Reduce every answer to lowest terms.

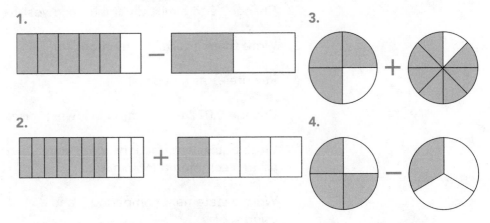

1.

3.

2.

4.

Directions: Write the missing numerators. Then find the sum or difference. Reduce every answer to lowest terms.

5. $\dfrac{2}{3} = \dfrac{10}{15}$

$-\dfrac{1}{5} = \dfrac{}{15}$

7. $\dfrac{1}{8} = \dfrac{}{24}$

$+\dfrac{2}{3} = \dfrac{}{24}$

9. $\dfrac{3}{10} = \dfrac{}{30}$

$-\dfrac{1}{6} = \dfrac{}{30}$

11. $\dfrac{3}{16} = \dfrac{3}{16}$

$\dfrac{1}{2} = \dfrac{}{16}$

$+\dfrac{1}{4} = \dfrac{}{16}$

6. $\dfrac{1}{6} = \dfrac{2}{12}$

$+\dfrac{1}{2} = \dfrac{}{12}$

8. $\dfrac{3}{4} = \dfrac{}{28}$

$-\dfrac{3}{7} = \dfrac{}{28}$

10. $\dfrac{11}{12} = \dfrac{}{60}$

$-\dfrac{4}{15} = \dfrac{}{60}$

12. $\dfrac{4}{15} = \dfrac{4}{15}$

$\dfrac{1}{3} = \dfrac{}{15}$

$+\dfrac{1}{5} = \dfrac{}{15}$

Directions: Find the sum or difference. Reduce every answer to lowest terms.

13. $\dfrac{3}{8}$

$+\dfrac{1}{2}$

16. $\dfrac{3}{4}$

$+\dfrac{2}{5}$

19. $\dfrac{3}{5}$

$+\dfrac{5}{6}$

14. $\dfrac{13}{16}$

$-\dfrac{5}{32}$

17. $\dfrac{5}{8}$

$-\dfrac{1}{6}$

20. $\dfrac{8}{9}$

$-\dfrac{3}{4}$

15. $\dfrac{4}{5}$

$+\dfrac{3}{10}$

18. $\dfrac{11}{12}$

$-\dfrac{3}{4}$

21. $\dfrac{1}{3}$

$+\dfrac{1}{4}$

Answers are on page 274.

EXERCISE 9

1. Rewrite $5\frac{7}{8}$ as an improper fraction.

2. Change $\frac{54}{10}$ to a mixed number in lowest terms.

3. Write three equivalent fractions for $\frac{5}{6}$.

4. Rewrite $\frac{5}{12}$ as a decimal.

5. Change 0.072 to a fraction in lowest terms.

6. Write equivalent fractions for $\frac{7}{10}$ and $\frac{5}{8}$ using a common denominator.

7. Write a statement comparing $\frac{4}{5}$ and $\frac{3}{4}$ using < or >.

Directions: Solve each addition or subtraction problem below using any method. Reduce every answer to lowest terms.

8. Nelida ordered carpet that was $\frac{11}{16}$-inch thick. The pad underneath it was $\frac{5}{8}$-inch thick. How much thicker is the carpet than the pad?

9. It rained $\frac{5}{8}$ of an inch last Saturday. The next day it rained another $\frac{7}{8}$ inch. How much rain fell during those two days?

10. According to the blueprint, a spring should be $\frac{9}{32}$-inch long. When Lars measured it, the spring was $\frac{5}{16}$-inch long. Is the actual spring longer or shorter than the blueprint measure and by how much?

Answers are on page 275.

Adding Mixed Numbers

To add mixed numbers, look at the denominators. If they are different, rename them using a common denominator. Next, add the whole number parts first; then add all the fractional parts of each mixed number. If the sum of the fractions results in an improper fraction, change it to a mixed number. Add the whole number part of the mixed number to the whole number part of the original sum.

Example   Add $2\frac{4}{5}$ and $1\frac{1}{3}$.

STEP 1   Look at the denominators. They are different (5 and 3).

STEP 2   Find equivalent fractions
for $\frac{4}{5}$ and $\frac{1}{3}$ with 15
as the denominator.

$$2\frac{4}{5} = 2\frac{12}{15}$$
$$+ 1\frac{1}{3} = 1\frac{5}{15}$$
$$\overline{\phantom{+ 1\frac{1}{3} = } 3\frac{17}{15}}$$

STEP 3   Add the whole numbers.

STEP 4   Add the renamed fractions.

STEP 5   Reduce the answer to lowest terms.

Since $\frac{17}{15}$ is an improper fraction, think:

$$3\frac{17}{15} = 3 + 1 + \frac{2}{15} = 4\frac{2}{15}.$$

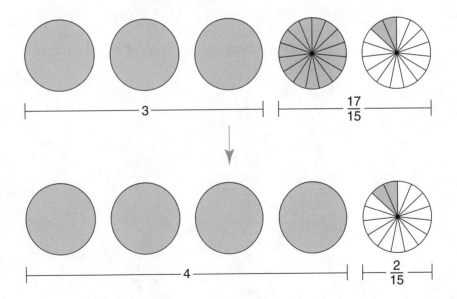

SUMMARY FOR ADDING MIXED NUMBERS

To add mixed numbers:

1) Rename the fractions using a common denominator.

2) Add the whole numbers, and add the new fractions.

3) Simplify the fraction, changing any improper fraction to a mixed number.

4) Add the whole number part of the mixed number to the whole number part of the original sum.

EXERCISE 10

Directions: Fill in any missing blanks and add.

1. $5\frac{7}{10}$

    $+\,3\frac{1}{10}$

    _____ $\frac{}{10}$ = _____ _____

2. $1\frac{1}{4}$ = _____ $\frac{}{4}$

    $+\,2\frac{1}{2}$ = _____ $\frac{}{4}$

    _____ $\frac{}{4}$

3. $6\frac{5}{9}$ = _____ $\frac{}{18}$

    $+\,8\frac{5}{6}$ = _____ $\frac{}{18}$

    _____ $\frac{}{18}$ = _____ $\frac{}{18}$

4. $7\frac{2}{3}$ = _____ $\frac{}{9}$

    $+\,5\frac{4}{9}$ = _____ $\frac{}{9}$ =

    _____ $\frac{}{9}$ = _____ $\frac{}{9}$

Directions: Add each set of mixed numbers.

5. $8\frac{2}{3}$

    $+\,4\frac{3}{8}$

6. $7\frac{4}{5}$

    $+\,9\frac{3}{4}$

7. $5\frac{5}{6}$

    $+\,4\frac{7}{8}$

8. $12\frac{9}{10}$

    $+\;\;8\frac{2}{3}$

9. $9\frac{7}{12}$

    $+\,10\frac{4}{5}$

10. $20\frac{3}{4}$

    $+\,16\frac{19}{25}$

Answers are on page 275.

Subtracting Mixed Numbers

To subtract mixed numbers, we sometimes have to rename mixed numbers.

Example   Subtract $1\frac{3}{4}$ from $3\frac{1}{6}$.

STEP 1   Look at the denominators. They are different (4 and 6).

STEP 2   Find equivalent fractions for $\frac{3}{4}$ and $\frac{1}{6}$ with 12 as the denominator.

$$3\frac{1}{6} = 3\frac{2}{12}$$
$$-1\frac{3}{4} = 1\frac{9}{12}$$

STEP 3   Subtract the fractional parts and whole numbers. If this is not possible, rename the first mixed number.

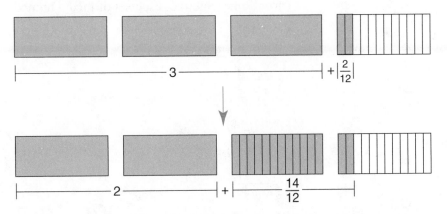

STEP 4   Subtract renamed fractions and the new whole numbers.

STEP 5   Simplify the answer if necessary.

$$3\frac{1}{6} = 3\frac{2}{12} = 2\frac{14}{12}$$
$$-1\frac{3}{4} = 1\frac{9}{12} = 1\frac{9}{12}$$
$$\phantom{-1\frac{3}{4} = 1\frac{9}{12} = }1\frac{5}{12}$$

SUMMARY FOR SUBTRACTING MIXED NUMBERS

To subtract mixed numbers:

1) Rename the fractions using a common denominator.

2) Rename the first mixed number if the first numerator is less than the second numerator.

3) Subtract the new fractions and the whole numbers. Simplify the fractional part of the difference, if necessary.

EXERCISE 11

Directions: Fill in the missing blanks and subtract.

1. $5\frac{9}{10} = \underline{\quad}\frac{9}{10}$

   $-3\frac{1}{2} = \underline{\quad}\frac{}{10}$

   $\underline{\quad}\frac{}{10} = \underline{\quad}\underline{\quad}$

2. $3\frac{1}{6} = \underline{\quad}\frac{}{12} = \underline{\quad}\frac{}{12}$

   $-1\frac{3}{4} = \underline{\quad}\frac{}{12} = \underline{\quad}\frac{}{12}$

   $\underline{\quad}\frac{}{12}$

3. $9\frac{1}{3} = \underline{\quad}\frac{}{12} = \underline{\quad}\frac{}{12}$

   $-6\frac{5}{12} = \underline{\quad}\frac{}{12} = \underline{\quad}\frac{}{12}$

   $\underline{\quad}\frac{}{12}$

4. $8\frac{3}{8} = \underline{\quad}\frac{}{24} = \underline{\quad}\frac{}{24}$

   $-4\frac{5}{6} = \underline{\quad}\frac{}{24} = \underline{\quad}\frac{}{24}$

   $\underline{\quad}\frac{}{24}$

Directions: Subtract each set of mixed numbers.

5. $10\frac{4}{5}$

   $-\ 6\frac{3}{4}$

6. $15\frac{3}{10}$

   $-\ 9\frac{7}{12}$

7. 14

   $-\ 8\frac{18}{25}$

8. $39\frac{7}{20}$

   $-10\frac{4}{5}$

Directions: Solve each problem below.

9. Janelle made a fruit salad with $1\frac{1}{4}$ pounds of grapes, $2\frac{3}{8}$ pounds of apples, and $1\frac{2}{3}$ pounds of strawberries. How much fruit did she use?

10. Ravi bought two rolls of 100 stamps. If stamps cost 34 cents each, estimate the cost of the stamps. Exactly how much did he spend on stamps?

11. In the 1992 Summer Olympic Games, Michael Stulze from the United States won the shot put event with a throw of 71 feet $2\frac{1}{2}$ inches. Sixty years earlier, the event was won by American John Kuck with a throw of 52 feet $11\frac{11}{16}$ inches. Who threw the shot put farther and by how much?

Answers are on page 276.

Multiplying Fractions and Mixed Numbers

Two fractions can be multiplied by simply multiplying the numerators and denominators and simplifying the answer. Look at the following example.

Example 1   Multiply $\frac{5}{8}$ and $\frac{3}{4}$.

STEP 1   Multiply the numerators.

Multiply the denominators.

$$\frac{5}{8} \times \frac{3}{4} = \frac{5 \times 3}{8 \times 4} = \frac{15}{32}$$

STEP 2   Rewrite the answer in lowest terms if necessary. In this case, the answer is already in lowest terms.

SUMMARY FOR MULTIPLYING FRACTIONS

To multiply fractions:

1) Multiply the numerators and multiply the denominators.

2) Simplify the result, if necessary.

When multiplying mixed numbers, change the mixed numbers to improper fractions. Then follow the steps for multiplying fractions.

Example 2   Multiply $1\frac{2}{3}$ and $2\frac{1}{5}$.

STEP 1   Change the mixed numbers to improper fractions.

$$1\frac{2}{3} = \frac{(1 \times 3) + 2}{3} = \frac{5}{3}; \ 2\frac{1}{5} = \frac{(2 \times 5) + 1}{5} = \frac{11}{5}$$

STEP 2   Multiply the improper fractions by multiplying the numerators and the denominators.

$$1\frac{2}{3} \times 2\frac{1}{5} = \frac{5}{3} \times \frac{11}{5} = \frac{55}{15}$$

STEP 3   Change the improper fraction to a mixed number, and simplify the fraction.

$$\frac{55}{15} = 3\frac{10}{15} = 3\frac{2}{3}$$

SUMMARY FOR MULTIPLYING MIXED NUMBERS

To find a product involving mixed numbers:

1) Change all mixed numbers to improper fractions.

2) Multiply the numerators and multiply the denominators.

3) Simplify the result, if necessary.

EXERCISE 12

Directions: Find each product. Reduce all mixed numbers or fractions to lowest terms.

1. $\frac{1}{5} \times \frac{3}{8}$

4. $\frac{4}{5} \times \frac{11}{20}$

7. $5\frac{9}{10} \times 4$

2. $\frac{7}{12} \times \frac{2}{3}$

5. $\frac{3}{8} \times \frac{12}{50}$

8. $4\frac{4}{15} \times 6\frac{5}{9}$

3. $\frac{9}{10} \times \frac{5}{6}$

6. $1\frac{2}{5} \times \frac{3}{8}$

9. $9\frac{11}{18} \times 3\frac{2}{3}$

Directions: Solve each problem.

10. To convert temperature measured as Fahrenheit to Celsius, subtract 32 and then multiply by $\frac{5}{9}$. What is the Celsius temperature if the Fahrenheit temperature is 104 degrees?

11. Kieron's exercise workout takes him $1\frac{1}{2}$ hours to complete. If he exercises three days a week, how much time does he spend exercising in a week?

Answers are on page 276.

Dividing Fractions and Mixed Numbers

To divide fractions or mixed numbers, you must invert the divisor and multiply. The divisor is the number that goes into the other number.

<u>Example 1</u>　Find $3 \div \frac{1}{16}$.

Divide 3 into sixteenths. Think "How many sixteenths are in 3 wholes?"

 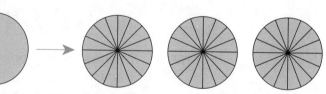

1 whole is the same as 16 (1 × 16) sixteenths.

2 wholes is the same as 32 (2 × 16) sixteenths.

3 wholes is the same as 48 (3 × 16) sixteenths.

Therefore, $3 \div \frac{1}{16}$ is the same as 3 × 16.

$3 \div \frac{1}{16} = 3 \times \frac{16}{1} = 48$

By studying this example, we notice that *dividing by $\frac{1}{16}$ became multiplying by 16 or $\frac{16}{1}$*. The divisor, $\frac{1}{16}$, was inverted to become $\frac{16}{1}$.

<u>**Example 2**</u>   Find $1\frac{3}{8} \div \frac{1}{2}$.

STEP 1   Change any mixed numbers to improper fractions.

$$1\frac{3}{8} \div \frac{1}{2} = \frac{11}{8} \div \frac{1}{2}$$

STEP 2   Change the division symbol to multiplication and invert the second fraction (the divisor).

$$\frac{11}{8} \div \frac{1}{2} = \frac{11}{8} \times \mathbf{\frac{2}{1}}$$

STEP 3   The problem is now a multiplication problem. Complete the problem.

$$\frac{11}{8} \times \frac{2}{1} = \frac{22}{8} = \frac{11}{4} = 2\frac{3}{4}$$

STEP 4   Check by estimating. Think: "How many $\frac{1}{2}$s are in $1\frac{3}{8}$?"

By drawing a number line, we can determine that the answer is about 3. Since $2\frac{3}{4}$ is about 3, the answer is reasonable.

SUMMARY FOR DIVIDING FRACTIONS AND MIXED NUMBERS

To divide fractions and mixed numbers:

1) Change any mixed numbers to improper fractions.

2) Invert the divisor and multiply.

3) Simplify the result, if necessary, by writing the answer in lowest terms.

4) Change any improper fraction to a mixed or whole number.

EXERCISE 13

Directions: Write the inverse of each fraction, mixed number, or whole number.

1. $\frac{5}{12}$ 2. 3 3. $6\frac{9}{10}$ 4. 27

Directions: Use the number line below to answer the following questions.

5. How many fourths are in 3?

6. How many eighths are in $2\frac{1}{2}$?

7. How many sixteenths are in $1\frac{3}{4}$?

8. How many $\frac{3}{4}$-inch pieces are in $2\frac{1}{4}$ inches?

9. How many $\frac{1}{8}$-inch pieces are in $1\frac{5}{16}$ inches?

Directions: Find each quotient.

10. $\frac{3}{8} \div \frac{2}{3} = \frac{3}{8} \times$ _____ $=$ _____

11. $\frac{5}{6} \div \frac{10}{17} =$ _____ $\times$ _____ $=$ _____ $=$ _____ $=$ _____

12. $2\frac{1}{3} \div \frac{4}{9} = \frac{}{3} \div \frac{4}{9} = \frac{}{3} \times \frac{}{} =$ _____ $=$ _____ $=$ _____

13. $1\frac{3}{4} \div 2\frac{7}{18} = \frac{}{4} \div \frac{}{18}$ 15. $6 \div 2\frac{9}{25}$

14. $4\frac{7}{12} \div 3\frac{1}{10}$ 16. $10\frac{23}{40} \div 5$

Directions: Solve each problem.

17. A pica is a measure of $\frac{1}{6}$ inch. If a length is measured as 21 picas, how many inches is this length?

18. Horsepower is defined to be the power needed to lift 33,000 pounds a distance of one foot in one minute. If this is about $1\frac{1}{2}$ times the power an average horse can exert, how much would a horse be expected to lift one foot in one minute?

Answers are on page 276.

Using a Number Grid with Fractions

You may be asked to write your fraction answer in a number grid.

Example Ray used $3\frac{1}{4}$ pounds of the original 4 pounds of hamburger he purchased. How much hamburger is left over? Write your answer on the number grid.

STEP 1 Set up the problem.

STEP 2 Subtract.

$$4 = 3\frac{4}{4}$$
$$\underline{-3\frac{1}{4} = -3\frac{1}{4}}$$
$$\frac{3}{4}$$

Write the correct answer in the blank boxes at the top of the grid. Use a separate column for each digit and a slash for the fraction bar. Fill in the circles below each box.

This grid is filled in correctly. Remember, your answer can be centered (like this example), shifted to the right, or shifted to the left.

EXERCISE 14

Directions: Solve each problem and write your answer on the number grid.

1. $\frac{3}{4} \times \frac{1}{2}$

2. $\frac{5}{6} - \frac{3}{4}$

3. $\dfrac{2}{5} + \dfrac{1}{2}$

6. $3\dfrac{1}{2} - 2\dfrac{2}{3}$

4. $\dfrac{1}{3} \div \dfrac{1}{2}$

7. $\dfrac{1}{9} \times \dfrac{1}{3}$

5. $\dfrac{3}{4} - \dfrac{1}{2}$

8. $1\dfrac{1}{3} \div 3\dfrac{1}{2}$

Answers are on page 277.

Using a Calculator with Fractions

The Casio *fx*-260 solar calculator has a fraction key. Follow these examples to learn how to work fraction problems on your calculator.

Example 1 Reduce $\frac{8}{10}$ to lowest terms.

STEP 1 First press `AC`.

STEP 2 Press `8` `a b/c` `1` `0` `=`.

The display should read [4⌐5.].

$\frac{8}{10}$ reduced to lowest terms is $\frac{4}{5}$.

Example 2 Solve $2\frac{1}{2} + 4\frac{3}{8}$.

STEP 1 Press `AC`.

STEP 2 Press `2` `a b/c` `1` `a b/c` `2` `+` `4` `a b/c` `3` `a b/c` `8` `=`.

The display should read [6⌐7⌐8.].

$2\frac{1}{2} + 4\frac{3}{8} = 6\frac{7}{8}$

EXERCISE 15

Directions: Use your calculator to reduce each fraction to lowest terms.

1. $\frac{3}{9}$

2. $\frac{4}{10}$

3. $\frac{6}{18}$

4. $\frac{20}{25}$

5. $\frac{75}{100}$

6. $\frac{80}{120}$

7. $\frac{14}{42}$

8. $\frac{20}{48}$

Directions: Use your calculator to solve each problem.

9. $1\frac{2}{3} + 3\frac{1}{4}$

13. $3\frac{1}{3} \times 2\frac{1}{2}$

10. $1\frac{1}{2} + 3\frac{3}{4} + 2\frac{2}{3}$

14. $1\frac{3}{4} \times 3\frac{1}{4}$

11. $4\frac{1}{3} - 2\frac{1}{2}$

15. $6 \div 1\frac{3}{4}$

12. $7\frac{3}{4} - 2\frac{8}{9}$

16. $2\frac{1}{2} \div 3\frac{1}{2}$

17. Luis bought $2\frac{1}{2}$ pounds of apples and $1\frac{3}{4}$ pounds of oranges. How many pounds of fruit did he buy?

18. Kami used $12\frac{3}{4}$ yards from the 15 yards of fabric she bought. How much fabric is left?

19. Jared used $2\frac{2}{3}$ cups of sugar to make a batch of cookies. If he wants to make a batch and a half, how much sugar must he use?

20. A restaurant has only $6\frac{1}{2}$ gallons of a special sauce. A recipe uses $\frac{3}{4}$ gallon. How many recipes can be made with this sauce?

Answers are on page 278.

Fractions Review

Directions: In questions 1–10, solve each problem. Show your work at the right.

1. What fraction is represented by the decimal .81?

2. What improper fraction is the equivalent of $5\frac{9}{10}$?

3. What mixed number is the equivalent of $\frac{49}{12}$?

4. Name three fractions equal to $\frac{6}{23}$.

5. What fraction with a denominator of 90 is the equivalent of $\frac{11}{18}$?

6. How many thirds are in 4?

7. Change the fraction $\frac{17}{25}$ to a decimal.

8. Change 4.96 to a mixed number in lowest terms.

9. Name a common denominator of $\frac{3}{10}$ and $\frac{11}{15}$.

10. Write a statement using < or > comparing $1\frac{7}{12}$ to $1\frac{9}{16}$.

Directions: Use your calculator to answer questions 11–15.

11. Joyce studied for two and a half hours. Luis made the claim that he studied three times as long. For how long would Luis have studied?

12. Martin lives $\frac{7}{8}$ of a mile from school. If Christy rides the bus for another $1\frac{3}{4}$ miles after Martin gets off, how far away from school does Christy live?

13. Rewrite the fraction $\frac{63}{72}$ in lowest terms.

14. Subtract $\frac{7}{16}$ from $1\frac{3}{8}$.

15. Find $\frac{9}{10} \div 1\frac{7}{8}$.

Directions: Questions 16–25 include whole numbers, decimals, and fractions. Choose the correct answer to each problem. Remember the problem-solving skills you have learned.

16. Last week Kevin worked 40 hours for his usual pay rate of $8 an hour. For the next 6 hours of work, he was paid one and a half times his usual rate. Which expression would you use to find his total pay for the week?

    (1) $(40 \times \$8) + (6 \times 1.5)$
    (2) $(40 \times \$8) + (\$8 \times 1.5)$
    (3) $(40 \times \$8) + (6 \times \$8 \times 1.5)$
    (4) $(46 \times \$8) + (6 \times 1.5)$
    (5) $(46 \times \$8) + (8 \times 1.5)$

17. Which of the following is in order from least to greatest?

    (1) .87, 8.7, 8.07, 8.77
    (2) $\frac{3}{10}, \frac{3}{8}, \frac{3}{4}, \frac{3}{2}$
    (3) .1, .01, .001, .0001
    (4) $8\frac{1}{7}, 8\frac{1}{8}, 8\frac{1}{9}, 8\frac{1}{10}$
    (5) $\frac{10}{3}, \frac{8}{3}, \frac{4}{3}, \frac{2}{3}$

18. Which of the following represents the largest amount?

    (1) $3.52
    (2) three and a half dollars
    (3) three dollars and two quarters
    (4) two dollars and three quarters
    (5) $3.50

19. A recipe calls for 1 cup shortening, $1\frac{1}{2}$ cups sugar, $1\frac{3}{4}$ cups flour, and 1 cup of raisins. If Bryan doubles the recipe, how many cups of flour should he use?

    (1) $2\frac{1}{2}$
    (2) $5\frac{1}{4}$
    (3) $1\frac{3}{4}$
    (4) $3\frac{1}{2}$
    (5) $\frac{7}{8}$

20. How many pieces $\frac{3}{4}$ inch long can be cut from a foot-long cord?

    (1) 9
    (2) 36
    (3) 16
    (4) 20
    (5) 12

21. If lean hamburger is $\frac{1}{5}$ fat, how many ounces of fat are in a 12-ounce hamburger?

    (1) $\frac{5}{12}$
    (2) $\frac{12}{5}$
    (3) 60
    (4) 5
    (5) 12

22. What would you do to add $\frac{2}{5}$ and $\frac{5}{12}$?

    (1) Multiply both $\frac{2}{5}$ and $\frac{5}{12}$ by some form of 1.

    (2) Find equivalent fractions for $\frac{2}{5}$ and $\frac{5}{12}$.

    (3) Determine a common denominator and add renamed numerators.

    (4) all of the above

    (5) none of the above

23. Which expression represents the correct comparison of $\frac{30}{5}$, 6.00, and 4.2 divided by .7?

    (1) $\frac{30}{5} < 6.00 < 4.2$ divided by .7

    (2) $\frac{30}{5} > 6.00 > 4.2$ divided by .7

    (3) $\frac{30}{5} = 6.00$ and both are less than 4.2 divided by .7

    (4) $\frac{30}{5} = 6.00$ and both are greater than 4.2 divided by .7

    (5) They all are equal.

24. Which is cheaper: 4 items for $1.60 or $5 for 12 items?

    (1) Four items for $1.60 is slightly cheaper.

    (2) Five dollars for 12 items is considerably cheaper.

    (3) They are the same.

    (4) Four items for $1.60 is considerably cheaper.

    (5) Five dollars for 12 items is slightly cheaper.

25. One rod is $8\frac{15}{16}$ inches long. Another rod is $7\frac{5}{8}$ inches long. If the two rods are placed end to end, what is their total length in inches?

    (1) $15\frac{20}{24}$

    (2) $1\frac{5}{16}$

    (3) $16\frac{20}{24}$

    (4) $16\frac{9}{16}$

    (5) $16\frac{9}{24}$

Directions: Solve each problem and write each answer on the number grid.

26. Maria has 8 eggs. What fraction of a dozen does she have?

27. Jackie has 2 pieces of fabric. One is $\frac{1}{5}$ yard and the other is $\frac{1}{2}$ yard. How much of a yard of fabric does she have altogether?

Answers are on page 278.

Chapter 6

Ratios and Proportions

Understanding Ratios

A **ratio** is a comparison of two numbers. For example, you can use a ratio to compare the numbers 2 and 7. There are three different ways to write the ratio:

by using the word *to*	by using a colon	by writing a fraction
2 to 7	2 : 7	$\frac{2}{7}$

Think of a ratio as a fraction. Just as the fractions $\frac{2}{7}$ and $\frac{7}{2}$ are not the same, the ratios "2 to 7" and "7 to 2" are not the same. So the *order* of the two numbers in a ratio is important. A ratio must be reduced to lowest terms.

Example 1   In Bob's family, there are 2 boys and 4 girls. What is the ratio of boys to girls in Bob's family?

STEP 1   Write the ratio in one of these three ways.

Use the word *to*.	Use a colon.	Write a fraction.
2 boys to 4 girls	2 boys : 4 girls	$\frac{2 \text{ boys}}{4 \text{ girls}}$
2 to 4	2 : 4	$\frac{2}{4}$

STEP 2   Reduce to lowest terms.

Use the word *to*.	Use a colon.	Write a fraction.
1 boy to 2 girls	1 boy : 2 girls	$\frac{1 \text{ boy}}{2 \text{ girls}}$
1 to 2	1 : 2	$\frac{1}{2}$

STEP 3   Make a statement about the ratio.

The following statements are all appropriate.
The ratio of boys to girls in Bob's family is 1 to 2.
The ratio of boys to girls in Bob's family is 1 : 2.
The ratio of boys to girls in Bob's family is $\frac{1}{2}$.

SUMMARY FOR WRITING RATIOS

To write a ratio comparing two numbers:

1) Use the word *to*, use a colon, or write a fraction.

2) The order of the numbers is important.

3) Reduce the ratio to lowest terms.

Some ratio problems require calculation before you write the ratio. See the example below.

Example 2   In a class of 30 students, there are 14 boys. What is the ratio of boys to girls in the class?

STEP 1   Calculate the number of girls in the class since this number is not given.

30 students – 14 boys = 16 girls

STEP 2   Write the ratio of boys to girls.

$\frac{14}{16}$

STEP 3   Reduce the ratio to lowest terms.

$\frac{14}{16} = \frac{7}{8}$

STEP 4   Make a statement about the ratio.

The ratio of boys to girls in the class is 7 to 8.

EXERCISE 1

Directions: Write each ratio in two other ways.

1. 6 to 7

2. 1 : 50

3. $\frac{7}{3}$

4. $\frac{10}{19}$

5. 13 : 1

6. 2 to 5

Directions: Write a ratio for each situation described.

7. To make orange juice, combine 1 can of concentrate with 3 cans of water. Write the ratio of concentrate to water.

8. Drew takes home $2,000 a month. He saves $200 and spends the rest. Write a ratio of the amount Drew spends to the amount Drew saves each month.

9. The Bobcats lost 9 games and won 2 games this season. Write the ratio of wins to losses.

10. Pam sleeps 8 hours every night. Write a ratio of Pam's time spent sleeping to Pam's time spent not sleeping.

11. To make lemonade, add 4 cans of water to every can of concentrate. Write the ratio of water to concentrate.

12. A ski resort advertised that it had 23 snow days during January. Write a ratio of snow days to no-snow days.

13. In a local election, Marshall received 582 votes while Hawks received 366 votes. Write a ratio of the number of votes for Hawks to the number of votes for Marshall.

14. Write the ratio of vowels to consonants in the word *extravagant*.

Directions: Results from three survey questions are given in the table below. Use these results to write the ratios indicated in problems 15–20.

	Yes	No
Question 1	76	32
Question 2	100	8
Question 3	25	83

15. Yes : No for Question 1

16. No : Yes for Question 2

17. Yes for Question 3 : Yes for Question 2

18. No for Question 1 : No for Question 2

19. Total Yes : Total No for Questions 1–3

20. Yes for Question 2 : Yes for Questions 1 and 3 combined

Directions: Choose the best answer.

21. Which statement does not have the same meaning as "the ratio of males to females is 1 to 2"?
    (1) Half are male, and half are female.
    (2) There are twice as many females as males.
    (3) For each male, there are two females.
    (4) Two out of three are female.
    (5) One out of three is male.

22. Three of Hannah's answers on a test of 30 problems were wrong. Which of the following is a ratio of right answers to wrong answers?
    (1) 30 to 3
    (2) 3 to 27
    (3) 27 to 30
    (4) 10 to 1
    (5) 9 to 1

Answers are on page 279.

Understanding Rates

A **rate** shows a relationship between two quantities measured in different units. Rates are a commonly used type of ratio. A **unit rate** is the rate for one unit of a quantity. To find a unit rate, you divide the two numbers in the ratio.

Example 1   Ken and Barbara used 16 gallons of gasoline to drive 500 miles. Find the unit rate of gas mileage (miles per gallon).

STEP 1   Write the ratio of miles to gallons: $\frac{500 \text{ miles}}{16 \text{ gallons}}$.

Note that this is a rate, but not a unit rate.

STEP 2   Divide so that you have a unit rate.

500 miles ÷ 16 gallons = 31.25 miles per gallon

A **unit price** is the price per unit of an item. Divide to find a unit price.

Example 2   Soap is priced at $1.19 for 4 bars. Find the unit price.

STEP 1   Write the ratio of price to number of bars: $\frac{\$1.19}{4 \text{ bars}}$.

STEP 2   Divide so that you have a unit price: $1.19 ÷ 4 bars = $0.2975

STEP 3   Round to the nearest cent: $0.2975 → $0.30.

The unit price is about $.30 per bar.

SUMMARY FOR FINDING RATES AND UNIT PRICES

To find a unit rate:

1) Write a ratio of the two quantities.

2) Divide to find the unit rate.

3) To find a unit price, divide price by the number of units.

EXERCISE 2

Directions: Write the unit rate for each situation described.

1. On a 15-minute typing test, Neysa typed 825 words. What was Neysa's typing rate (words per minute)?

2. This week, Ravi worked 20 hours and earned $130. What is his earning rate (dollars per hour)?

3. Louisa and Won drove 135 miles and used 6 gallons of gasoline. Find the gas mileage rate of their car (miles per gallon).

4. Les and Erna drove 210 miles in $3\frac{1}{2}$ hours. Find their rate of travel (miles per hour).

Directions: Write each unit price.

5. 5 pounds of potatoes for $1.49

6. 10 pencils for $.99

7. 3 rolls of film for $8

8. A dozen eggs for $1.09

Directions: Solve each problem.

9. Consuela's car used 12 gallons of gasoline for 330 miles of highway driving. Bill's car used 10 gallons for 300 miles of highway driving. Which car has better gas mileage?

10. Robin ran a 10-kilometer race in 42 minutes 30 seconds. What was her average rate (kilometers per minute)?

11. Brian ran 6 miles in 50 minutes. On average, did he run *faster* or *slower* than 8 minutes per mile?

12. Lorenzo normally types 80 words per minute. On his last test, he typed 416 words in 5 minutes. Is this *faster* or *slower* than his normal typing rate?

13. Suppose your favorite shampoo is sold in two sizes. The 15-oz bottle costs $2.79, and the 12-oz bottle costs $1.99. Is the bigger bottle the better buy?

14. You have three choices for buying soda: a 6-pack for $2.19, a 12-pack for $3.99, or a 24-pack for $8.49. Which is the best buy? Which is the worst buy?

Answers are on page 280.

Understanding Proportions

A **proportion** is made up of two equal ratios. If you think of ratios as fractions, then the two ratios in a proportion are equivalent fractions.

Example 1   Write a proportion, using 3 to 4 as one of the ratios.

STEP 1   Write the given ratio as a fraction: $\frac{3}{4}$

STEP 2   Write an equivalent fraction.

$$\frac{3}{4} = \frac{3 \times 2}{4 \times 2} = \frac{6}{8}$$

STEP 3   Write the proportion.

$$\frac{3}{4} = \frac{6}{8}$$

Sometimes you can use the idea of equivalent fractions to decide if two ratios form a proportion or not. "Do the two ratios form a proportion?" is the same as asking, "Are the two fractions equivalent?"

Example 2   Do the two ratios $\frac{4}{10}$ and $\frac{5}{12}$ form a proportion?

STEP 1   Find a common denominator: 60.

STEP 2   Write each as a fraction with denominator 60.

$$\frac{4}{10} = \frac{4 \times 6}{10 \times 6} = \frac{24}{60}$$

$$\frac{5}{12} = \frac{5 \times 5}{12 \times 5} = \frac{25}{60}$$

STEP 3   Are the two fractions equivalent? No, since $\frac{24}{60} \neq \frac{25}{60}$.

Do the two ratios form a proportion? No.

A quick way to see if two ratios form a proportion or not is to check their two cross products. A **cross product** is the numerator of one ratio multiplied by the denominator of the other ratio. If the cross products are equal, the ratios form a proportion. If the cross products are not equal, the ratios do not form a proportion.

Example 3   Do the two ratios $\frac{2}{15}$ and $\frac{3}{16}$ form a proportion?

STEP 1   Find cross products: $2 \times 16 = 32$, and $15 \times 3 = 45$

STEP 2   Are the cross products equal? No, since $32 \neq 45$.

Do the two ratios form a proportion? No.

You can use proportions to solve some rate problems.

Example 4   On Monday, Sam drove 100 miles in 2 hours. On Tuesday, he drove 125 miles in $2\frac{1}{2}$ hours. Did he drive the same rate on Tuesday as on Monday? If so, write a proportion showing that the two ratios (rates) are equal.

STEP 1   Divide to find each rate.

100 miles $\div$ 2 hours = 50 miles per hour

125 miles $\div$ $2\frac{1}{2}$ hours = 50 miles per hour

STEP 2   Answer the question.

Yes, Sam drove the same rate on Tuesday as on Monday (50 miles per hour).

STEP 3   Write a proportion showing that the rates are equal.

$$\frac{100}{2} = \frac{125}{2.5}$$

STEP 4   Use cross products to check your answer.

$100 \times 2.5 = 250$; $2 \times 125 = 250$

The cross products are equal, so the rates are equal.

TIP
The two ratios that form a proportion must be equal. So the two ratios must be equivalent fractions or equivalent rates. Also, their cross products must be equal.

EXERCISE 3

Directions: Do the two ratios form a proportion? If so, write the proportion.

1. $\frac{2}{3}, \frac{10}{15}$

2. $\frac{1}{4}, \frac{2}{9}$

3. $\frac{16}{3}, \frac{8}{1}$

4. $\frac{5}{5}, \frac{3}{3}$

5. 3 to 4, 5 to 8

6. 50 to 20, 10 to 4

7. 1 : 2, 6 : 9

8. 8 : 3, 24 : 9

Directions: Form a proportion, using the ratio given. There is more than one correct answer.

9. $\frac{1}{9}$

10. $\frac{25}{20}$

11. 12 to 13

12. 6 : 3

13. 13 to 1

14. $\frac{17}{3}$

15. 5 : 11

16. 10 : 3

Directions: Solve each problem.

17. Photographs measure either 3 inches by 5 inches, or 4 inches by 6 inches. Do the width ratios of $\frac{width}{length}$ form a proportion? Show your work.

18. Barb mixed three parts of blue paint with one part of yellow paint to make green paint. Bonnie mixed five parts of blue paint with two parts of yellow paint to make green paint. Will the two shades of green paint be the same? Why or why not?

19. Tessa typed 650 words in 10 minutes. Suzie typed 780 words in 12 minutes. Do the two rates form a proportion? Is their typing speed the same?

20. A dozen large eggs cost $1.09. At the same rate, how much should two dozen large eggs cost? Express this as a proportion.

Directions: Choose the best answer.

21. Which of the following is the correct pair of cross products for the proportion $\frac{5}{6} = \frac{20}{24}$?

    (1) $5 \times 20, 6 \times 24$
    (2) $5 \times 24, 6 \times 20$
    (3) $5 \times 6, 20 \times 24$
    (4) $5 \times 4 = 20, 6 \times 4 = 24$
    (5) none of the above

22. Which ratio will not form a proportion with the ratio 1 to 5?

    (1) 5 to 25
    (2) 2 to 10
    (3) 5 to 1
    (4) 1.5 to 7.5
    (5) 24 to 120

23. Which statement is true of the proportion $\frac{3}{4} = \frac{9}{12}$?

    (1) $3 : 4$ and $9 : 12$ are equal ratios.

    (2) $\frac{9}{12}$ and $\frac{3}{4}$ are equivalent fractions.

    (3) Cross products 3×12 and 4×9 are equal.

    (4) The ratios $\frac{3}{4}$ and $\frac{9}{12}$ form a proportion.

    (5) All the statements above are true.

24. The unit price of toothpaste is $.16 per ounce. Which of the following is a proportion that shows this?

    (1) $\frac{\$1.60}{10 \text{ oz}}$

    (2) $\frac{\$1.00}{16 \text{ oz}}$

    (3) $\frac{\$1.20}{10 \text{ oz}} = \frac{\$1.68}{14 \text{ oz}}$

    (4) $\frac{\$1.28}{8 \text{ oz}} = \frac{\$1.92}{12 \text{ oz}}$

    (5) all of the above

Answers are on page 280.

Problem Solving with Proportions

To solve a proportion, you find the missing value in the proportion. You can use what you have already learned about proportions to solve them.

Example 1   Solve the proportion $\frac{5}{8} = \frac{\square}{10}$.

STEP 1   Find whichever cross product you can.

$5 \times 10 = 50$

STEP 2   Divide by the number not yet used.

$50 \div 8 = 6.25$

STEP 3   Write the value into the proportion, and check cross products.

$\frac{5}{8} = \frac{6.25}{10}$; $5 \times 10 = 50$; $8 \times 6.25 = 50$; cross products are equal.

STEP 4   Write the missing value: 6.25

For many problems, you can write and solve a proportion.

Example 2   A college advertises a 4 : 5 ratio of male students to female students. If there are about 1,200 male students, how many female students are there?

STEP 1   Write a proportion. Make sure the order of the numbers is the same for each of the two ratios. Leave a blank for the missing value (in this case, the number of female students).

$\frac{\text{male}}{\text{female}} = \frac{4}{5} = \frac{1,200}{\square}$

STEP 2   Solve the proportion.

$5 \times 1,200 \div 4 = 1,500$ female students

STEP 3   Check cross products in the proportion $\frac{4}{5} = \frac{1,200}{1,500}$.

$4 \times 1,500 = 6,000$; $5 \times 1,200 = 6,000$

STEP 4   State your answer.

There are about 1,500 female students.

EXERCISE 4

Directions: Solve the proportion (find the missing value).

1. $\dfrac{1}{13} = \dfrac{10}{\square}$

2. $\dfrac{10}{3} = \dfrac{\square}{150}$

3. $\dfrac{\square}{42} = \dfrac{6}{7}$

4. $\dfrac{7}{\square} = \dfrac{5}{12}$

5. $\dfrac{4}{1} = \dfrac{16}{\square}$

6. $\dfrac{9}{2} = \dfrac{\square}{12}$

7. $\dfrac{\square}{5} = \dfrac{5}{25}$

8. $\dfrac{30}{\square} = \dfrac{4}{15}$

9. $\dfrac{9}{10} = \dfrac{\square}{36}$

10. $\dfrac{5}{7} = \dfrac{1}{\square}$

Directions: Solve each problem.

11. Etu earned $100 mowing 8 lawns. At this rate, how much will he earn mowing 10 lawns?

12. To make punch, combine 5 parts juice with 2 parts ginger ale. How much ginger ale should you add to 8 liters of juice?

13. The scale on a highway map is 1 in. : 50 miles. What is the distance between two cities that are $2\frac{1}{2}$ inches apart on the map?

14. Brendan's car gets 32 miles to the gallon. How many miles can Brendan drive on a full tank, which is about 12 gallons?

15. Gauri read on a cereal box that one serving, or $\frac{3}{4}$ cup of cereal, has 230 calories. But Gauri eats 1 cup as a serving. How many calories does 1 cup of the cereal have? Round to the nearest calorie.

16. Pat wants to use a copy machine to enlarge a small rectangular picture that measures $1\frac{1}{4}$ in. by 2 in. What is the largest Pat can make the picture and still have it fit on a piece of $8\frac{1}{2}$ in. by 11 in. paper?

Answers are on page 280.

Ratios and Proportions Review

Directions: In questions 1–15, solve each problem. Show your work at the right.

1. Solve the proportion $\frac{3}{7} = \frac{\square}{63}$.

2. $487 + 36$

3. $3,900 \div 1.3$

4. Form a proportion using the ratio 1 to 3.

5. What is the unit price of 12 bagels for $5?

6. A football team won 8 games and lost 2 games. Write the ratio of wins to losses.

7. Write the ratio $\frac{6}{7}$ in two other ways.

8. 26×18

9. $293 - 186$

10. The scale on a map is 1 cm : 100 km. What is the distance between 2 cities located 5 cm apart on the map?

11. Mina drove 130 miles in two hours. What was her average rate (miles per hour)?

12. 8.6×1.3

13. $2\frac{1}{4} \div \frac{3}{4}$

14. Do the two ratios $\frac{2}{5}$ and $\frac{3}{10}$ form a proportion? If so, write the proportion.

15. The ratio of men to women at a company is 2 : 3. If there are 60 men, how many women are there?

Directions: Choose the correct answer to each problem. Remember the problem-solving skills you have learned.

16. Each day Trinh buys a can of soda at a machine in her apartment building for 75¢. Instead, she could buy a 12-pack at the grocery store for $4.99. If she did this, how much money would she save in a month?

    (1) about $10
    (2) about $12
    (3) about $22
    (4) about $4
    (5) about $18

17. A majority is a number greater than half of the total. What is the majority for the House of Representatives, which has 435 voting members?

    (1) 222
    (2) 217
    (3) 218
    (4) 217.5
    (5) Not enough information is given.

18. Bess is planning a trip. She drives an average of 55 miles per hour. Her destination is 275 miles away. She wants to arrive by 4:00 P.M. and allow an extra hour for stops. By what time should she start driving?

    (1) 11:00 A.M.
    (2) 12:00 noon
    (3) 10:00 P.M.
    (4) 10:00 A.M.
    (5) Not enough information is given.

19. Recently 300 people in Monroe County took a civil service exam. For every 6 people who took the exam, 5 people passed. How many people passed the exam? Write your answers on the number grid.

20. On a test with 20 problems, Riley got 2 problems wrong. As a fraction reduced to lowest terms, what was the ratio of problems wrong to the total number of problems? Write your answer on the number grid.

Answers are on page 281.

Chapter 7

Percent

Understanding Percent

A **percent** is another means of expressing a number as part of a whole. The word **percent** means "of 100." For example, you can write the ratio 3 to 100 as 3% and read it as 3 percent.

Because a percent is a form of a ratio and you can write any ratio as a fraction, you can write a percent as a fraction. You can also write fractions and percents as decimals. It is very useful to be able to change among these three forms of a number: percents, fractions, and decimals.

Example 1   The 10-by-10 grid below has 100 squares. What portion of the grid is shaded? Write a percent, a fraction, and a decimal.

STEP 1   Write a percent.

40 of the 100 squares are shaded: 40%

STEP 2   Write a fraction in lowest terms.

$$\frac{40}{100} = \frac{40 \div 20}{100 \div 20} = \frac{2}{5}$$

STEP 3   Write a decimal.

"forty hundredths" = 0.40 = 0.4

STEP 4   Summarize.

So 40%, or $\frac{2}{5}$, or 0.4, of the grid is shaded.

To calculate with a percent, you first need to change the percent to a fraction or a decimal. The next two examples show you how to do this.

Example 2   Change 14% to a fraction.

STEP 1   Write the percent as a ratio that compares a number to 100 (a fraction with denominator 100).

$$14\% = \frac{14}{100}$$

STEP 2   Write the fraction in lowest terms.

$$\frac{14}{100} = \frac{14 \div 2}{100 \div 2} = \frac{7}{50}$$

STEP 3   Summarize.

$$14\% = \frac{7}{50}$$

Example 3   Change 14% to a decimal.

STEP 1   Write the percent as a ratio that compares a number to 100 (a fraction with denominator 100). Do not write the fraction in lowest terms.

$$14\% = \frac{14}{100}$$

STEP 2   Write the fraction as a decimal.

$$\frac{14}{100} = \text{fourteen hundredths} = 0.14$$

STEP 3   Summarize.

$$14\% = 0.14$$

Here's a shortcut. To change a percent to a decimal, move the decimal point two places to the *left* and drop the percent symbol. To change a decimal to a percent, move the decimal point two places to the *right* and write the percent symbol.

Example 4   Change 78% to a decimal.

STEP 1   Remember that the decimal point for a whole number is to the right of the ones digit.

78.

STEP 2   Move the decimal point two places to the left.

0.78

STEP 3   Summarize.

78% = 0.78

Example 5   Change 0.06 to a percent.

STEP 1   Move the decimal point two places to the right.

006.

STEP 2   Write the percent symbol (and remove unnecessary zeros).

6%

STEP 3   Summarize.

0.06 = 6%

To change a fraction to a percent, first divide to write the fraction as a decimal. Then write the decimal as a percent.

Example 6   Change $\frac{2}{5}$ to a percent.

STEP 1   Divide to write the fraction as a decimal.

$2 \div 5 = 0.4$

STEP 2   Write the decimal as a percent.

0.4 = 40%

STEP 3   Summarize.

$\frac{2}{5} = 40\%$

SUMMARY FOR CHANGING PERCENTS, FRACTIONS, AND DECIMALS

- To change a percent to a fraction: Write the percent as a ratio (a fraction with denominator 100) and reduce to lowest terms.

- To change a percent to a decimal: Write the percent as a fraction and then as a decimal. Or, move the decimal point two places to the left and drop the percent symbol.

- To change a decimal to a percent: Move the decimal point two places to the right, and write the percent symbol.

- To change a fraction to a percent: Divide the fraction to express as a decimal; then write it as a percent.

EXERCISE 1

Directions: Change each percent to a fraction and a decimal.

1. 25%
2. 8%
3. 10%

4. 66%
5. 1%
6. 90%

7. 37%
8. 3%
9. 50%

Directions: Change each fraction or decimal to a percent.

10. $\frac{3}{5}$
11. 0.09
12. 0.74
13. $\frac{1}{10}$

14. $\frac{3}{4}$
15. 0.7
16. 0.16
17. $\frac{7}{20}$

18. $\frac{1}{25}$
19. 0.02
20. 0.99
21. $\frac{3}{8}$

Directions: Which is greater?

22. $\frac{1}{4}$ or 20%

23. 85% or $\frac{4}{5}$

24. $\frac{1}{2}$ or 48%

25. 10% or 0.11

26. 100% or 0.01

27. $\frac{2}{10}$ or 22%

28. 0.35 or 39%

29. 42% or 0.7

Directions: Choose the best answer.

30. Which of the following is *not* equivalent to 65%?

    (1) $\frac{65}{100}$
    (2) $\frac{13}{20}$
    (3) 6.50
    (4) 0.65

31. Which of the following is the smallest?

    (1) 1%
    (2) 1
    (3) 0.1
    (4) 10%

Answers are on page 281.

Common Percents, Fractions, and Decimals

Some percents, fractions, and decimals are so commonly used that it's best to memorize them. Two of these fractions have decimals that repeat.

Example 1   Change $\frac{1}{3}$ to a percent.

STEP 1   Divide to write the fraction as a decimal.

$1 \div 3 = 0.33333\ldots$

Note that the 3 continues to repeat, indicated by the dots . . .

STEP 2   Write the decimal as a percent (move the decimal point).

$0.33333\ldots = 33.333\ldots\%$

STEP 3   Write 33.333 . . . as a mixed number. To the left of the decimal point is the whole number 33. To the right is 0.333 . . . , or $\frac{1}{3}$.

$33.333\ldots\% = 33\frac{1}{3}\%$

STEP 4   Summarize.

$\frac{1}{3} = 33\frac{1}{3}\%$

Example 2   Change $\frac{2}{3}$ to a percent.

STEP 1   Divide to write the fraction as a decimal.

$2 \div 3 = 0.66666\ldots$

STEP 2   Write the decimal as a percent.

$0.66666\ldots = 66.666\ldots\%$

STEP 3   Write 66.666 . . . as a mixed number.

$66.666\ldots\% = 66\frac{2}{3}\%$

STEP 4   Summarize.

$\frac{2}{3} = 66\frac{2}{3}\%$

EXERCISE 2

Directions: The table below includes commonly used percents, fractions, and decimals. Complete the table.

	Fraction	Percent	Decimal
1.	$\frac{1}{4}$		
2.	$\frac{1}{3}$		
3.	$\frac{1}{2}$		
4.	$\frac{2}{3}$		
5.	$\frac{3}{4}$		
6.		50%	
7.		$33\frac{1}{3}\%$	
8.		75%	
9.		25%	
10.		$66\frac{2}{3}\%$	
11.			0.75
12.			0.666 . . .
13.			0.25
14.			0.333 . . .
15.			0.5

Answers are on page 282.

Percent of a Number

A percent is a portion of some number. Often you want to figure out what that portion is. For example, if you decide to leave a 15% tip at a restaurant, you need to calculate the *amount of money* that is 15% of the bill.

Example 1   What is 15% of $25?

> **STEP 1**   Write the percent as a decimal.
>
> $15\% = 0.15$
>
> **STEP 2**   Multiply.
>
> $0.15 \times \$25 = \$3.75$
>
> **STEP 3**   Summarize.
>
> 15% of $25 is $3.75.

To calculate with percents, you first need to change the percent to either a decimal or a fraction. The example above uses a decimal, and the example below uses a fraction. You may use whichever form of the number is easier for you to work with, since they will both give you the same answer.

Example 2   What is 25% of $400?

> **STEP 1**   Write the percent as a fraction.
>
> $25\% = \frac{1}{4}$
>
> **STEP 2**   Multiply.
>
> $\frac{1}{4} \times \$400 = \$100$
>
> **STEP 3**   Summarize.
>
> 25% of $400 is $100.

SUMMARY FOR FINDING THE PERCENT OF A NUMBER

To find the percent of a number:

1) Change the percent to a decimal or a fraction.

2) Multiply.

Some problems require you to find the percent of a number. Before you do any calculations, remember to read the problem carefully. With percent problems, look for the word *of* since most percent problems ask you to find the percent of a number. When the answer you need is the percent *of* a number, multiply to find the answer.

Example 3   A state official predicts that 70% of the registered voters in Montana will vote on election day. If there are 514,000 registered voters in Montana, how many are predicted to vote?

STEP 1   Understand the question.

You must figure out how many of the 514,000 registered voters are predicted to vote on election day.

STEP 2   Decide what information is needed.

Use the percent of voters predicted to vote: 70%.
Also, use the number of registered voters: 514,000.

STEP 3   Choose the most appropriate operation.

This problem asks, "What is 70% of 514,000?"
The operation to use is multiplication.

STEP 4   Solve the problem.

70% of $514,000 = 0.70 \times 514,000 = 359,800$ voters

STEP 5   Check your answer.

To check, see if the ratio $\frac{359,800}{514,000}$ equals 70%.

$359,800 \div 514,000 = 0.7 = 70\%$

So 359,800 voters are predicted to vote.

Example 4   Use your calculator to find 72% of 600.

STEP 1   First press **AC**.

STEP 2   Press **6** **0** **0** **×** **7** **2** **SHIFT** **%**.

The display should read ⌐‾‾‾‾‾432.⌐.

EXERCISE 3

Directions: Calculate each of the following.

1. 10% of 870

2. 75% of 16

3. 12% of $100

4. $33\frac{1}{3}$% of 99

5. 80% of 1,064

6. 5% of $60,000

7. 47% of 100

8. 50% of $50

9. 65% of 44,500

10. 1% of $800

11. $66\frac{2}{3}$% of 180

12. 30% of $68

Directions: Use your calculator to solve each problem below.

13. 100% of 23

14. 2% of 8,750

15. 25% of 48

16. 98% of $1

Directions: Solve each problem.

17. The sales tax rate is 6%. Calculate the sales tax on an automobile purchase of $12,500.

18. Gerry wants to leave a 15% tip at a restaurant. His bill is $13.00. How much money should Gerry leave for a tip?

19. A store advertises "40% off" all shoes. How much money will you save on a pair of shoes priced at $45?

20. Christa is buying an $80 dress for "25% off." How much will the dress cost?

21. To pass an exam, you must get at least 70% of the 30 problems correct. How many problems must you get correct to pass?

22. A realtor earns 5% commission on the sale of a home sold for $108,000. How much commission does the realtor earn on this sale?

Directions: Use your calculator to solve each problem below.

23. A women's basketball coach reported that 80% of the team's 20 games were wins. How many games were wins? How many were losses?

24. Heather puts 10% of her gross earnings into a savings account. Each month she earns $2,500. How much will she put into savings in one year?

25. A manufacturer claims that only 2% of its products are defective. If 1,000 of its products are sold to a store in a month, how many of these are defective? How many are not?

26. Of 600 voters surveyed, 42% favored Brown, 51% favored Sanchez, and the rest were undecided. What percent of the voters surveyed were undecided? How many voters were undecided?

Answers are on page 282.

Interest Problems

When you put money into a savings account, the bank pays you **interest.** When you borrow money from a bank, you pay interest. The amount of the interest depends upon three things: principal, rate, and time. You can use the formula below to calculate interest.

$$\text{interest} = \text{principal} \times \text{rate} \times \text{time}$$

The **principal** is the amount of money invested or borrowed. The **rate** is the annual interest rate, usually given as a percent. The **time** is the length of time (years) the money is invested or borrowed.

Example Laurel put $1,000 into a savings account. The bank pays 3% interest annually on this account. How much interest will Laurel earn if she leaves the money in the account for 2 years?

STEP 1 Identify the principal, the rate, and the time.

Principal: $1,000 Rate: 3% = 0.03 Time: 2

STEP 2 Multiply.

$$\begin{aligned}\text{Interest} &= \text{principal} \times \text{rate} \times \text{time} \\ &= \$1,000 \times 0.03 \times 2 \\ &= \$60\end{aligned}$$

STEP 3 Summarize: Laurel will earn $60 in interest.

Make sure that time is expressed in terms of years.

$$4 \text{ months} = \frac{4}{12} \text{ years} \qquad 9 \text{ months} = \frac{9}{12} \text{ years}$$

$$200 \text{ days} = \frac{200}{365} \text{ years} \qquad 31 \text{ days} = \frac{31}{365} \text{ years}$$

EXERCISE 4

Directions: Calculate interest.

1. principal = $10,000
   rate = 8%
   time = 5 years

2. principal = $2,000
   rate = 10%
   time = 1 year

3. principal = $2,500
   rate = 4%
   time = 6 months

4. principal = $120,000
   rate = 9%
   time = 30 years

5. principal = $5,000
   rate = 11%
   time = 100 days

6. principal = $600
   rate = 5.5%
   time = 12 months

Directions: Solve each problem.

7. Kachina put $4,000 into a savings account that pays 4% annual interest. How much interest will she earn in 3 years?

8. Jamil borrowed $75,000 from a mortgage company to buy a house. He will repay the loan at 8% annual interest in 30 years. How much will he pay the mortgage company in interest?

9. On her eighteenth birthday, Veda put $1,500 into a savings account. The annual interest rate on the account is 6%. How much money will she have in the account on her twenty-first birthday?

10. A credit card company charges 12% annual interest on any balance due. If the balance due on Mimi's credit card is $150 and she waits 30 days to pay the bill, how much interest will she owe?

11. Zahur bought a car priced at $18,500. He made a 10% down payment and borrowed the rest of the money at a 9% annual interest rate. He will pay the balance due in five years. How much interest will he pay?

Answers are on page 282.

Using Proportion with Percent

One way to solve percent problems is to use proportions. You solve a proportion with the percent written as a ratio comparing a number to 100.

$$\frac{\text{part}}{\text{whole}} = \frac{\%}{100}$$

The next three examples show how to use this type of proportion to solve percent problems. By solving the proportion you find the missing value—the part, the whole, or the percent. The 100 is always in the proportion. Be careful to write the proportion correctly before you solve it. After solving the proportion, multiply to check your result.

Example 1 What is 30% of 90?

STEP 1 Identify the part, the whole, and the percent.

Part: (missing) Whole: 90 Percent: 30

STEP 2 Write the proportion $\frac{\text{part}}{\text{whole}} = \frac{\%}{100}$

$$\frac{\square}{90} = \frac{30}{100}$$

STEP 3 Solve the proportion.

$90 \times 30 \div 100 = 27$

STEP 4 Summarize.

30% of 90 is 27.

STEP 5 Use multiplication to check your answer.

30% of 90 = 0.3 × 90 = 27

Example 2 What percent of 90 is 18?

STEP 1 Identify the part, the whole, and the percent.

Part: 18 Whole: 90 Percent: (missing)

STEP 2 Write the proportion $\frac{\text{part}}{\text{whole}} = \frac{\%}{100}$.

$$\frac{18}{90} = \frac{\square}{100}$$

STEP 3 Solve the proportion.

$18 \times 100 \div 90 = 20$

STEP 4   Summarize.

20% of 90 is 18.

STEP 5   Use multiplication to check your answer.

20% of 90 = 0.2 × 90 = 18

Example 3   80% of what number is 20?

STEP 1   Identify the part, the whole, and the percent.

Part: 20 Whole: (missing) Percent: 80

STEP 2   Write the proportion $\frac{part}{whole} = \frac{\%}{100}$.

$$\frac{20}{\square} = \frac{80}{100}$$

STEP 3   Solve the proportion.

20 × 100 ÷ 80 = 25

STEP 4   Summarize.

80% of 25 is 20.

STEP 5   Use multiplication to check your answer.

80% of 25 = 0.8 × 25 = 20

You can also use this method when solving word problems that involve percents. Carefully decide what is missing—the part, the whole, or the percent. Then write the proportion with the numbers given, and solve for the missing value.

Example 4   In an election, 49% of the votes cast were against a constitutional amendment. This was 158,071 votes. How many votes were cast?

STEP 1   Understand the question.

You must figure out the total number of votes cast, for and against the amendment.

STEP 2   Decide what information is needed.

The percent of votes cast against the amendment: 49%.
The number of votes cast against the amendment: 158,071.

STEP 3   Write the proportion $\frac{part}{whole} = \frac{\%}{100}$.

Part: 158,071 Whole: (missing) Percent: 49

$$\frac{158,071}{\square} = \frac{49}{100}$$

STEP 4   Solve the proportion.

$158,071 \times 100 \div 49 \approx 322,594$ votes

STEP 5   Summarize.

49% of 322,594 is about 158,071.

STEP 6   Use multiplication to check your answer.

$49\% \times 322,594 = 0.49 \times 322,594 \approx 158,071$

So, 322,594 votes were cast.

EXERCISE 5

Directions: Answer each question.

1.   What number is 25% of 80?

2.   3 is 75% of what number?

3.   What percent of 44 is 11?

4.   16% of what number is 200?

5.   3% of 500 is what number?

6.   12 is what percent of 24?

7.   What percent of 16 is 12?

8.   What number is 90% of 1,000?

9.   10% of what number is 8?

10.   6 is 25% of what number?

11.   9 is what percent of 100?

12.   50% of 62 is what number?

13.   7 is 1% of what number?

14.   17 is what percent of 51?

15.   What is 100% of 49?

16.   15% of what number is 6?

Answers are on page 282.

EXERCISE 6

Directions: Solve each problem. If necessary, round to the nearest percent or whole number.

1. Americans consume 340 million pounds of cranberries a year. They consume about 73 million pounds during Thanksgiving week alone. What percent of American cranberry consumption is attributed to Thanksgiving?

2. There are about 93 million households in America. Living in about 8% of the households are single parents with children. Find the number of households in America of single parents with children.

3. Adams received 52% of the votes to win an election. There were 215,405 voters. How many people voted for Adams?

4. Rivera got 13,407 votes while his opponent got 6,309 votes. What percent of the votes did Rivera get?

5. One serving of wheat cereal provides 5 grams of dietary fiber. This is 21% of the daily value recommended for a 2,000-calorie diet. How many grams of dietary fiber are recommended daily for a person on a 2,000-calorie diet?

6. Barbara bought some mittens on sale for $12. She paid only 80% of the original price. What was the original price of the mittens? How much money did she save by buying the mittens on sale?

7. A baby's head is about 25% the length of its body, while an adult's head is about 17% the length of its body. Abigail is 4 months old and measures 24 inches long. About how long is her head?

8. A child's height at age 2 is usually about 50% of its full adult height. Eric is 2 years old and 32 inches tall. About how tall will Eric be as an adult?

9. A newborn baby sleeps an average of 16 hours in a 24-hour period. What percent of its time does a newborn baby spend sleeping?

10. Diana says that she spends about 30% of her time sleeping. How many hours does she sleep in a 24-hour period?

Directions: Choose the best answer.

11. Which of the following proportions could you use to find what percent 5 is of 8?

 (1) $\frac{5}{\square} = \frac{8}{100}$

 (2) $\frac{5}{8} = \frac{\square}{100}$

 (3) $\frac{\square}{8} = \frac{5}{100}$

 (4) none of the above

12. Which of the following proportions could you use to find what percent of 25 is 10?

 (1) $\frac{10}{25} = \frac{\square}{100}$

 (2) $\frac{10}{100} = \frac{25}{\square}$

 (3) $\frac{10}{\square} = \frac{25}{100}$

 (4) none of the above

13. Which calculation will *not* give 25% of 80?

 (1) 0.25×80

 (2) $\frac{1}{4} \times 80$

 (3) $80 \times 25 \div 100$

 (4) $80 \times 100 \div 25$

Answers are on page 283.

Percent Review

Directions: In questions 1–15, solve each problem. Show your work at the right.

1. Change 0.23 to a percent.

2. Change 70% to a decimal.

3. Calculate 85% of 120.

4. Change $\frac{2}{3}$ to a percent.

5. Write the fraction and decimal that equals 25%.

6. What percent of 60 is 6?

7. Change 2% to a fraction.

8. How much is a 15% tip on a restaurant bill of $7?

9. 90% of what number is 18?

10. Change $\frac{1}{5}$ to a percent.

11. Calculate the interest earned on $2,000 invested for 2 years at an annual rate of 6%.

12. What number is 30% of 40?

13. 35 is what percent of 70?

14. $6\frac{1}{2} - 2\frac{7}{8}$

15. 52.9 – 16.75

Directions: Use your calculator to solve each problem. Write each answer on the number grid.

16. 36% of 420

17. 2% of 8,460

18. 91% of 75

Directions: Choose the correct answer to each problem. Remember the problem-solving skills you have learned.

19. Daniel's bill at a restaurant was $19. He wants to leave a 15% tip. He will write a check for the total. For what amount should he write the check?

(1) $ 2.85
(2) $21.85
(3) $28.50
(4) $16.15
(5) Not enough information is given.

20. A meteorologist reported that 17 days in Boston during June were rainy. What percent of days in Boston during June were rainy?

(1) 17%
(2) about 17%
(3) about 55%
(4) about 57%
(5) Not enough information is given.

21. Hwa is buying four items at a store priced at $4.99, $2.49, $0.98, and $6.29. Each item is subject to 4% sales tax. If he pays with a $20 bill, how much change should he receive?

(1) $ 4.66
(2) $15.34
(3) $ 5.25
(4) $14.75
(5) $ 0.59

22. Lanelle found the pair of jeans she wants at five different stores. The original price of the jeans at each store is $35. Which of the following will give Lanelle the best deal on the jeans?

(1) 25% off
(2) $\frac{1}{3}$ off
(3) pay 70% of the original price
(4) $10 off
(5) Not enough information is given.

23. Alfredo is planning to invest some money in order to earn some interest. The annual interest rate is 5%. With which of the following investments will he earn the most money?

    (1) $3,000 for 2 years

    (2) $4,000 for 1 year

    (3) $3,500 for 18 months

    (4) $2,000 for 3 years

    (5) $2,500 for $2\frac{1}{2}$ years

24. Daniel decided to save 5% of his weekly salary. If he earned $340 last week, how much should he save?

    (1) $ 68
    (2) $ 17
    (3) $ 34
    (4) $ 45
    (5) $170

25. The sales tax rate in Omaha is $6\frac{1}{2}$%. If Jay bought a car for $12,500, how much sales tax will he pay?

    (1) $125
    (2) $625
    (3) $750
    (4) $812.50
    (5) $650.50

Answers are on page 283.

Chapter 8

Working with Data

Mean, Median, Mode, and Range

Data is information that is collected and analyzed. It is often, but not always, numerical. Statisticians use many different methods for collecting and analyzing data. Two important characteristics of a set of data are its center and its spread. The **center** of a data set can be described by three different measures: mean, median, and mode. One of these measures might be more appropriate than another for a given data set. The **spread** of a data set can be described by its range. Here are some definitions of these measures.

- The **mean** is the average value of a data set.

- The **median** is the middle value of a data set listed in order from least to greatest.

- The **mode** is the item that occurs most often in a data set.

- The **range** is the difference between the greatest and least items of a data set.

The examples show how to find these measures. They use Robin's Running Data, given below.

Example 1   **Robin's Running Data**

Robin is training for a 5-kilometer race. Each day she runs 5 kilometers and records her time to the nearest minute. Here is the data she collected one week: 20, 24, 22, 22, 21, 20, 25.

Refer to Robin's Running Data. Find the mean.

STEP 1   Find the sum of all the items in the data set.

20 + 24 + 22 + 22 + 21 + 20 + 25 = 154

STEP 2   Count the number of items in the data set.

7 items

STEP 3   Divide the sum by the number of items in the data set.

154 ÷ 7 = 22
The mean is 22 minutes.

SUMMARY FOR FINDING THE MEAN

To find the mean:

1) Add all the items in the data set.

2) Divide by the number of items.

Example 2 Refer to Robin's Running Data. Find the median.

STEP 1 List items in order from least to greatest.

20, 20, 21, 22, 22, 24, 25

STEP 2 Count the number of items in the data set.

7 items

STEP 3 If the number of items is odd, identify the middle value in the ordered list.

The middle value is 22.
The median is 22 minutes.

Sometimes there is an even number of items in a data set. In this case, the median is the average of the two middle values.

Example 3 Find the median of this data: 20, 24, 22, 22, 21, 20.

STEP 1 List items in order from least to greatest.

20, 20, 21, 22, 22, 24

STEP 2 Count the number of items in the data set.

6 items

STEP 3 If the number of items is even, identify the two middle values in the ordered list.

The two middle values are 21 and 22.

STEP 4 Find the average (mean) of the two middle values.

$21 + 22 = 43$; $43 \div 2 = 21.5$
The median is 21.5.

SUMMARY FOR FINDING THE MEDIAN

To find the median:

1) List all the items in the data set in order from least to greatest.

2) Find the middle value.

3) If there is an even number of items, find the average of the two middle values.

Example 4   Refer to Robin's Running Data. Find the mode(s), if any.

STEP 1   Group items in the data set that are the same.

20, 20   21   22, 22   24   25

STEP 2   Find the item that occurs most often. A set of data might have one mode, more than one mode, or no modes.

The items 20 and 22 both occur most often (twice).

The modes are 20 minutes and 22 minutes.

SUMMARY FOR FINDING THE MODE

To find the mode:

1) Group items in the data set that are the same.

2) Find the item that occurs most often. A set of data might have one mode, more than one mode, or no modes.

Example 5   Refer to Robin's Running Data. Find the range.

STEP 1   Identify the items with the greatest value and the least value.

25   20

STEP 2   Subtract the item with least value from the item with greatest value.

25 − 20 = 5

The range is 5 minutes.

SUMMARY FOR FINDING THE RANGE

To find the range:

Subtract the item with the least value from the item with the greatest value.

EXERCISE 1

Directions: Refer to Barbara's Running Data. Find each measure. Round to the nearest minute, if necessary.

Barbara's Running Data

Barbara is training for a 10-kilometer race. Each day she runs 10 kilometers and records her time to the nearest minute. Here is the data she collected one week: 42, 41, 45, 40, 46, 42, 44.

---

1. Mean : 43

2. Median : 42 min

3. Mode - 42 min.

4. Range : 6

Directions: Find the measure for the given data.

5. Find the median.
   House prices: $85,000; $108,000; $95,500; $120,000; $105,000; $99,900; $124,000

6. Find the mode(s), if any.
   Favorite water sport: swimming, skiing, scuba diving, swimming, skiing, fishing, rafting, skiing, sailing

7. Find the mean.
   High temperatures (°F) for February in Milwaukee: 10, 12, 30, 38, 22, 6, 2, 0, 0, 18, 22, 25, 16, 33, 40, 38, 32, 35, 10, 8, 5, 5, 9, 12, 15, 21, 30, 19 = 513 ÷ 28 = 18

8. Find the mode(s), if any.
   Number of siblings in a family: 2, 1, 4, 3, 1, 2, 1, 3, 3, 2, 4, 2

9. Find the range.
   Ages of employees in a department: 24, 40, 58, 22, 33, 35, 29, 28, 64, 48 = 42

10. Find the median.
    Shoe sizes of women: 7, $6\frac{1}{2}$, $8\frac{1}{2}$, 9, 10, 5, 7, 8 = $\frac{15}{2}$ = $7\frac{1}{2}$

11. Find the mean.
    Test scores: 75%, 72%, 88%, 90%, 85%, 100%, 77%, 86%
    673 ÷ 8 = 84

12. Find the range.
    Prices for a new toaster: $39.99; $60; $24.50; $54.99; $64.99; $45; $41.49 $40.49

Directions: Solve each problem.

13. Garry's bank statement listed his electronic withdrawals for the month: $40, $80, $100, $20, $50, $60, $20, $80, $60, $40, $30, $100, $60. What amount does he withdraw most often? 60

14. Employees of a small company have the following salaries: $24,000; $15,000; $100,000; $30,000; $12,000. Find the average salary and the median salary. Why do you think there is such a big difference in the two?

15. On March 31 in San Diego, a meteorologist reported 60°F as the high temperature for the day for the first time during March. The meteorologist also reported 60°F as the median high temperature for San Diego for the month. On how many March days in San Diego was the high temperature lower than 60°F?

16. Tim collected data on his height (to the nearest inch) and that of four of his friends, but he lost the data. Tim was the tallest, measuring 72 inches. Also, no two friends had the same height. Tim had calculated the following measures: median = 68, mean = 68, range = 7. Figure out what the original data was.

17. The age range for players on a soccer team is 10 years. The youngest player is 15 years old. What is the age of the oldest player?

18. Bill's test scores are 70%, 85%, 78%, and 80%. What score must Bill get on his next test in order to have an 80% average?

Directions: Choose the best answer to define each word on the left.

19. ____4____ median   (1) average

20. ____3____ range   (2) most frequent

21. ____2____ mode   (3) middle

22. ____1____ mean   (4) difference

Answers are on page 284.

Bar Graphs

Data can be displayed in many different ways. A **graph** gives a visual picture of the data. With a graph you can often "see" things about the data that are difficult to see by looking only at the numbers.

A **bar graph** can help you make visual comparisons among numerical data. A bar graph is made up of rectangular bars that extend upward or lengthwise. The height of each bar corresponds to one number in the data. The higher the bar, the greater the number.

The bar graph below displays the data given in the table.

AVERAGE MONTHLY TEMPERATURES IN ANCHORAGE, ALASKA

Month	Temperature (°F)
January	13
April	35
July	58
October	35

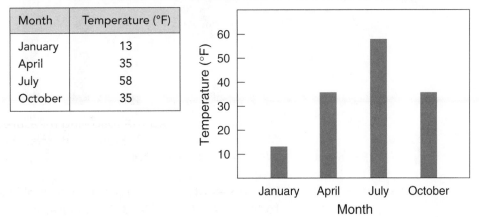

The table and the graph provide the same information, but the graph makes comparisons quick and easy. For example, you can see that April and October have the same average monthly temperature because their bars are the same height.

Here are some things to notice about the bar graph above. This information will help you to read, interpret, and draw bar graphs.

- Along the **horizontal axis,** the bottom of the graph, the months being compared are listed: January, April, July, and October.

- Along the **vertical axis,** the left side of the graph, numbers representing temperatures from 10°F to 60°F are listed.

- The top of each bar aligns with the correct number on the vertical axis. In this graph, a bar for each of the four months gives the average temperature for the month.

The next three examples show how to read the bar graph below to answer questions about the data displayed.

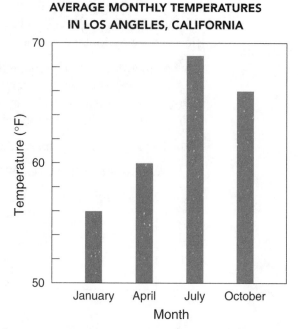

**AVERAGE MONTHLY TEMPERATURES
IN LOS ANGELES, CALIFORNIA**

Example 1   What is the average temperature in Los Angeles in April?

Find the bar for April. Trace a horizontal line from the top of this bar to the vertical axis. Read the number on the axis: 60.

The average temperature in Los Angeles in April is 60°F.

Example 2   In what month is the average temperature in Los Angeles 69°F?

Since 69 does not appear on the vertical axis, determine that each mark represents 2 degrees. Trace a horizontal line from where 69 would be (halfway between 70 and the mark directly below it) to the top of a bar. Read the month for that bar: July.

The average temperature in Los Angeles is 69°F in July.

TIP
When the number you are working with does not appear on an axis, determine the amount covered between marks and find its approximate location.

Example 3   What is the range of average monthly temperatures in Los Angeles?

STEP 1   Read from the graph the lowest temperature, shown by the lowest bar: 56°F. Read from the graph the highest temperature, shown by the highest bar: 69°F.

STEP 2   Subtract to find the range: 69°F – 56°F = 13°F.

SUMMARY FOR READING A BAR GRAPH

To read a bar graph:

1) Find the bar that displays the information you seek.

2) Trace a line from the top of the bar to the vertical axis.

3) Read the number on the axis. (Or, do the opposite. Find the number, then the bar.)

EXERCISE 2

Directions: Use the bar graph below to answer each question.

NUMBER OF SPECIES IN SELECTED FAMILIES OF MAMMALS

1. How many species are there in the horse family? 6

2. Which family of mammals has almost 20 species? Seal

3. Which family has about the same number of species as the cat family? dog/fox

4. Which two families have the fewest number of species?
   noise and pig

5. How many more species are there in the rabbit family than in the seal family? *21*

6. Which family has about twice as many species as the seal family?
   Rabbit

7. How many times more species are there in the rabbit family than in the pig family? *5*

Directions: Refer to the bar graph below to answer each question.

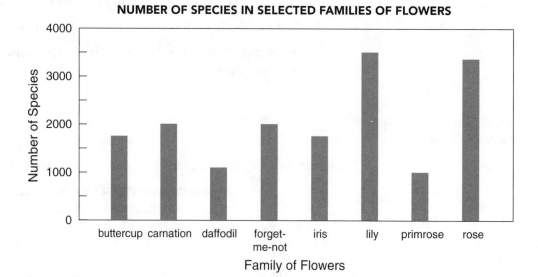

NUMBER OF SPECIES IN SELECTED FAMILIES OF FLOWERS

8. How many species are there in the forget-me-not family?

9. Which family has 2,500 more species than the primrose family?

10. List the families in order from least number of species to greatest number of species; then find the median number of species for these families.

11. Which statement is *not* true?

   (1) The carnation family and the forget-me-not family have about the same number of species.
   (2) The buttercup and iris families combined have about the same number of species as the lily family.
   (3) The primrose and daffodil families combined have about the same number of species as the carnation family.
   (4) The rose family has about twice as many species as the daffodil family.
   (5) The iris family has about half as many species as the lily family.

Answers are on page 284.

Drawing Bar Graphs

Drawing a bar graph is another important skill to learn. Remember that a bar graph can help you make comparisons among numerical data. The lengths of the bars must be different enough so that someone reading the graph can quickly see the differences and make the important comparisons.

Example   In the 1994 Winter Olympics, the U.S. won 6 gold, 5 silver, and 2 bronze medals. Draw a bar graph to display this data.

STEP 1   Draw a horizontal axis. Along the axis, write the types of medals: Gold, Silver, and Bronze. Label the axis: Type of Medal.

STEP 2   Draw a vertical axis. Along the axis, write numbers that at least cover the range of the data. Label the axis: Number of Medals.

STEP 3   For each type of medal, draw a bar that shows the number of medals won. The heights of the bars should match the data. Shade the bars.

STEP 4   Give the bar graph a title: Medals Won by the U.S. in the 1994 Winter Olympics.

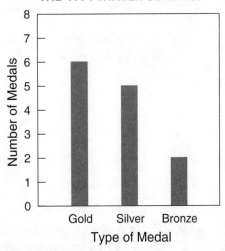

MEDALS WON BY THE U.S. IN THE 1994 WINTER OLYMPICS

SUMMARY FOR DRAWING BAR GRAPHS

To create a bar graph:

1) Draw and label horizontal and vertical axes.

2) Draw and shade bars to display the data.

3) Give the graph a title.

EXERCISE 3

Directions: Refer to the data in the table below to draw the bar graphs described.

Country	Gold Medals	Silver Medals	Bronze Medals	Total Medals
Top Medal Winners in the 1994 Winter Olympics, Lillehammer, Norway				
Norway	10	11	5	26
Germany	9	7	8	24
Russia	11	8	4	23
Italy	7	5	8	20
United States	6	5	2	13
Canada	3	6	4	13
Switzerland	3	4	2	9
Austria	2	3	4	9
South Korea	4	1	1	6
Finland	0	1	5	6

1. Draw a bar graph that displays the types and numbers of medals won by Norway.

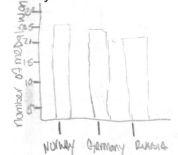

2. Draw a bar graph that displays the number of gold medals won by the top five countries listed in the table.

3. Draw a bar graph that displays the types and numbers of medals won by the United States.

4. Draw a bar graph that displays the total number of medals won by the countries listed in the table.

5. Draw your own bar graph, displaying some of the data given in the table.

Answers are on page 285.

Line Graphs

A **line graph** can help you see patterns and trends in data. A line graph is made up of points that are connected by line segments. Line graphs are often used to display data over a period of time.

The line graph below displays the data given in the table.

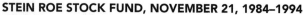

STEIN ROE STOCK FUND, NOVEMBER 21, 1984–1994

Year	Price of One Share
1984	$13.63
1985	$16.74
1986	$19.87
1987	$16.64
1988	$13.91
1989	$18.68
1990	$ 8.14
1991	$23.01
1992	$26.29
1993	$25.33
1994	$23.58

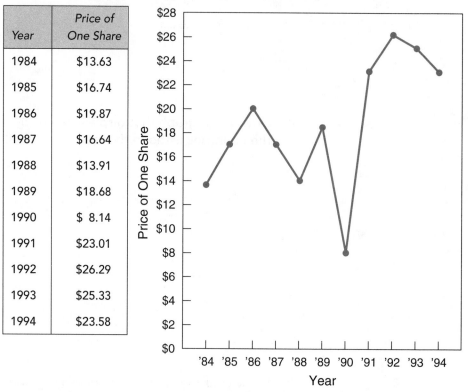

The table and the graph provide the same information, but the graph shows, visually, the dramatic decrease in the price in 1990 and the increase in 1991.

Like bar graphs, line graphs have a horizontal and vertical axis.

- Along the **horizontal axis,** the years refer to annual dates from November 21, 1984 to November 21, 1994.

- Along the **vertical axis,** numbers that fall within the range of the data represent the price of one share of the Stein Roe Stock Fund. Prices range from about $8 to about $27.

- In the body of the graph, the **points** display the data. Points connected by **line segments** show how the price changes (increases or decreases) from year to year.

The next three examples show how to read the line graph below.

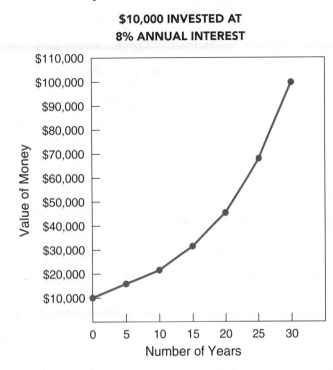

**$10,000 INVESTED AT
8% ANNUAL INTEREST**

<u>Example 1</u>   If you invest $10,000 at an 8% annual interest rate, what will be its value in 25 years?

Find 25 years on the horizontal axis. Find the point directly above 25. Trace a line across to the vertical axis: about $68,000.

In 25 years, the value of the money will be about $68,000.

<u>Example 2</u>   If you invest $10,000 at an 8% annual interest rate, how long will it take for your money to be worth $40,000?

Find $40,000 on the vertical axis. Trace directly across to the graph. Where you intersect the line graph, draw a point. From this point, trace down to the horizontal axis: about 18.

It will take about 18 years for the money to be worth $40,000.

Sometimes you can make predictions from a line graph. Look for a pattern or a trend in the line, and extend it to make the prediction.

<u>Example 3</u>   If you invest $10,000 at an 8% annual interest rate, estimate the value of the money in 40 years.

Extend the horizontal axis across to 40 years. Extend the vertical axis up to at least $200,000, and list more values along the axis. Now notice the upward trend in the data, shown by the line. Also, each line segment is steeper than the one before it. Extend the line graph, following this pattern. On the line graph, draw a point for 40 years. From this point, trace across to the vertical axis.

In 40 years, the value of the money will be about $200,000.

SUMMARY FOR READING A LINE GRAPH

To read a line graph:

1) Find the given information on the horizontal axis.

2) Directly above, find the point on the line graph.

3) Trace a line across to the vertical axis.

4) Read the number. (Or, do the opposite. Start with the vertical axis, trace to the line graph, and read the number from the horizontal axis.)

EXERCISE 4

Directions: Refer to the line graph below to answer each question.

HOURLY TEMPERATURES IN GREAT FALLS, MONTANA ON NOVEMBER 21, 1994

1. What was the temperature in Great Falls at 4:00 P.M.?

2. At what time was the hourly temperature 12°F?

3. At what time was the hourly temperature the highest? What was the temperature?

4. At what time was the hourly temperature the lowest? What was the temperature?

5. At what four times was the hourly temperature 18°F?

6. At what time was the hourly temperature the same as it was at 8:00 A.M.?

7. Was the temperature higher at 6:00 A.M. or at 6:00 P.M.?

8. What was the median hourly temperature for the 24-hour period?

9. What was the range of hourly temperatures in the 24-hour period?

10. Which hour had the greatest increase in temperature? By how much did the temperature rise?

11. Which hour had the greatest decrease in temperature? By how much did the temperature drop?

12. Sunset was at about 5:00 P.M., and sunrise was at about 7:30 A.M. Which statement is *not* true?

    (1) The temperature rose from sunrise until mid-afternoon.
    (2) The temperature dropped dramatically at sunset.
    (3) The temperature did not drop in the afternoon until sunset.
    (4) The temperature dropped during the early morning hours until sunrise.
    (5) The temperature at sunset and midnight was about the same.

13. Which statement is true?

    (1) The graph shows 48 temperature readings.
    (2) The hourly temperature was never lower than 10°F.
    (3) The hourly temperature was never higher than 24°F.
    (4) The temperature changed by the same number of degrees each hour.
    (5) none of the above

Answers are on page 286.

Drawing Line Graphs

Example   The table below gives the price of one share of the Stein Roe Special Fund on November 21 for ten years. Draw a line graph to display this data.

STEIN ROE SPECIAL FUND, NOVEMBER 21, 1984–1994

Year	Price
1984	$14.39
1985	$17.38
1986	$20.03
1987	$15.55
1988	$14.46
1989	$20.20
1990	$16.45
1991	$19.08
1992	$22.23
1993	$24.89
1994	$23.10

STEP 1   Draw a horizontal axis. Along the axis, write the years: 1984 to 1994. Label the axis: Date (November 21 each year).

STEP 2   Draw a vertical axis. Along the axis, write numbers that at least cover the range of the data. Label the axis: Price of One Share.

STEP 3   For each year, draw a point that shows the approximate price of one share. Connect the points with line segments.

STEP 4 Give the line graph a title: Stein Roe Special Fund, November 21, 1984–1994.

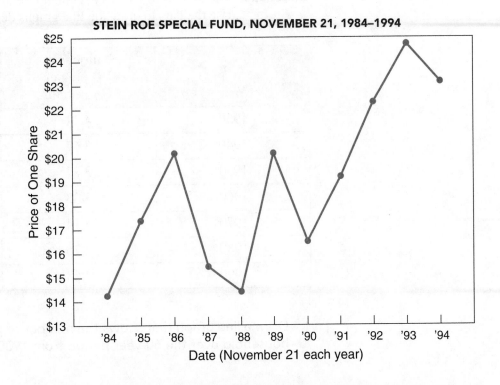

STEIN ROE SPECIAL FUND, NOVEMBER 21, 1984–1994

SUMMARY FOR DRAWING LINE GRAPHS

To draw a line graph:

1) Draw and label horizontal and vertical axes.

2) Draw points to display the data.

3) Connect the points with line segments.

4) Give the graph a title.

EXERCISE 5

Directions: The table below gives data on households in the United States. Use the data to draw the line graphs described.

Year	Number of People per Household	Number of Households (millions)
1930	4.11	30
1940	3.67	35
1950	3.37	44
1960	3.33	53
1970	3.14	63
1980	2.76	81
1990	2.63	93

1. Draw a line graph that shows the number of people per U.S. household over the 60-year period from 1930 to 1990.

2. Draw a line graph that shows the number of households (in millions) in the United States over the 60-year period from 1930 to 1990.

Directions: The table below gives consumer data for the United States. Use the data to draw the line graphs described.

Year	Consumer Price Index	Purchasing Power of the Dollar
1985	323.4	$.31
1986	325.7	$.31
1987	340.2	$.29
1988	357.9	$.28
1989	371.1	$.27
1990	399.4	$.25
1991	404.7	$.25
1992	416.3	$.24
1993	423.1	$.24

3. Draw a line graph that displays the Consumer Price Index in the United States from 1985 to 1993.

4. Draw a line graph that displays the Purchasing Power of the Dollar in the United States from 1985 to 1993.

Answers are on page 286.

Circle Graphs

A **circle graph** shows parts of a whole. The circle is the whole, or 100%. The circle is divided into parts, and all the parts add up to 100%. So circle graphs are often used to display data given as percents.

The circle graph below displays the data given in the table. The graph shows that air exhaled by the human body contains parts of nitrogen, oxygen, carbon dioxide, and water. It also shows the size of each part. For example, nitrogen has the largest part of the circle (75%) because nitrogen is the largest part of exhaled air (75%).

EXHALED AIR

nitrogen	75%
oxygen	15%
carbon dioxide	4%
water	6%

EXHALED AIR

The next five examples show how to read a circle graph to answer questions about the data displayed. The examples are based on the circle graph above.

Example 1   What percent of exhaled air is oxygen?

Find oxygen in the circle graph. Read the percent: 15%.

Exhaled air is 15% oxygen.

Example 2   What makes up 6% of exhaled air?

Find 6% in the circle graph. Read the label: water.

Water makes up 6% of exhaled air.

Example 3   What fraction of exhaled air is nitrogen?

Find nitrogen in the circle graph. Read the percent: 75%.

Write 75% as a fraction: $\frac{75}{100} = \frac{75 \div 25}{100 \div 25} = \frac{3}{4}$

Exhaled air is $\frac{3}{4}$ nitrogen.

Example 4   List the parts of exhaled air in order from least to greatest.

Write the percents given in the circle graph in order from least to greatest: 4%, 6%, 15%, 75%.

Write the parts in order from least to greatest:
4%, carbon dioxide; 6%, water; 15%, oxygen; 75%, nitrogen.

The list is: carbon dioxide, water, oxygen, nitrogen.

Example 5   Suppose the amount of exhaled air is 760 millimeters of mercury (mmHg). Find the amount of carbon dioxide in the exhaled air.

Find carbon dioxide in the circle graph. Read the percent: 4%.

Write a proportion: $\frac{part}{whole} = \frac{\%}{100}$.

$$\frac{h}{760} = \frac{4}{100}$$

Multiply to find the cross products, and divide:
$760 \times 4 \div 100 \approx 30$

The amount of carbon dioxide in the exhaled air is about 30 mmHg.

SUMMARY FOR READING A CIRCLE GRAPH

To read a circle graph:

1) Find the category you seek, and read the percent.

2) Or, do the opposite: Find the percent you seek, and read the category.

EXERCISE 6

Directions: The circle graph below shows the portion of miles of general coastline of each of the states along the U.S. Pacific coastline. Refer to this data to answer each question.

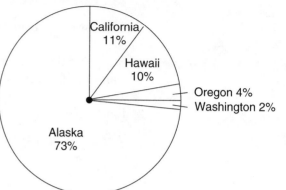

U.S. PACIFIC COASTLINE

1. What percent of the U.S. Pacific coastline lies in Oregon?

2. Which state makes up 11% of the U.S. Pacific coastline?

3. Which state makes up almost $\frac{3}{4}$ of the U.S. Pacific coastline?

4. What fraction of the U.S. Pacific coastline lies in Hawaii?

5. How many states make up part of the U.S. Pacific coastline?

6. What percent of the U.S. Pacific coastline lies in the lower 48 states?

7. Which state has twice as much U.S. Pacific coastline as Washington?

8. The U.S. Pacific coastline is 7,623 miles long. Find the approximate length of the coastline in each state.

Directions: Exit polls were conducted on Election Day 1994 for how Americans voted in the race for the House of Representatives. The circle graphs below display some of the data collected. Refer to them to answer each question.

HOW AMERICANS VOTED IN THE RACE FOR THE HOUSE, 1994

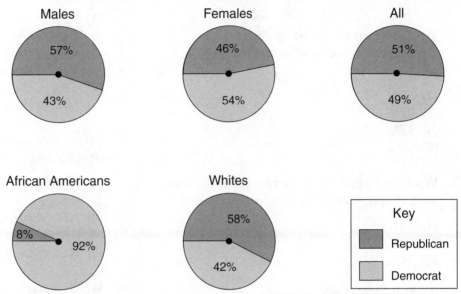

9. Which group showed the most support for Democrats? What percent of this group voted Democratic?

10. Which group showed the most support for Republicans? What percent of this group voted Republican?

11. Was the race between the Republicans and Democrats closer with the males or with the females?

12. Did the Democrats or the Republicans receive more votes? Which data did you use to answer this question?

Answers are on page 287.

EXERCISE 7

Directions: Refer to the circle graphs on page 167. Choose the best answer.

1. What percent of the males voted Democratic in the race for the House?

   (1) 43%
   (2) 57%
   (3) 92%
   (4) 42%
   (5) 49%

2. What percent of the African American females voted Republican in the race for the House?

   (1) 46%
   (2) 8%
   (3) 54%
   (4) 38%
   (5) Not enough information is given.

3. A total of 10,210 voters participated in the exit poll. How many of these voters did not vote Republican?

   (1) 51% of voters
   (2) 5,003 voters
   (3) 54% of voters
   (4) 5,207 voters
   (5) Not enough information is given.

4. Which of the following is not shown by the graphs?

   (1) 92% of the African Americans voted Democratic.
   (2) 46% of the females voted Republican.
   (3) 49% of the voters voted Democratic.
   (4) 43% of the males voted Democratic.
   (5) 58% of the whites are Republicans.

5. Which group cast the greatest number of votes for Republicans?

   (1) males
   (2) females
   (3) African Americans
   (4) whites
   (5) Not enough information is given.

6. Which statement is true?

   (1) More males voted Republican than voted Democrat.
   (2) More females voted Democrat than voted Republican.
   (3) More African Americans voted Democrat than voted Republican.
   (4) More whites voted Republican than voted Democrat.
   (5) all of the above

Answers are on page 287.

Drawing Circle Graphs

To draw a circle graph, you need to use some geometry skills. Recall that a **central angle** of a circle is an angle formed at the center. The graph at the right shows a central angle of a circle. To divide a circle graph into parts, you need to find the central angle for each part. The sum of all the central angles of a circle is 360°.

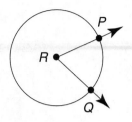

central angle *PRQ*

Example 1 Data from an exit poll taken on Election Day 1994 is as follows: In the race for the House of Representatives, non-high school graduates voted 40% Republican and 60% Democratic. Draw a circle graph to display this data.

STEP 1 Calculate the central angle for each part. To do this, write the percent as a decimal and multiply by 360°. Round to the nearest degree, if necessary. Check the sum of the central angles (360°).

40% Republican: $0.40 \times 360° = 144°$
60% Democratic: $0.60 \times 360° = 216°$

Sum of central angles: $144° + 216° = 360°$

STEP 2 Use a compass to draw a circle. Draw a point at the center of the circle. Use a protractor to draw each central angle.

STEP 3 Label each part of the circle graph with a name and a percent. Give the circle graph a title.

**NON-HIGH SCHOOL GRADUATES'
VOTES FOR THE HOUSE, 1994**

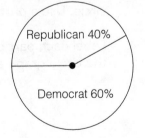

Sometimes data is given as numbers instead of percents. To draw the circle graph, you calculate a percent for each part.

Example 2 The entire coastline of the United States is 12,383 miles long. It includes these four coasts: Atlantic, 2,069 miles; Gulf of Mexico, 1,631 miles; Pacific, 7,623 miles; Arctic, 1,060 miles. Draw a circle graph to display this data.

STEP 1 Calculate the percent for each part. Round to the nearest percent, if necessary. Check the sum of the percents (100%).

Atlantic: $2,069 \div 12,383 \approx 0.17 = 17\%$
Gulf: $1,631 \div 12,383 \approx 0.13 = 13\%$
Pacific: $7,623 \div 12,383 \approx 0.62 = 62\%$
Arctic: $1,060 \div 12,383 \approx 0.09 = 9\%$

Sum of the percents: $17\% + 13\% + 62\% + 9\% = 101\%$
The sum should be 100%, so adjust either by rounding Pacific to 61% or Arctic to 8%.

STEP 2 Calculate the central angle for each part. To do this, write the percent as a decimal and multiply by 360°. Round to the nearest degree, if necessary. Check the sum of the central angles (360°).

Atlantic: $0.17 \times 360° \approx 61°$
Gulf: $0.13 \times 360° \approx 47°$
Pacific: $0.61 \times 360° \approx 220°$
Arctic: $0.09 \times 360° \approx 32°$

Sum of the central angles: $61° + 47° + 220° + 32° = 360°$

STEP 3 Use a compass to draw a circle. Draw a point at the center of the circle. Use a protractor to draw each central angle.

STEP 4 Label each part of the circle graph with a name and a percent. Give the circle graph a title.

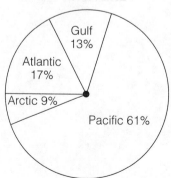

U.S. COASTLINE

SUMMARY FOR DRAWING CIRCLE GRAPHS

To draw a circle graph:

1) Calculate the percent for each part, if necessary. The sum of the percents should be 100%.

2) Calculate the central angle for each part. The sum of the central angles should be 360°.

3) Draw a circle, mark the center, and draw each central angle.

4) Label each part and give the graph a title.

EXERCISE 8

Directions: Use the data below to draw the circle graphs described.

1. On November 8, 1994, California voters passed Proposition 187 by a vote of 59% to 41%. This action bars illegal immigrants from receiving many state benefits. Draw a circle graph to display this data. Give the graph a title.

2. A telephone poll of 800 adult Americans was taken after Election Day 1994. The question asked was, "Now that the Republicans control Congress, is this a new era of government in Washington, or will there be a continuation of politics as usual?" The response was as follows: Politics as usual, 63%; New era, 32%; Not sure, 5%. Draw a circle graph that displays this data. Give the graph a title.

3. The U.S. House of Representatives, voted into office on November 8, 1994, includes 230 Republicans, 204 Democrats, and 1 Independent. Draw a circle graph that displays this data.

4. The coastline of the Gulf coast of the United States is 1,631 miles long. The five states bordering the Gulf coast, along with their respective miles of coastline, are shown below. Draw a circle graph that displays this data.

State	Coastline (miles)
Florida	770
Alabama	53
Mississippi	44
Louisiana	397
Texas	367

Answers are on page 287.

MAY 19th = POP QUIZ

Probability

Probability is the chance of something happening. It does not guarantee that something will happen, but it gives a measure of how likely it is that something will happen.

You can calculate the probability of an event using the fraction below.

$$\text{Probability of an event} = \frac{\text{number of favorable outcomes}}{\text{total number of possible outcomes}}$$

Example 1   A number cube has faces numbered 1 to 6. When you roll a cube, what is the probability of rolling a 4?

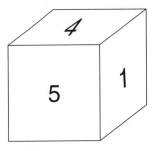

STEP 1   Find the total number of possible outcomes.

There are 6 different faces, so the total number of possible outcomes is 6.

STEP 2   Find the number of favorable outcomes.

The favorable outcome in this case is that the number cube lands on the face numbered 4, so there is 1 favorable outcome.

STEP 3   Calculate the probability.

$$\frac{\text{favorable outcomes}}{\text{total outcomes}} = \frac{1}{6}$$

The probability of rolling a 4 is $\frac{1}{6}$.

Example 2   When you roll a cube, what is the probability of rolling an even number?

STEP 1   Find the total number of possible outcomes.

There are 6 different faces, so the total number of possible outcomes is 6.

STEP 2   Find the number of favorable outcomes.

The favorable outcome in this case is that the cube lands on 2, 4, or 6. There are 3 different favorable outcomes.

STEP 3   Calculate the probability.

$$\frac{\text{favorable outcomes}}{\text{total outcomes}} = \frac{3}{6} = \frac{1}{2}$$

The probability of rolling an even number is $\frac{1}{2}$.

You can express a probability as a fraction, a decimal, or a percent. Always write the fraction in lowest terms. The highest a probability can be is 1, or 100%. The lowest a probability can be is 0, or 0%.

Example 3   What is the probability that the sun will set in the west the next time it sets?

The sun always sets in the west, so the probability is $\frac{1}{1}$, or 1, or 100%.

Example 4   What is the probability that the sun will set in the east the next time it sets?

The sun never sets in the east, so the probability is $\frac{0}{1}$, or 0, or 0%.

EXERCISE 9

Directions: Solve each problem. Write each probability as a fraction, a decimal, and a percent. Refer to the spinner below for numbers 1–4.

1. What is the probability of spinning $10?

2. What is the probability of spinning at least $10?

3. Which two amounts of money are the least likely to be spun?

4. Which amount of money has a 50% probability of being spun?

5. When you flip a coin, what is the probability of flipping "heads"?

6. When you flip a coin, what is the probability of flipping "heads" or "tails"?

7. A standard deck of cards has 52 cards, including 4 Kings, 4 Queens, and 4 Jacks. When you draw one card, what is the probability of drawing a King?

8. When you roll a number cube, what is the probability of rolling a 4?

9. A meteorologist reports a 10% chance of rain. What is the probability of no rain?

10. A winning number appears on one of 10,000 baseball programs. If you buy a program, what are your chances of getting the winning number?

11. The Lopez family draws names for holiday presents. Each of the 10 family members puts his or her own name into a hat. What is the probability that someone will draw his or her own name?

12. One hundred raffle tickets are sold. The holder of the winning ticket will win a new car. If you buy five tickets for $3, what is the probability that you will win the new car?

13. A bag contains the following colored jelly beans: 10 red, 7 green, and 1 black. You pick one jelly bean without looking. What is the probability the jelly bean is red?

14. A bag contains the following colored jelly beans: 10 red, 7 green, and 1 black. You pick one jelly bean without looking. What is the probability the jelly bean is yellow?

Answers are on page 288.

EXERCISE 10

Directions: Choose the best answer.

1. Suppose you roll a number cube. Which outcome is most likely?

   (1) an odd number
   (2) a number less than 5
   (3) 6
   (4) 1 or 2
   (5) a number greater than 3

2. A hat contains 26 small pieces of paper labeled with a letter from the alphabet. The letters are equally likely to be drawn. Suppose you draw one letter from the hat. Which outcome is least likely?

   (1) a vowel
   (2) a consonant
   (3) a letter in the second half of the alphabet
   (4) the first letter of your first name
   (5) A or Z

3. Which event has probability equal to 1?

   (1) Tuesday will immediately follow Wednesday.
   (2) Tuesday will be a rainy day.
   (3) Wednesday will not be a rainy day.
   (4) Wednesday will immediately follow Tuesday.
   (5) Tuesday and Wednesday will be rainy days.

4. Which event has probability closest to 0?

   (1) You will win a lottery.
   (2) You will sleep.
   (3) You will spend some money.
   (4) You will earn some money.
   (5) You will drink some water.

5. Which of the following is *not* a possible value for the probability of an event?

   (1) 0
   (2) $\frac{1}{2}$
   (3) $\frac{100}{101}$
   (4) 1
   (5) 1.21

6. Which of the following best describes an event that has 0 probability?

   (1) The event cannot happen.
   (2) The event may happen.
   (3) The event has already happened.
   (4) The event will happen regularly.
   (5) not enough information is given

Answers are on page 288.

Favorable Outcomes

Sometimes it is helpful to make a table or draw a tree diagram when finding the number of favorable outcomes. With either method, you generate a list of all the possible outcomes. Then you can see which of these are favorable and find the probability you seek.

Example 1   Suppose you flip two coins. What is the probability of flipping two heads?

STEP 1   One way to solve this problem is to make a table. Let H = head, and let T = tail. The two possibilities for one coin are given in the top row: H and T. The two possibilities for the other coin are given in the left column: H and T.

	H	T
H		
T		

STEP 2   Complete the table. This gives all the possible outcomes.

	H	T
H	HH	HT
T	TH	TT

STEP 3   Find the total number of possible outcomes.

The possible outcomes are HH, HT, TH, and TT. There are 4 possible outcomes.

STEP 4   Find the number of favorable outcomes.

The favorable outcome is HH. There is 1 favorable outcome.

STEP 5   Calculate the probability.

$$\frac{\text{favorable outcomes}}{\text{total outcomes}} = \frac{1}{4} = 0.25 = 25\%$$

When you flip two coins, the probability of flipping two heads is $\frac{1}{4}$, or 0.25, or 25%.

Example 2   Suppose you flip three coins. What is the probability of flipping exactly two heads?

STEP 1   One way to solve this problem is to draw a tree diagram. Let H = head, and let T = tail. The two possibilities for a coin are H and T. Each branch of the tree leads to a possible outcome.

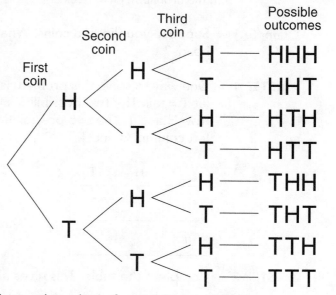

STEP 2   Find the total number of possible outcomes.

The possible outcomes are HHH, HHT, HTH, HTT, THH, THT, TTH, and TTT. There are 8 possible outcomes.

STEP 3   Find the number of favorable outcomes.

The favorable outcomes are HHT, HTH, and THH. There are 3 favorable outcomes.

STEP 4   Calculate the probability.

$$\frac{\text{favorable outcomes}}{\text{total outcomes}} = \frac{3}{8} = 0.375 = 37.5\%$$

When you flip three coins, the probability of flipping two heads is $\frac{3}{8}$, or 0.375, or 37.5%.

EXERCISE 11

Directions: The table below gives all possible outcomes for rolling two number cubes. Complete the table, then refer to it for numbers 1–6.

	1	2	3	4	5	6
1	1, 1	1, 2	1, 3	1, 4		
2	2, 1	2, 2				
3	3, 1					
4	4, 1					
5						
6						

1. How many possible outcomes are there?

2. Often when you roll two number cubes, you add the two numbers to find the sum. How many different sums are possible?

3. List the three favorable outcomes for rolling a sum of 4. What is the probability of rolling a sum of 4?

4. What is the probability of rolling a sum of 8?

5. Which sum is most likely to be rolled?

6. What is the probability of rolling doubles (the two cubes have the same number)?

Directions: Choose the best answer.

7. Suppose you flip some coins. Which event has the lowest probability?

   (1) Flip 1 head.
   (2) Flip 2 heads in a row.
   (3) Flip 3 heads in a row.
   (4) Flip 4 heads in a row.
   (5) Flip 5 heads in a row.

8. Suppose you roll two number cubes. Which outcome is most likely?

   (1) sum of 12
   (2) sum of 7
   (3) doubles
   (4) at least one 6
   (5) (1,5) or (5,1)

Directions: The tree diagram below gives all possible outcomes for three children in a family, with B = boy and G = girl. Assume boy and girl are equally likely outcomes. Complete the tree diagram, then refer to it for numbers 9–16.

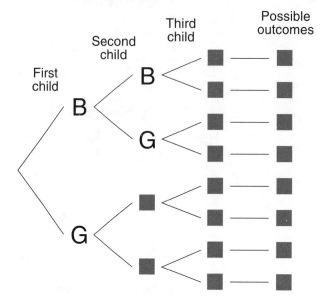

9. List all possible outcomes for three children in a family.

10. What is the probability of three girls?

11. What is the probability of two girls and one boy, in any order?

12. What is the probability of two girls and one boy, in that order?

13. What is the probability of no girls?

14. What is the probability of all girls or all boys?

15. List all favorable outcomes for one girl and two boys.

16. What is the probability of having a boy, then a girl, then a boy?

Answers are on page 288.

Working with Data Review

Directions: In Questions 1–18, solve each problem. Show your work at the right.

Refer to the table below for problems 1–4.

NAMES AND AGES OF EMPLOYEES

Name	Age	Name	Age
Tyson	28	Jade	22
Tat	37	Lin	40
Heidi	19	Rosa	63
Carlos	51	Chung	40
Pedro	40	Luisa	25
Carmen	31		

1. Find the mean age of the employees.

2. Find the median age of the employees.

3. Find the mode(s), if any.

4. Find the age range of the employees.

5. List all possible gender outcomes for two children in a family. Let B = boy, and let G = girl.

6. When you roll two number cubes, what is the probability of a sum of 3?

7. Each letter of the alphabet is written on a piece of paper and put into a hat. You will keep drawing letters from the hat until you get Z. The first letter you draw is A. What is the probability that the next letter you draw is Z?

Refer to the bar graph below for problems 8 and 9.

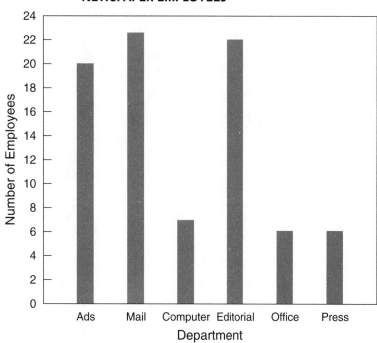

NEWSPAPER EMPLOYEES

8. How many newspaper employees are there in the computer department?

9. Which departments have at least 20 employees?

10. Draw a bar graph that displays the data given in the table below.

NUMBER OF SPECIES IN SELECTED FAMILIES OF BIRDS

Family of Birds	Number of Species
Parrots	243
Pheasants	214
Finches	153
Ducks	140
Larks	75
Falcons	60

Refer to the line graph below for problems 11 and 12.

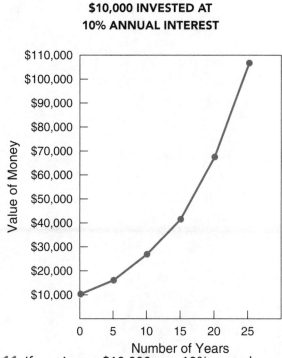

$10,000 INVESTED AT 10% ANNUAL INTEREST

11. If you invest $10,000 at a 10% annual interest rate, what will be the value of the money in 10 years?

12. If you invest $10,000 at a 10% annual interest rate, how long will it take for the money to be worth $80,000?

13. Draw a line graph that displays the data given in the table below.

DAILY LOW TEMPERATURE FOR ONE WEEK

Day	Temp. (°F)
Sunday	20
Monday	16
Tuesday	14
Wednesday	10
Thursday	10
Friday	15
Saturday	19

Refer to the circle graph below for problems 14 and 15.

THE WONG FAMILY BUDGET

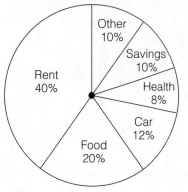

14. Which budget item costs twice as much as the amount of money the Wongs put into savings?

15. If the Wongs' total monthly budget is $2,000, how much money do they spend on rent?

16. Blood is made up of 55% plasma and 45% cells. Draw a circle graph that displays this data.

17. When you roll a number cube, what is the probability of rolling an odd number?

18. If you spin the spinner shown below once, what is the probability of winning $100?

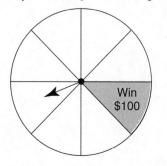

Directions: Choose the correct answer to each problem. Remember the problem-solving skills you have learned.

19. The ratio of males to females at a party is 1 to 4. There is a total of 20 people at the party. How many are female?

    (1) 4
    (2) 15
    (3) 12
    (4) 16
    (5) 5

20. Which is the best buy for donuts?

    (1) 2 for $.69
    (2) 5 for $2
    (3) $.35 each
    (4) 4 for $1.50
    (5) 3 for $1

21. Which of the following is a set of equivalent numbers?

    (1) $\frac{8}{10}$, 8%, 0.08
    (2) 0.8, $\frac{4}{5}$, 8%
    (3) 80%, $\frac{80}{100}$, 0.08
    (4) $\frac{4}{5}$, 80%, 0.8
    (5) 8%, $\frac{8}{100}$, 0.8

22. Whitney wants to graph the price of a U.S. postage stamp for the last 20 years. What type of graph would work the best?

    (1) bar graph
    (2) line graph
    (3) circle graph
    (4) tree diagram
    (5) any of the above

23. Fingernails grow about $1\frac{1}{2}$ inches per year. At this rate, how much have the fingernails of a 48-year-old grown?

    (1) 6 inches
    (2) 2 feet
    (3) 32 inches
    (4) 6 feet
    (5) 70 inches

24. A scale drawing of a new storage shed is shown below. The scale for the drawing is 1 centimeter : 2 meters. Which proportion would you solve to find the actual length of the longer side of the shed?

    Shed   2 cm

    4.5 cm

    (1) $\frac{1\ cm}{2\ m} = \frac{2\ cm}{h}$

    (2) $\frac{1\ cm}{h} = \frac{2\ m}{4.5\ cm}$

    (3) $\frac{1\ cm}{4.5\ cm} = \frac{h}{2\ m}$

    (4) $\frac{4.5\ cm}{h} = \frac{2\ m}{1\ cm}$

    (5) $\frac{1\ cm}{2\ m} = \frac{4.5\ cm}{h}$

25. Gerrard has a lump sum of money to invest. With which investment will Gerrard earn the most money?

    (1) 8% for 2 years
    (2) 3% for 8 years
    (3) 5% for 5 years
    (4) 12% for 1 year
    (5) The amount to be invested must be known.

26. Which pair of fractions has a sum that is greater than 1?

(1) $\frac{1}{3} + \frac{1}{6}$

(2) $\frac{1}{2} + \frac{1}{10}$

(3) $\frac{3}{7} + \frac{4}{9}$

(4) $\frac{2}{5} + \frac{4}{10}$

(5) $\frac{3}{5} + \frac{4}{7}$

27. Holly bought a box of popsicles. Of the popsicles, 3 are orange, 5 are grape, and 4 are cherry. If Holly takes a popsicle without looking, what is the probability that the popsicle will be cherry? Write the probability as a fraction on the number grid.

28. Hailey earns $375 a week. She budgets 25% of her monthly salary for rent. How much rent does Hailey pay per month? Write your answer on the number grid.

29. Heather paid for a $34.99 sweater with a $50 bill. With the change, she has decided to buy as many $3 bottles of shampoo as she can. How many bottles is she able to buy? Write your answer on the number grid.

Answers are on page 288.

Chapter 9

Basic Algebra

Exponents and Square Roots

In the expression 2^4, 2 is called the **base,** and 4 is called the **exponent.** To find the value, you multiply the base times itself the number of times indicated by the exponent. The expression 2^4 is the same as the product of $2 \times 2 \times 2 \times 2 = 16$.

Example 1 Find the value of 3^5.

STEP 1 Identify the base and the exponent.

Base: 3
Exponent: 5

STEP 2 Write the base as many times as the exponent indicates.

$3 \times 3 \times 3 \times 3 \times 3$

STEP 3 Multiply.

$3 \times 3 \times 3 \times 3 \times 3 = 243$
The value of 3^5 is 243.

Example 2 Find the value of 1^3.

STEP 1 Identify the base and the exponent.

Base: 1
Exponent: 3

STEP 2 Write the base as many times as the exponent indicates.

$1 \times 1 \times 1$

STEP 3 Multiply.

$1 \times 1 \times 1 = 1$
The value of 1^3 is 1.

<u>Example 3</u>   Find the value of 9^1.

STEP 1   Identify the base and the exponent.

Base: 9
Exponent: 1

STEP 2   Write the base as many times as the exponent indicates.

9

Notice that you do not need to multiply, because 9 is written just once.

The value of 9^1 is 9.

SUMMARY FOR FINDING THE VALUE OF EXPRESSIONS WITH EXPONENTS

To find the value of expressions with exponents:

1) Identify the base and the exponent.

2) Write the base as many times as the exponent indicates.

3) Multiply.

To find the value of an expression that has 0 as an exponent, use the following tip.

TIP
When the exponent is 0, the value of the expression is 1.

<u>Example 4</u>   Find the value of 9^0.

STEP 1   Identify the base and the exponent.

Base: 9
Exponent: 0

STEP 2   Use the tip above.

The exponent is 0, so the value of the expression is 1.
The value of 9^0 is 1.

The expression 7^2 is sometimes called "7 squared" or "the square of 7." The exponent 2 indicates that the base is squared. Recall that 7^2 is the same as 7×7, so the value of 7^2 is 49.

The expression $\sqrt{49}$ is read, "the square root of 49." Finding the square root of a number is the opposite of finding the square of a number. A number's square root is the one number that, multiplied by itself, will yield the square.

Example 5   Use the calculator to find 38^2.

STEP 1   Press AC.

STEP 2   Press 3 8 x^2.

The display should read ☐ 1444. .

$38^2 = 1,444$

Example 6   Use the calculator to find 6^5.

STEP 1   Press AC.

STEP 2   Press 6 x^y 5 = .

The display should read ☐ 7776. .

$6^5 = 7,776$

Example 7   Find the value of $\sqrt{49}$.

STEP 1   Think: "What number multiplied by itself is 49?"

$h \times h = 49$
$7 \times 7 = 49$

STEP 2   Write the square root.

$\sqrt{49} = 7$

The value of $\sqrt{49}$ is 7.

Example 8   Find the value of $\sqrt{100}$.

STEP 1   Think: "What number multiplied by itself is 100?"

$h \times h = 100$
$10 \times 10 = 100$

STEP 2   Write the square root.

$\sqrt{100} = 10$

The value of $\sqrt{100}$ is 10.

SUMMARY FOR FINDING A SQUARE ROOT

To find a square root:

1) Think: "What number multiplied by itself is the number found under the square root symbol?"

2) Write the square root.

3) Many square roots are memorized as part of the multiplication facts.

Example 9   Use the calculator to find $\sqrt{169}$.

STEP 1   Press `AC`.

STEP 2   Press `1` `6` `9` `SHIFT` `x²`

The display should read [13.].

The square root of 169 is 13.

EXERCISE 1

Directions: Find the value of each of the following.

1. 7^4 = 2,401
2. 12^0 = 1
3. 4^5 = 1024
4. 3^4 = 81

5. 7^3 = 343
6. 0^6 = 1
7. $\sqrt{25}$ = 5
8. $\sqrt{144}$ = 12

9. $\sqrt{16}$ 4
10. $\sqrt{64}$ = 8
11. $\sqrt{9}$ = 3
12. $\sqrt{225}$ = 15

Directions: Use your calculator to solve each problem.

13. 23.5^3 = 12,977.875

14. $\sqrt{256}$ = 16

15. 2.4^4 = 33.1776

16. $\sqrt{2.25}$ 1.5

17. 48^3 = 110,592

18. $\sqrt{.81}$ .9

19. 396^2 = 156,816

20. $\sqrt{56.25}$ 7.5

Directions: Complete each table.

21.

Number	Square
1	$1^2 =$
2	$2^2 =$
3	$3^2 = 9$
4	$4^2 = 16$
5	$5^2 = 25$
6	$6^2 = 36$
7	$7^2 = 49$
8	$8^2 = 64$
9	$9^2 = 81$
10	$10^2 = 100$
11	$11^2 = 121$
12	$12^2 = 144$
13	$13^2 = 169$
14	$14^2 = 196$
15	$15^2 = 225$
20	$20^2 = 400$

22.

Number	Square Root
1	$\sqrt{1} = 1$
4	$\sqrt{4} = 2$
9	$\sqrt{9} = 3$
16	$\sqrt{16} = 4$
25	$\sqrt{25} = 5$
36	$\sqrt{36} = 6$
49	$\sqrt{49} = 7$
64	$\sqrt{64} = 8$
81	$\sqrt{81} = 9$
100	$\sqrt{100} = 10$
121	$\sqrt{121} = 11$
144	$\sqrt{144} = 12$
169	$\sqrt{169} = 13$
196	$\sqrt{196} = 14$
225	$\sqrt{225} = 15$
400	$\sqrt{400} = 20$

Directions: Solve each problem.

23. The value of $\sqrt{20}$ lies between what two consecutive whole numbers? 4 and 5

25. The value of $\sqrt{150}$ lies between what two consecutive whole numbers? 144 and 169

26. What whole number is between $\sqrt{60}$ and $\sqrt{70}$? 8

Answers are on page 290.

EXERCISE 2

Directions: Choose the best answer.

1. Which of the following is the same as 4^5?

    (1) $5 \times 5 \times 5 \times 5$
    (2) $4 \times 4 \times 4 \times 4 \times 4$
    (3) 4×5
    (4) 5×4
    (5) 5^4

2. Which of the following is *not* the same as 2^8?

    (1) $2 \times 2 \times 2 \times 2 \times 2 \times 2 \times 2 \times 2$
    (2) 256
    (3) 8×8
    (4) 4^4
    (5) 16^2

3. If the square root of a number is 9, what is the number?

    (1) 3
    (2) $\sqrt{81}$
    (3) $\sqrt{9}$
    (4) $\sqrt{3}$
    (5) 81

4. If the square of a number is 25, what is the number?

    (1) 5
    (2) 625
    (3) 5^2
    (4) $\sqrt{5}$
    (5) 25^2

5. Evaluate $(1 + 2 + 3)^2$

    (1) 14
    (2) 123
    (3) 36
    (4) 12
    (5) 32

6. Evaluate $\sqrt{17^2 - 15^2}$

    (1) 4
    (2) 8
    (3) 64
    (4) 255
    (5) none of the above

7. What is the difference between 5^2 and 6^2?

    (1) 1
    (2) 61
    (3) 121
    (4) 72
    (5) 11

8. What is the sum of $\sqrt{49}$ and $\sqrt{64}$?

    (1) $\sqrt{113}$
    (2) 15
    (3) 56
    (4) $\sqrt{15}$
    (5) 1

Answers are on page 291.

Order of Operations

An arithmetic expression often includes more than one operation. When finding the value of an arithmetic expression, you need to know the proper order to perform the operations. For example, the expression $8 - 4 \times 2$ suggests two possible ways to solve the problem. Working from left to right, you would subtract first and get $8 - 4 = 4$; $4 \times 2 = 8$, an incorrect answer. But if you multiply first, you would get $4 \times 2 = 8$; $8 - 8 = 0$, the correct answer.

Use the following set of rules whenever you find the value of an arithmetic expression.

SUMMARY FOR ORDER OF OPERATIONS

To find the value of an arithmetic expression, follow these steps in the order indicated. If an expression includes more than one operation of the same type, work from left to right.

1) Do operations within parentheses.

2) Do exponents and square roots.

3) Do multiplication and division.

4) Do addition and subtraction.

Example 1   Find the value of the expression $5 \times (6 - 2) \div 2 - 2^3$.

STEP 1   Do operations within parentheses.

$5 \times 4 \div 2 - 2^3$

STEP 2   Do exponents and square roots.

$5 \times 4 \div 2 - 8$

STEP 3   Do multiplication and division. Work from left to right.

$20 \div 2 - 8$
$10 - 8$

STEP 4   Do addition and subtraction.

2

The value of the expression is 2.

If an expression does not include all the operations listed in the rules, just skip a step and go on to the next step.

<u>Example 2</u>   Find the value of the expression $3 \times 4 - (8 + 1)$.

STEP 1   Do operations within parentheses.

$3 \times 4 - 9$

STEP 2   Do exponents and square roots.

(There are none, so skip this step.)

STEP 3   Do multiplication and division.

$12 - 9$

STEP 4   Do addition and subtraction.

3

The value of the expression is 3.

If an expression includes a set of parentheses inside another set, work from the inside to the outside.

<u>Example 3</u>   Find the value of the expression $100 - [2 \times (9 - 2)] \times \sqrt{9}$.

STEP 1   Do operations within parentheses.

$100 - [2 \times 7] \times \sqrt{9}$
$100 - 14 \times \sqrt{9}$

STEP 2   Do exponents and square roots.

$100 - 14 \times 3$

STEP 3   Do multiplication and division.

$100 - 42$

STEP 4   Do addition and subtraction.

58

The value of the expression is 58.

EXERCISE 3

Directions: Find the value of each of the following.

1. $(12 + 4) \div (1 + 7)$

2. $3^2 + 6^2 \div 3$

3. $\sqrt{25} + 6 \times 4 - 10$

4. $[(30 - 8) \div 2] + 5$

5. $24 \div (1^5 + 5)$

6. $(2^3 + 3^3) \div 7$

7. $13 + 6 \times 2 \div 4 - 9$

8. $3 \times (10 - 4) \div 9 + 4^2$

9. $9 \times 8^0 + (6 - 1)$

10. $60 - [25 - (13 - 4)]$

Answers are on page 291.

PRE-GED PRACTICE

EXERCISE 4

Directions: Choose the best answer.

1. Which has the greatest value?

    (1) $10 \times (4 - 1) + 5$
    (2) $10 \times 4 - 1 + 5$
    (3) $10 \times (4 - 1 + 5)$
    (4) $10 \times 4 - (1 + 5)$
    (5) $(10 \times 4 - 1) + 5$

2. Which has the least value?

    (1) $3^2 + 6 \times 4 - 2$
    (2) $(3^2 + 6) \times (4 - 2)$
    (3) $(3^2 + 6) \times 4 - 2$
    (4) $3^2 + (6 \times 4) - 2$
    (5) $3^2 + 6 \times (4 - 2)$

3. What is the value of the expression
   $14 - 2^3 + 6 \times 2$?

    (1) 20
    (2) 18
    (3) 28
    (4) 24
    (5) 14

4. Which expression does *not* have the same value as the expression $40 + 12 \div 6$?

    (1) $6 + 4 \times 3 + 12$
    (2) $(3 \times 7) \times 2$
    (3) $\sqrt{36} \times (6 + 1)$
    (4) $15 \times (3 + 2) - 33$
    (5) $4 \times 8 + 2 \times 5$

5. Which expression has the same value as
   $(5) \times (8 - 2) \div (4)$?

    (1) $(5 \times 8) - (2 \div 4)$
    (2) $5 \times 8 - 2 \div 4$
    (3) $5 \times (8 - 2) \div 4$
    (4) $(5 \times 8) - 2 \div (4)$
    (5) Not enough information is given.

6. Which two expressions are equal?

    (1) $3^2 + 4^2$ and 5^2
    (2) $10^2 - 8^2$ and 6^2
    (3) $8^2 + 15^2$ and 17^2
    (4) $13^2 - 12^2$ and 5^2
    (5) all of the above

Answers are on page 291.

Variables and Simple Equations

An **equation** is a statement that two amounts are equal. In algebra, an equation usually has at least one variable. A **variable** is a letter used to represent an unknown amount. A **solution** to an equation is the value of the variable that makes the equation a true statement.

Example 1   Is 8 a solution to the equation $n + 7 = 15$?

STEP 1   Substitute the value for the variable in the equation. In this case, substitute 8 for n.

$8 + 7 = 15$

STEP 2   Decide whether or not the equation is a true statement.

$8 + 7 = 15$ is a true statement. Yes, 8 is a solution.

Example 2   Is 8 a solution to the equation $\frac{x}{3} = 5$?

STEP 1   Substitute the value for the variable in the equation. In this case, substitute 8 for x.

$\frac{8}{3} = 5$

STEP 2   Decide whether or not the equation is a true statement.

$\frac{8}{3} = 5$ is not a true statement. No, 8 is not a solution.

To solve an equation, you can use the **inverse operations** listed below:

- The inverse of addition is subtraction.
- The inverse of subtraction is addition.
- The inverse of multiplication is division.
- The inverse of division is multiplication.

Example 3   Solve the equation $y + 4 = 21$.

STEP 1   Identify the operation used in the equation.

There is a plus sign, so the operation is addition.

STEP 2   Identify the inverse operation.

The inverse of addition is subtraction.

STEP 3 Use the inverse operation to solve the equation. In this case, subtract 4 from the numbers on each side of the equal sign.

$$
\begin{array}{r}
y + 4 = 21 \\
\underline{-4 \quad -4} \\
y \ = 17
\end{array}
$$

STEP 4 Check the solution, as in Examples 1 and 2.

$17 + 4 = 21$ is a true statement. The solution is 17. $y = 17$

<u>Example 4</u> Solve the equation $3a = 24$.

STEP 1 Identify the operation used in the equation.

$3a$ means $3 \times a$, so the operation is multiplication.

STEP 2 Identify the inverse operation.

The inverse of multiplication is division.

STEP 3 Use the inverse operation to solve the equation. In this case, divide the numbers on each side of the equal sign by 3.

$3a = 24$ $\qquad \dfrac{3a}{3} = \dfrac{24}{3}$ $\qquad a = 8$

STEP 4 Check the solution, as in Examples 1 and 2.

$3 \times 8 = 24$ is a true statement. The solution is 8. $a = 8$

<u>Example 5</u> Solve the equation $x - 8 = 18$.

STEP 1 Identify the operation used in the equation.

There is a minus sign, so the operation is subtraction.

STEP 2 Identify the inverse operation.

The inverse of subtraction is addition.

STEP 3 Use the inverse operation to solve the equation. In this case, add 8 to the numbers on each side of the equal sign.

$$
\begin{array}{r}
x - 8 = \ 18 \\
\underline{+8 \quad +8} \\
x \ = 26
\end{array}
$$

STEP 4 Check the solution, as in Examples 1 and 2.

$26 - 8 = 18$ is a true statement. The solution is 26. $x = 26$

Example 6   Solve the equation $\frac{z}{6} = 5$.

STEP 1   Identify the operation used in the equation.

$\frac{z}{6}$ means $z \div 6$, so the operation is division.

STEP 2   Identify the inverse operation.

The inverse of division is multiplication.

STEP 3   Use the inverse operation to solve the equation. In this case, multiply the numbers on each side of the equal sign by 6.

$$\frac{z}{6} = 5$$

$$\frac{z}{6} \times 6 = 5 \times 6$$

$$z = 30$$

STEP 4   Check the solution, as in Examples 1 and 2.

$\frac{30}{6} = 5$ is a true statement. The solution is 30. $z = 30$

SUMMARY FOR SOLVING SIMPLE EQUATIONS

To solve a simple equation, follow these steps:

1) Identify the operation used in the equation.

2) Identify the inverse operation.

3) Use the inverse operation to solve the equation. Whatever operation you perform on one side of the equal sign, do the same on the other side.

4) Check the solution by substituting the answer for the variable in the equation, and see if the equation is true.

EXERCISE 5

Directions: Is the value given for the variable a solution to the equation? Write *yes* or *no*.

1. $9y = 27$; $y = 3$

2. $x + 3 = 7$; $x = 10$

3. $n - 14 = 10$; $n = 24$

4. $4z = 32$; $z = 8$

5. $\frac{x}{2} = 11$; $x = 22$

6. $\frac{a}{5} = 20$; $a = 4$

Directions: Solve each equation.

7. $5y = 35$

8. $n - 1 = 10$

9. $y + 20 = 21$

10. $\frac{z}{3} = 2$

11. $8n = 32$

12. $n + 1 = 8$

13. $\frac{x}{4} = 9$

14. $a - 17 = 11$

15. $z - 4 = 5$

16. $10a = 200$

17. $\frac{y}{2} = 16$

18. $x + 9 = 19$

19. $a + 3 = 37$

20. $9z = 54$

21. $y - 8 = 6$

22. $\frac{a}{7} = 1$

23. $x - 15 = 3$

24. $2x = 50$

25. $\frac{n}{6} = 6$

26. $z + 14 = 23$

Directions: Choose the best answer.

27. Which equation has 3 as the solution?

    (1) $2x = 9$
    (2) $8x = 30$
    (3) $4x = 12$
    (4) $3x = 15$
    (5) $5x = 18$

28. Which equation does *not* have 6 as the solution?

    (1) $y + 6 = 12$
    (2) $y + 10 = 16$
    (3) $y - 2 = 4$
    (4) $y - 6 = 12$
    (5) $y + 5 = 11$

Answers are on page 291.

Formulas

A **formula** is an equation with more than one variable. It is an equation that is always true. It is a useful tool for solving problems. To use a formula, you substitute into the equation all the values you know, then solve for the value you do not know.

<u>Example 1</u>   The formula for distance is: rate × time, or $d = rt$.

distance = 200 miles; time = 4 hours; rate = _____

STEP 1   Write the formula you will use.

$d = rt$

STEP 2   Identify the values you know and the value you do not know.

Values you know: $d = 200$, and $t = 4$

Value you do not know: r

STEP 3   Substitute into the formula all the values you know.

$200 = r \times 4$

STEP 4   Solve for the value you do not know.

The equation $200 = r \times 4$ is the same as the equation $4r = 200$. To solve, divide the numbers on each side of the equal sign by 4.

$$\frac{4r}{4} = \frac{200}{4}$$

$r = 50$

The rate is 50 miles per hour.

You can use formulas to solve many word problems. Here are some formulas and two examples.

Interest = principal × rate × time ($i = prt$)
Distance = rate × time ($d = rt$)
Total cost = number of units × cost per unit ($c = nr$)
Fahrenheit temperature = 1.8 × Celsius temperature + 32
   ($F = 1.8C + 32$)
Batting average = number of hits ÷ number of times at bat
   ($a = \frac{h}{n}$)

Example 2   Mei bought 3 rolls of film for $10.50. How much did each roll of film cost?

STEP 1   Write the formula you will use.

$c = nr$

STEP 2   Identify the values you know and the value you do not know.

Values you know: $c = \$10.50$, and $n = 3$
Value you do not know: r

STEP 3   Substitute into the formula all the values you know.

$\$10.50 = 3r$

STEP 4   Solve for the value you do not know.

$\$10.50 = 3r$ is the same as $3r = \$10.50$.

$$\frac{3r}{3} = \frac{\$10.50}{3}$$

$r = \$3.50$

Each roll of film cost $3.50.

Example 3   If the Celsius temperature is 14°, what is the equivalent Fahrenheit temperature?

STEP 1   Write the formula you will use.

$F = 1.8C + 32$

STEP 2   Identify the values you know and the value you do not know.

Value you know: $C = 14$
Value you do not know: F

STEP 3   Substitute into the formula all the values you know.

$F = 1.8 \times 14 + 32$

STEP 4   Solve for the value you do not know.

$F = 1.8 \times 14 + 32$
$ = 25.2 + 32$
$ = 57.2°$

The Fahrenheit temperature is 57.2°.

SUMMARY FOR SOLVING PROBLEMS USING FORMULAS

To solve problems using a formula:

1) Write the formula you will use.

2) Identify the values you know and the value you do not know.

3) Substitute into the formula all the values you know.

4) Solve for the value you do not know.

EXERCISE 6

Directions: Use the formula given, and find the unknown value.

1. Formula: $c = nr$
   total cost = $28
   price per item = $7
   number of items = _____

2. Formula: $i = prt$
   interest = $360
   rate = 6%
   time = 3 years
   principal = _____

3. Formula: $a = \frac{h}{n}$
   batting average = 0.300
   number of times at bat = 50
   number of hits = _____

4. Formula: $F = 1.8C + 32$
   Celsius temperature = 10°
   Fahrenheit temperature = _____

5. Formula: $d = rt$
   distance = 100 miles
   time = 1 hour 45 minutes
   rate = _____

6. Formula: $i = prt$
   principal = $10,000
   rate = 8%
   time = 5 years
   interest = _____

Directions: Solve each problem.

7. Patty bought 4 tires at $37.99 each. What was the total cost of the tires?

8. Raffi earned $80 in interest by investing $1,000 for 2 years. What was the interest rate?

9. If the Celsius temperature is 30°, what is the equivalent Fahrenheit temperature?

10. If Angelo drives 55 miles per hour for 6 hours, how far will he have driven?

11. During the softball season, Tasha had 12 hits in 40 times at bat. What was her batting average?

12. How long will it take to drive 300 miles at an average of 60 miles per hour?

13. Saul's batting average is 0.380. In the next 5 times at bat, about how many hits would you expect Saul to make?

14. Peder bought 12 gallons of gasoline for $14.94. What was the price per gallon of the gasoline?

15. Maria invested $5,000 at a 5% interest rate. She earned $750 in interest. For how long was the money invested?

16. In one hour, the temperature dropped from 20°C to 15°C. How much was the drop in temperature (in °F)?

Answers are on page 291.

The Coordinate Plane

A **coordinate plane** is formed by two number lines perpendicular to each other at 0. The horizontal number line is called the **x-axis,** and the vertical number line is called the **y-axis.** The point where the two lines meet is called the **origin.**

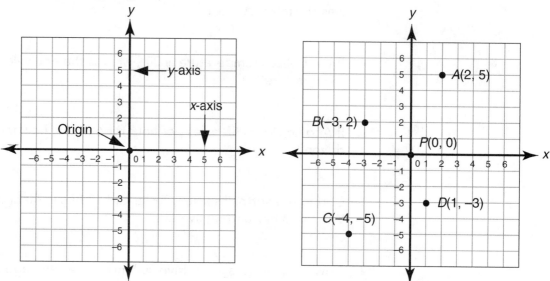

A point in the coordinate plane is named by two coordinates, an **x-coordinate** and a **y-coordinate.** Together the coordinates form an **ordered pair.** The pair is *ordered* because the *order* of the two coordinates matters. The x-coordinate is always first in the pair, and the y-coordinate is always second. The ordered pair tells exactly where the point lies in the coordinate plane.

The coordinate plane above shows five points in the coordinate plane. Point P is the origin, which has ordered pair (0, 0). The x-coordinate tells how far the point is—right or left—from the origin. The y-coordinate tells how far the point is—up or down—from the origin. Point A has ordered pair (2, 5), which means that point A is 2 units right and 5 units up from the origin. Point B is at (–3, 2), or 3 units left and 2 units up from the origin. Point C is at (–4, –5), or 4 units left and 5 units down from the origin. Point D is at (1, –3), or 1 unit right and 3 units down from the origin.

TIP
A positive coordinate is right or up from the origin, while a negative coordinate is left or down from the origin.

Use the coordinate plane below for the examples that follow.

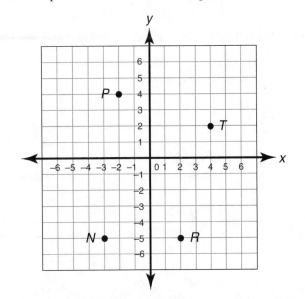

Example 1   What is the letter of the point at (2, –5)?

STEP 1   Start at the origin. Count 2 units right and 5 units down.

STEP 2   Identify the point: *R*.

The point at (2, –5) is *R*.

Example 2   What is the ordered pair for point *T*?

STEP 1   Start at the origin. Count the number of units to the right until *T* is directly above: 4. Count the number of units up to *T*: 2.

STEP 2   Write the ordered pair: (4 right, 2 up) = (4, 2).

The ordered pair for point *T* is (4, 2).

Example 3   What is the ordered pair for point *N*?

STEP 1   Start at the origin. Count the number of units to the left until *N* is directly below: 3. Count the number of units down to *N*: 5.

STEP 2   Write the ordered pair: (3 left, 5 down) = (–3, –5)

The ordered pair for point *N* is (–3, –5).

EXERCISE 7

Directions: Write the letter of the point at each ordered pair.

1. (3, –2) J
2. (8, 5) H
3. (–9, –4) M
4. (8, –4) A
5. (–3, 6) L
6. (9, 2) C
7. (–6, –5) G
8. (–4, 2) Z

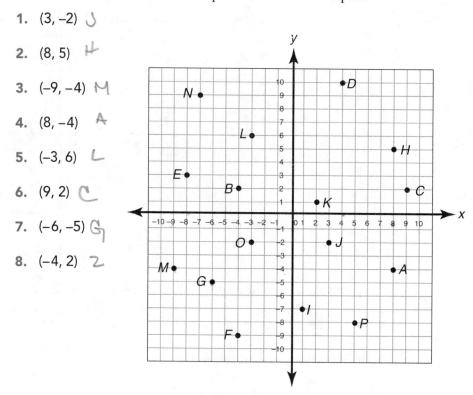

Directions: Write the ordered pair for each point on the coordinate plane above.

9. K (2 , 1)
10. O (3 , -2)
11. E (-8 , 3)
12. D (4 , 10)
13. I (1 , -7)
14. P (5 , -8)
15. N (-8 9)
16. F (-4 , -9)

Directions: Refer to the coordinate plane above.

17. Which points have a positive *x*-coordinate and a positive *y*-coordinate? K, D, H, C

18. Which points have a negative *x*-coordinate and a negative *y*-coordinate? O, M, G, 7

19. Which points have a positive *x*-coordinate and a negative *y*-coordinate? J, A, P, I

20. Which points have a negative *x*-coordinate and a positive *y*-coordinate? N, L, E, B

Directions: Graph and label each point on the coordinate plane below.

21. *A* (1, 1)

22. *B* (4, –2)

23. *C* (–2, 3)

24. *D* (5, 4)

25. *E* (–3, –2)

26. *F* (–1, 4)

27. *G* (2, –5)

28. *H* (–4, –4)

Directions: Show each segment on the coordinate plane below.

29. Show the line segment with endpoints (4, 2) and (–3, 5).

30. Show the line segment with endpoints (4, 0) and (–4, –3).

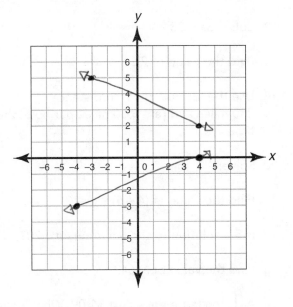

Answers are on page 292.

GED PRACTICE
Basic Algebra Review

Directions: For Questions 1–17, solve each problem. Show your work at the right.

1. Find the value of $\sqrt{25}$. $5 \times 5 = 25$

2. Is 3 a solution to the equation $\frac{m}{8} = 24$? $\frac{3}{8} = 24 = NO$

3. Solve: $y - 7 = 4$ $Y = 11$
   $7 + 4 = 11 \quad -7 = 4$

4. Use the formula $F = 1.8C + 32$. If $C = 9°$, then $F =$ $48.2°$.

5. Find the value of $3^2 + 6 \times 2 - 15$.
   $9 \quad 15 \times 30 - 15 = 15$

6. How much money must you invest to earn $900 interest in 3 years with an 8% interest rate? (Use the formula $i = prt$.)

7. Solve: $3z = 33$ $z = 11$

8. Find the value of 2^5. $= 32$

9. Use the formula $d = rt$. If distance = 250 miles and rate = 50 miles per hour, then time = _____.

10. Solve: $\frac{x}{2} = 15$

11. Find the value of $(4 + 5) \times (6 - 3)$.
    $9 \quad \times \quad 3 = 27$

12. Is 5 a solution to the equation $4a = 20$?   yes

13. Find the value of $\sqrt{64}$. 8

14. A dozen large eggs cost $1.09. What is the cost of each egg? (Use the formula $c = nr$.)

15. Solve: $n + 19 = 27$ $27 - 19 = 8 \quad n = 8$

16. Use your calculator to find the value of 17.5^2. 306.25

17. Use your calculator to find the value of $\sqrt{3844}$. 62

Directions: Choose the correct answer to each problem. Remember the problem-solving skills you have learned.

18. Ralph got $10 worth of unleaded gasoline priced at $1.347 per gallon. How many gallons did Ralph get?

    (1) about 8
    (2) about 13
    (3) about 14
    (4) about 10
    (5) about 7

19. Jon wanted to borrow $2,500 for 18 months at $7\frac{1}{4}$% interest. How much must he repay? (Use your calculator.)

    (1) $ 181.25
    (2) $ 271.88
    (3) $2,500
    (4) $2,771.88
    (5) $3,750

20. Zaida's current annual salary is $18,000. Next month, a 4% raise will become effective. At that time, what will be Zaida's monthly salary?

    (1) $ 720
    (2) $ 1,560
    (3) $18,720
    (4) $ 1,500
    (5) $ 6,000

21. The blood that circulates in the human body accounts for about 7% of body weight. About what percent of body weight is *not* accounted for by blood?

    (1)   7%
    (2) 70%
    (3) 93%
    (4)   3%
    (5) Not enough information is given.

22. Five homes recently sold in a neighborhood at these prices: $109,000; $85,500; $74,000; $99,900; $115,000. Which of the following statements are true of this data?

    (1) The range is $41,000.
    (2) The median is $99,900.
    (3) There are no modes.
    (4) The mean is $96,680.
    (5) All of the statements above are true.

23. Which of the following has the greatest value?

    (1) 200^1
    (2) 5^4
    (3) 1^{200}
    (4) 2^{10}
    (5) 20^2

24. A book club advertises 8 books for $1.99. In small print, you read, "plus shipping and handling," which is $4.95. You also read, ". . . when you agree to take 4 more shipments of 2 books each." These shipments will be sent every 4 weeks for only $4.99 per book, plus $2.95 shipping and handling. If you join the club, which of the statements are true?

    (1) You will spend $58.66 for 16 books.
    (2) You will spend $16.75 on shipping and handling alone.
    (3) You will end up with at least 16 books.
    (4) You will pay about $3.67 per book, including shipping and handling.
    (5) All of the statements above are true.

25. Geraldo has $20 worth of nickels. How many nickels does Geraldo have?

    (1)   100
    (2) 1,000
    (3)   400
    (4)   40
    (5)   800

26. Melanie bought 6.37 pounds of brisket at $2.48 per pound. How much will she pay for the brisket? Use your calculator and write your answer on the number grid.

27. The ratio of white keys to black keys on a piano is $\frac{13}{9}$. There are 36 black keys on a piano. How many black keys and white keys are there altogether? Write your answer on the number grid.

28. The circle graph below shows the Smiths' monthly budget. If the Smiths make $2,450 a month, how much do they spend on utilities and car expenses combined? Use your calculator and write your answer on the number grid.

29. If you graph the three given points on a coordinate plane, then connect the points in the order given, which set of points forms a triangle that is upside down?

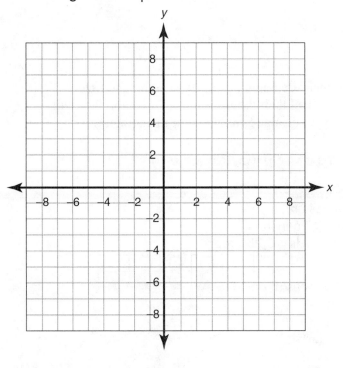

(1) (3, 7), (3, 3), (8, 3)
(2) (−4, −1), (−4, −5), (−6, −5)
(3) (1, −3), (−2, −3), (−2, 2)
(4) (−5, 5), (0, 0), (2, 2)
(5) (4, −1), (4, −6), (8, −1)

30. The ratio of males to females at a meeting was 2 : 3, with 12 men and 18 women. Later another man and woman joined the meeting. Which of the following statements is true about the ratio now?

(1) The ratio of men to women stayed the same, since one of each joined the meeting.
(2) The ratio of men to women is 3 : 4.
(3) The ratio of men to women is 2 : 3.
(4) The ratio of men to women is 13 : 19.
(5) The ratio of women to men is 13 : 19.

31. A store advertised, "Buy one sweater, and get the second for half price!" Assuming you buy 2 sweaters, this is the same as which of the following deals?

(1) 50% off

(2) 25% off

(3) $\frac{1}{3}$ off

(4) 2 for the price of 3

(5) 3 for the price of 4

Answers are on page 292.

Chapter 10

Measurement and Geometry

Customary Measures

We use different **units** to measure length, capacity, weight, and time. Customary units of measure and their relationships are given in the chart below. Use this information to change from one unit to another.

CUSTOMARY UNITS OF MEASURE

Length
1 foot (ft) = 12 inches (in.)
1 yard (yd) = 3 feet = 36 inches
1 mile (mi) = 1,760 yards = 5,280 feet

Capacity
1 cup (c) = 8 fluid ounces (fl oz)
1 pint (pt) = 2 cups
1 quart (qt) = 2 pints
1 gallon (gal) = 4 quarts

Weight
1 pound (lb) = 16 ounces (oz)
1 ton (T) = 2,000 pounds

Time
1 minute (min) = 60 seconds (sec)
1 hour (hr) = 60 minutes
1 day = 24 hours
1 week (wk) = 7 days
1 year (yr) = 365 days

Example 1   Change 105 days to weeks.

STEP 1   Find the relationship between the two units.

There are 7 days in 1 week.

STEP 2   To change from a smaller unit (days) to a larger unit (weeks), divide.

105 days ÷ 7 = 15 weeks

Example 2   Change 3 gallons to cups.

STEP 1   Find the relationship between the two units.

There are 4 quarts in 1 gallon, 2 pints in 1 quart, and 2 cups in 1 pint. Use these relationships.

STEP 2   To change from a larger unit to a smaller unit, multiply.

3 gallons × 4 = 12 quarts   12 quarts × 2 = 24 pints

24 pints × 2 = 48 cups

SUMMARY FOR CHANGING UNITS OF MEASURE

To change units of measure:

1) Find the relationship between the two units.

2) To change from a smaller unit to a larger unit, divide.

3) To change from a larger unit to a smaller unit, multiply.

EXERCISE 1

Directions: Circle the larger unit.

1. cups or pints

2. pounds or ounces

3. inches or feet

4. gallons or quarts

5. minutes or seconds

6. yards or miles

7. days or hours

8. quarts or pints

9. days or weeks

10. yards or feet

Directions: Change each measurement to the unit indicated. Refer to the chart on page 212, if necessary.

11. 12 gallons = _____ quarts

12. 84 days = _____ weeks

13. 30 feet = _____ yards

14. 5 tons = _____ pounds

15. 3 pounds = _____ ounces

16. 60 inches = _____ feet

17. 240 seconds = _____ minutes

18. 6 cups = _____ pints

19. 12 miles = _____ feet

20. 300 minutes = _____ hours

Directions: Answer each question below.

21. How many inches are in 3 yards?

22. How many hours are in 1 week?

23. How many cups are in 6 quarts?

24. How many tons are in 8,000 pounds?

25. How many ounces are in 5 pounds?

26. How many seconds are in 1 day?

27. How many miles are in 15,840 feet?

28. How many gallons are in 32 cups?

29. Which unit is *not* smaller than a quart?

   (1) pint
   (2) cup
   (3) gallon
   (4) fluid ounce

30. Which unit is *not* larger than a minute?

   (1) hour
   (2) second
   (3) day
   (4) week

Answers are on page 293.

Mixed Units

Some measurements are given in mixed units. For example, a person's height is given as 5 feet 4 inches. Changing from mixed units or to mixed units is an important skill.

Example 1   Change 5 feet 4 inches to inches.

Use the relationship: 12 inches = 1 foot.

5 feet 4 inches = (5 feet) + (4 inches)
$$= (5 \text{ feet} \times 12) + (4 \text{ inches})$$
$$= 60 \text{ inches} + 4 \text{ inches}$$
$$= 64 \text{ inches}$$

Example 2   Change 200 minutes to hours and minutes.

Use the relationship: 60 minutes = 1 hour.
200 minutes = 200 ÷ 60 = 3 r20 or 3 hours and 20 minutes

EXERCISE 2

Directions: Change each measurement to the unit(s) indicated.

1. 6 feet 2 inches = _____ inches

2. 54 inches = _____ feet _____ inches

3. 2 hours 15 minutes = _____ minutes

4. 300 minutes = _____ hours _____ minutes

5. 11 cups = _____ quarts _____ cups

6. 10,000 feet = _____ miles _____ feet

7. $3\frac{1}{3}$ minutes = _____ minutes _____ seconds

8. 1 year = _____ weeks _____ days

9. 50 ounces = _____ pounds _____ ounces

10. 7 minutes 35 seconds = _____ seconds

Directions: Solve each problem below.

11. Enrique is 6 feet 1 inch tall. Simon is 70 inches tall. Who is taller?

12. Ria worked 8 hours 45 minutes. Sue worked 600 minutes. Who worked longer?

13. Can A contains 10 fluid ounces of sauce. Can B contains 1 cup of sauce. Which can contains more sauce?

14. Nadia made 20 cups of punch and filled a 1-gallon container. How many cups of punch are left?

Answers are on page 294.

The Metric System

The **metric system** of measurement is used widely throughout the world. It is based on the decimal system of numbers. The basic units of metric measure are **meter** for length, **liter** for liquid capacity, and **gram** for mass. Prefixes used with these units form other units. The common prefixes are **milli-** for $\frac{1}{1000}$ or 0.001, **centi-** for $\frac{1}{100}$ or 0.01, and **kilo-** for 1,000 times the basic unit.

<u>Example 1</u>   Use the prefixes to find the number of millimeters in 1 meter.

Millimeter is the smaller unit, and 1 millimeter is $\frac{1}{1000}$ or 0.001 of a meter. So there are 1,000 millimeters in 1 meter.

The diagram below can help you change from one metric unit to another.

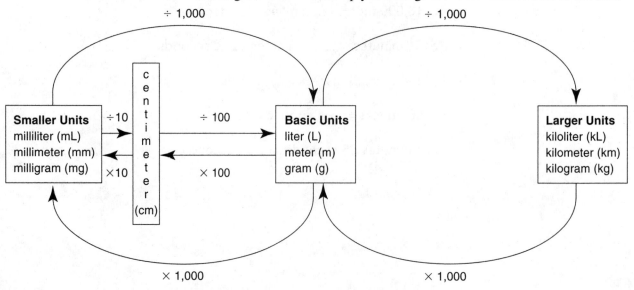

Example 2   Change 70 centimeters to meters.

As with standard units of measure, divide to change from a smaller unit to a larger unit.

There are 100 centimeters in 1 meter, so divide by 100.

70 cm ÷ 100 = 0.70 m = 0.7 m

Example 3   Change 5.2 liters to milliliters.

Multiply to change from a larger unit to a smaller unit. Since 1,000 milliliters are in 1 liter, multiply by 1,000.

5.2 L × 1,000 = 5,200 mL

> **TIP**
>
> When multiplying or dividing by a multiple of 10, just move the decimal point the same number of places as the number of zeros in the multiple of 10.

EXERCISE 3

Directions: Complete the chart below.

Length

1. 1 meter (m) = _____ centimeters (cm)

2. 1 meter = _____ millimeters (mm)

3. 1 centimeter = _____ millimeters

4. 1 kilometer (km) = _____ meters

Liquid Capacity

5. 1 liter (L) = _____ milliliters (mL)

6. 1 kiloliter (kL) = _____ liters

Mass

7. 1 gram (g) = _____ milligrams (mg)

8. 1 kilogram (kg) = _____ grams

Directions: Change each measurement to the unit indicated.

9. 320 cm = _____ m

10. 40 cm = _____ mm

11. 0.4 kL = _____ L

12. 5,500 g = _____ kg

13. 6 m = _____ cm

14. 89 mm = _____ cm

15. 6.5 L = _____ mL

16. 2 km = _____ m

17. 342,000 mg = _____ g

18. 1.4 kL = _____ L

19. 10 kg = _____ g

20. 750 mL = _____ L

21. 5kg = _____ g

22. 600 cm = _____ m

23. 7.2g = _____ mg

24. 240m = _____ km

25. 2,000 L = _____ kL

26. 512 mL = _____ L

Directions: Solve each problem below.

27. Write four metric units for length in order from smallest to largest.

28. Write three metric units for mass in order from largest to smallest.

29. How many milliliters of liquid are in a half-liter bottle?

30. A glass holds 250 milliliters of water. How many liters of water are needed to fill 10 glasses?

31. The mass of a person is about 70 kilograms. How many grams is this?

32. An orange contains about 60 milligrams of protein. How many grams is this?

Answers are on page 294.

Measuring Line Segments

To measure a given distance or length, you can use a meter stick or a centimeter ruler. A centimeter ruler is shown below. Centimeters are labeled 1, 2, 3, . . . , 15. The shorter lines are millimeters.

Example   Write the length of segments *AB*, *CD*, and *EF* shown above.

STEP 1   Count millimeters from 0 to the end of segment *AB*: 8 mm, or 0.8 cm.

STEP 2   Read centimeters from 0 to the end of segment *CD*: 7 cm.

STEP 3   Read centimeters, then count millimeters, from 0 to the end of segment *EF*: 10 cm + 4 mm, or 10.4 cm.

TIP
Remember that the metric system is based on decimals. Use decimal numbers to write metric measurements.

EXERCISE 4

Directions: Write the length of each segment shown below.

1. *AB*   2. *CD*   3. *EF*

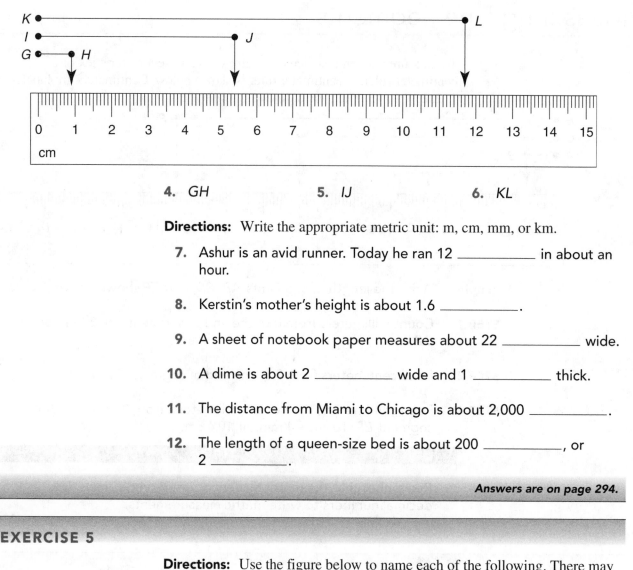

4. GH   **5.** IJ   **6.** KL

Directions: Write the appropriate metric unit: m, cm, mm, or km.

7. Ashur is an avid runner. Today he ran 12 _____ in about an hour.

8. Kerstin's mother's height is about 1.6 _____.

9. A sheet of notebook paper measures about 22 _____ wide.

10. A dime is about 2 _____ wide and 1 _____ thick.

11. The distance from Miami to Chicago is about 2,000 _____.

12. The length of a queen-size bed is about 200 _____, or 2 _____.

Answers are on page 294.

EXERCISE 5

Directions: Use the figure below to name each of the following. There may be more than one correct answer.

1. a ray

2. a segment

3. a line

4. a right angle

5. a circle

6. perpendicular lines

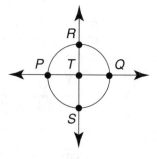

Directions: Use the figure below to name each of the following. There may be more than one correct answer.

7. a square

8. parallel segments

9. a triangle

10. perpendicular segments

11. an angle that is not a right angle

12. a rectangle that is not a square

13. three segments having the same length

14. three angles having the same measure

Directions: Circle *T* if the statement is true, or *F* if it is false.

15. **T F** A square has perpendicular sides.

16. **T F** A 30° angle is larger than a right angle.

17. **T F** Parallel lines are always the same distance from each other.

18. **T F** A rectangle is a square.

19. **T F** A rectangle has parallel sides.

20. **T F** A triangle can have parallel sides.

21. **T F** A triangle can have more than one right angle.

22. **T F** Perpendicular lines do not intersect.

23. **T F** Lines in the same plane either intersect or are parallel.

24. **T F** Two perpendicular lines form four 90° angles.

Answers are on page 294.

Geometric Definitions

In the study of geometry there are many definitions to learn. Skills of geometry include drawing shapes, identifying shapes, and understanding relationships among shapes. You will learn some basic definitions and practice these skills in this section. First, carefully study the definitions and figures below.

Line: a set of points continuing in opposite directions

Segment: a set of points forming the shortest path between two points

Ray: a set of points continuing in one direction only

line *AB*   segment *CD*   ray *EF*

Angle: a figure made of two rays extending from the same point

Right angle: an angle that measures 90°

angle *XYZ*

right angle *GMB*

Parallel lines: lines that run in the same direction and that do not cross or intersect

Perpendicular lines: lines that intersect to form right angles

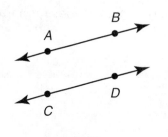

parallel lines
AB and *CD*

perpendicular lines
RS and *TU*

Rectangle: a four-sided figure with four right angles

Square: a four-sided figure with four right angles and four equal sides

rectangle *JTLC*

square *JKLM*

Triangle: a three-sided figure

Circle: a curved flat figure every point of which is the same distance from the center

triangle *GRV*

circle *O*

EXERCISE 6

Directions: Draw and label each figure described.

1. Segment *MN*

4. Perpendicular lines intersecting at point *B*

2. Circle *C*

5. Right angle *RST*

3. An angle formed by rays *FG* and *FK*

6. Ray *PQ*

7. Parallel lines *AB* and *CD*

10. A triangle that has a right angle

8. Line *ST*

11. Square *WXYZ*

9. A triangle no two sides of which have the same length

12. Rectangle *ABCD* with parallel sides *AB* and *DC*

Directions: Fill in each blank with the appropriate word.

13. A right angle is an angle that measures _____.

14. A _____ is a curved flat figure every point of which is the same distance from the center.

15. A _____ is a set of points continuing in opposite directions.

16. A rectangle is a four-sided figure with four _____ angles.

17. A _____ is a set of points forming the shortest path between two points.

18. Lines that run in the same direction and that do not cross or intersect are _____.

19. An _____ is a figure made of two rays extending from the same point.

20. _____ lines intersect to form right angles.

Answers are on page 295.

Perimeter and Circumference

The distance around a figure such as a triangle, rectangle, or square is its **perimeter.** To find the perimeter of a figure, simply add the lengths of all the sides.

Example 1   Find the perimeter of the rectangle shown.

Perimeter = 28 + 10 + 28 + 10 = 76 cm

Example 2   Find the perimeter of a square with sides 5 feet long.

STEP 1   Draw a diagram.

STEP 2   A square has four equal sides, so each side is 5 feet long.

Perimeter = 5 + 5 + 5 + 5 = 20 ft

The distance around a circle is its **circumference.** This measure depends on the radius or diameter of the circle. The **radius** of a circle is the distance from the center to any point on the curve of the circle. The **diameter** is a line segment that crosses the circle through its center from one side to the other.

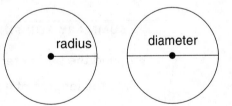

If you know the radius of a circle, multiply by 2 to find its diameter. If you know the diameter of a circle, divide by 2 to find its radius.

Example 3   Find the radius and diameter of the circle shown.

The radius is labeled: 10 in.
The diameter is twice the radius: 10 in. × 2 = 20 in.

To find the circumference of a circle, multiply its diameter by π (pi), which is about 3.14 or $\frac{22}{7}$.

TIP
Use $\pi \approx \frac{22}{7}$ when the diameter or radius is a multiple of 7. Otherwise, use $\pi \approx 3.14$.

Example 4   Find the circumference of a circle with a diameter of 21 feet. Since the diameter is a multiple of 7, use $\pi \approx \frac{22}{7}$.

Circumference $= \pi \times d \approx \frac{22}{7} \times 21 = 66$ ft

Example 5   Find the circumference of a circle with a radius of 12 centimeters.

STEP 1   Find the diameter.

$d = 12$ cm $\times 2 = 24$ cm

STEP 2   Since the diameter is not a multiple of 7, use $\pi \approx 3.14$.

Circumference $= \pi \times d \approx 3.14 \times 24 = 75.36$ cm

Example 6   Use your calculator to find the circumference of a circle with a 12 inch diameter.

STEP 1   Press `AC`.

STEP 2   Press `3` `.` `1` `4` `×` `1` `2` `=`.

The display should read | 37.68 |.

The circumference is 37.68 inches.

SUMMARY FOR FINDING PERIMETER AND CIRCUMFERENCE

To find the perimeter of a triangle, square, or rectangle:
Add the lengths of its sides.

To find the circumference of a circle:
Multiply its diameter by π (pi).

EXERCISE 7

Directions: Find the perimeter or circumference of each figure shown.

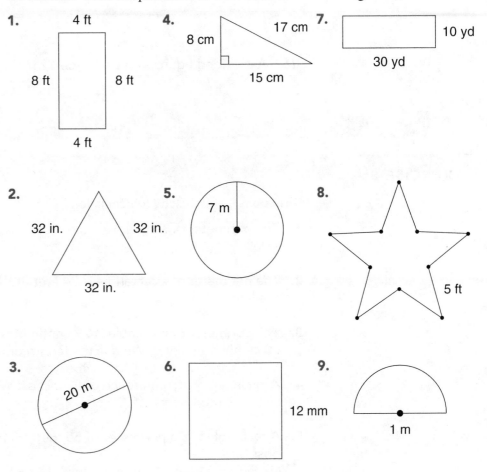

1.
4 ft
8 ft   8 ft
4 ft

4.
17 cm
8 cm
15 cm

7.
10 yd
30 yd

2.
32 in.   32 in.
32 in.

5.
7 m

8.
5 ft

3.
20 m

6.
12 mm

9.
1 m

Directions: Find the perimeter or circumference of each figure described.

10. A square with sides 9 in.

11. A rectangle with length 8 mm and width 11 mm

12. A triangle with each side 15 cm

13. A circle with radius 3 ft

14. A triangle with sides 30 cm, 40 cm, and 50 cm

Directions: Use your calculator to find the circumference of each figure.

15. A circle with diameter 42 mm

16. A six-sided figure with each side 12 m

Answers are on page 295.

EXERCISE 8

Directions: Solve each problem below.

1. The perimeter of a square is 16 meters. What is the length of each side?

2. The perimeter of a rectangle is 24 feet. If the width is 7 feet, what is the length?

3. The perimeter of a triangle is 29 centimeters. Two of the sides are 10 centimeters long. What is the length of the third side?

4. A circle has a circumference of 22 inches. What is the radius of the circle? (**Hint:** Use $\pi \approx \frac{22}{7}$.)

5. A rectangle has a perimeter of 50 feet. Which dimensions are not possible?
   (1) sides: 11 feet, 12 feet, 13 feet, 14 feet
   (2) sides: 5 feet, 20 feet, 5 feet, 20 feet
   (3) length 8 feet, width 17 feet
   (4) length 1 foot, width 24 feet

6. A circle has a circumference of 44 centimeters. Which dimension is possible?
   (1) radius 7.1 centimeters
   (2) radius 7 centimeters
   (3) diameter 15 centimeters
   (4) diameter 12 centimeters

Answers are on page 296.

Area

The **area** of a figure is the amount of surface covered by the figure. Area is measured in square units.

To find the area of a rectangle, multiply its length and width.

Example 1   Find the area of the rectangle shown.

Area = length × width = 28 cm × 10 cm = 280 sq cm (or cm²)

To find the area of a square, multiply its length and width.

Example 2   Find the area of a square with sides 5 feet long.

STEP 1   Draw a diagram.

5 ft

STEP 2   A square has four equal sides, so its length is 5 feet and its width is 5 feet.

Area = 5 ft × 5 ft = 25 ft²

To find the area of a triangle, first identify the base and height of the triangle. The base is always the side that the triangle rests on. The height is the length of the segment perpendicular to the base and extending to the "top" of the triangle. In each triangle shown below, the base is labeled *b* and the height is labeled *h*.

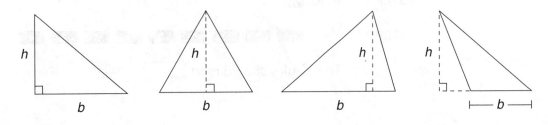

Example 3   Find the base and height of a triangle with right angle *ABC* and sides *AB* = 3 meters, *BC* = 4 meters, and *AC* = 5 meters.

STEP 1   Draw a diagram.

STEP 2   Since *AB* and *BC* are perpendicular, the height of the triangle is *AB* and has a measure of 3 meters. The base of the triangle is *BC* and has a measure of 4 meters.

TIP
Be careful to identify the base and height of a triangle before finding its area.

The area of a triangle is half its base times its height.

Example 4   Find the area of the triangle shown.

STEP 1   Identify the base and height.
base = 10 cm; height = 12 cm

STEP 2   Area = $\frac{1}{2}$ × base × height

$= \frac{1}{2}$ × 10 cm × 12 cm = 60 cm²

Example 5   Use your calculator to find the area of the triangle above.

STEP 1   Press **AC**.

STEP 2   Press **·** **5** **×** **1** **0** **×** **1** **2** **=**

The display should read [60.].

The area of a circle is π times the radius times the radius again. Use $\pi \approx \frac{22}{7}$ or $\pi \approx 3.14$.

Example 6   Find the area of the circle shown.

STEP 1   Find the radius.

Diameter ÷ 2 = 20 in. ÷ 2 = 10 in.

STEP 2   Since the radius is not a multiple of 7, use π ≈ 3.14.

Area = π × radius × radius
       ≈ 3.14 × 10 in. × 10 in. ≈ 314 in.²

Example 7   Use your calculator to find the area of the circle above.

STEP 1   Press **AC**.

STEP 2   Press **3** **.** **1** **4** **×** **1** **0** **×** **1** **0** **=**

The display should read | 314. |.

SUMMARY FOR FINDING AREA

Rectangle: Area = length × width

Triangle: Area = $\frac{1}{2}$ × base × height

Circle: Area = π × radius × radius

EXERCISE 9

Directions: Find the area of each figure shown.

1.   14 ft

11 ft   11 ft

14 ft

2.   7 in.

3.   9 mm

4. 30 m
   30 m   30 m
   30 m

5. 12 ft
   20 ft
   15 ft
   7 ft

6. 7 yd
   3 yd

7. 10 cm   10 cm
   8 cm
   12 cm

8. 45 cm
   27 cm
   36 cm

9. 15 cm

Directions: Find the area of each figure described.

10. A rectangle with length 9 millimeters and width 6 millimeters

11. A circle with radius 3 meters

12. A triangle with base 10 meters and height 3 meters

13. A square with sides 12 inches

14. A circle with diameter 28 yards

Directions: Use your calculator to find the area of each figure.

15. A triangle with base 4.26 inches and height 2.48 inches

16. A circle with diameter 42 yards

Answers are on page 296.

EXERCISE 10

Directions: Solve each problem below.

1. The area of a square is 16 square meters. What is the length of each side?

2. The area of a rectangle is 36 square feet. If the width is 4 feet, what is the length?

3. The area of a triangle is 30 square centimeters. Its base is 6 centimeters. What is its height?

4. A circle has an area of 120 square inches. Is its radius closer to 6 inches or 7 inches?

5. A rectangle has an area of 48 square feet. Which dimensions are *not* possible?
   (1) sides: 6 feet, 8 feet, 6 feet, 8 feet
   (2) sides: 2 feet, 24 feet, 2 feet, 24 feet
   (3) length 3 feet, width 16 feet
   (4) length 4 feet, width 13 feet

6. A triangle has an area of 12 square centimeters. Which dimensions are possible?
   (1) base 12 centimeters, height 1 centimeter
   (2) base 12 centimeters, height 2 centimeters
   (3) base 3 centimeters, height 4 centimeters
   (4) base 6 centimeters, height 2 centimeters

Answers are on page 296.

Volume

Volume is a measure of the space inside a three-dimensional figure. It is like capacity, the amount a container can hold. Volume is measured in cubic units.

The figure below is called a **rectangular solid** because it is made up of rectangles. We commonly call it a box.

To find the volume of a rectangular solid, multiply its length, width, and height.

Example 1   Find the volume of the rectangular solid shown below.

6 in.

8 in.

10 in.

Volume = length × width × height
        = 10 inches × 8 inches × 6 inches
        = 480 cubic inches (or in.³)

Example 2   Use your calculator to find the volume of the rectangular solid above.

STEP 1   Press `AC`.

STEP 2   Press `1` `0` `×` `8` `×` `6` `=`.

The display should read ⎹   **480.** ⎹.

A **cube** is a rectangular solid made up of squares. The length, width, and height of a cube are equal.

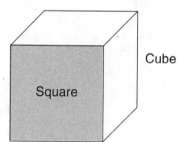

Cube

Square

Example 3   Find the volume of a cube with side 10 centimeters.

Volume = length × width × height
        = 10 centimeters × 10 centimeters × 10 centimeters
        = 1,000 cubic centimeters (or cm³)

SUMMARY FOR FINDING VOLUME

To find the volume of a rectangular solid:

Multiply its length, width, and height.

EXERCISE 11

Directions: Find the volume of each figure shown.

1. 10 m 4 m 4 m

2. 8 ft 5 ft 12 ft

3. 6 cm 6 cm 6 cm

4. 11 in. Cube

Directions: Use your calculator to find the volume of each figure described.

5. A rectangular solid with length 20 meters, width 5 meters, and height 1 meter

6. A cube with side 14 inches

Directions: Solve each problem below.

7. The volume of a cube is 27 cubic meters. Find its length, width, and height.

8. The volume of a rectangular solid is 126 cubic feet. If the length is 3 feet and the width is 7 feet, what is the height?

9. A rectangular solid has a volume of 72 cubic feet. Which dimensions are *not* possible?
   (1) length 2 feet, width 4 feet, height 9 feet
   (2) length 6 feet, width 6 feet, height 2 feet
   (3) length 9 feet, width 8 feet, height 0 feet
   (4) length 3 feet, width 6 feet, height 4 feet

10. A cube has a volume of 64 cubic centimeters. Which dimension is possible?
    (1) side 4 centimeters
    (2) side 16 centimeters
    (3) side 8 centimeters
    (4) side $21\frac{1}{3}$ centimeters

Answers are on page **296.**

Problem Solving with Measurement and Geometry

In this section you will combine your skills of measurement, geometry, and problem solving. Remember to use the five-step approach to solve each problem. With measurement and geometry problems, you need to pay attention to units. Also, if a diagram is not given, it may be helpful to draw your own.

Example 1   A bowling lane, from the foul line to the first pin, is 60 feet long. A bowling ball measures 27 inches around. If a bowling ball is rolled straight down a bowling lane and hits the first pin, how many revolutions will the ball make?

STEP 1   Understand the question.

You must figure out how many times the ball will "rotate" while rolling from the foul line to the first pin.

STEP 2   Decide what information is needed.

The distance the ball will roll is 60 feet. The distance around the ball is 27 inches. Draw a diagram showing this information.

STEP 3   Choose the most appropriate operation.

Change 60 feet to inches so that both measurements are inches. Divide by 27 inches for the number of revolutions.

STEP 4   Solve the problem.

60 feet × 12 = 720 inches; 720 inches ÷ 27 inches = $26\frac{2}{3}$ revolutions

STEP 5   Check your answer.

Use feet, rather than inches, to check your answer.

27 inches ÷ 12 = $2\frac{1}{4}$ feet;

$2\frac{1}{4}$ feet × $26\frac{2}{3}$ revolutions = 60 feet

EXERCISE 12

Directions: Solve each problem below.

1. The Russian space shuttle Buran has a wing-span of 79.2 feet. NASA's space shuttle wing-span is 78.6 feet. Which wing-span is greater? How much greater?

2. A pyramid near Cairo, Egypt, is approximately 450 feet high. Its square base has sides 755 feet long. What is the area of the base of the pyramid?

3. The Sears Tower in Chicago is 443 meters high. The Empire State Building in New York City is 381 meters high. How much higher is the Sears Tower than the Empire State Building?

4. A board foot is a unit used for lumber. It measures 12 inches by 12 inches by 1 inch. What is the volume (cubic inches) of one board foot?

5. A football field is $53\frac{1}{3}$ yards wide. Express the width of a football field in feet.

6. Which figure has the greater area, a circle with a diameter of 2 inches or a square with a side of 2 inches? Draw a diagram to show your result.

7. In 4 weeks, a baby gained 3 pounds. On average, how many ounces did the baby gain each day?

8. At birth, Abby weighed 6 pounds 9 ounces. At her 1-month doctor checkup, she weighed 8 pounds 13 ounces. Gaining at this rate, how much will she weigh at her 2-month checkup?

9. A brownie recipe suggests the use of two 8-inch square pans or one rectangular pan that measures 13 inches by 9 inches. Which will result in thicker brownies?

10. This sentence is printed on a 5-pound sack of flour: "There are about four cups of flour in one pound." A recipe for a loaf of bread requires $1\frac{3}{4}$ cups of flour. How many loaves of bread can you make with this sack of flour?

Answers are on page 296.

Perimeter, Circumference, Area, and Volume Problems

Many problems involve finding perimeter, circumference, area, or volume. Sometimes you need to decide which of these measures to calculate in order to solve a problem. Here are some useful hints.

- Perimeter and circumference are both distances around a figure. They are one-dimensional measures of length.

- Area is the amount of surface. Area is a two-dimensional measure, so use square units.

- Volume is the amount of space. Volume is a three-dimensional measure, so use cubic units.

Here's a problem that involves the three different types of measures. Suppose you buy a tiny present for someone and decide to wrap it in the box shown below. Refer to this box for the examples.

Example 1   How much styrofoam filling will the box hold?

STEP 1   Decide which measure to calculate and which units to use.

The problem asks for the amount of space in the box, a three-dimensional measure. Find the volume (cubic inches, or in.³).

STEP 2   Volume = length × width × height
            = 12 inches × 8 inches × 5 inches
            = 480 cubic inches
The box will hold 480 cubic inches (in.³) of styrofoam filling.

Example 2   How much wrapping paper will cover the box?

STEP 1   Decide which measure to calculate and which units to use.

The problem asks for the amount of surface on each rectangle of the box. Find its area (square inches).

STEP 2 Draw a diagram and calculate the area for each rectangle.

Top: Area = $12 \times 8 = 96$ in.^{2}
Bottom: Area = $12 \times 8 = 96$ in.^{2}

Front: Area = $12 \times 5 = 60$ in.^{2}
Back: Area = $12 \times 5 = 60$ in.^{2}

Left side: Area = $8 \times 5 = 40$ in.^{2}
Right side: Area = $8 \times 5 = 40$ in.^{2}

STEP 3 Add the areas: $96 + 96 + 60 + 60 + 40 + 40 = 392$ in.^{2}
Therefore, 392 square inches of wrapping paper will cover the box.

Example 3 How much ribbon will go around the box in two directions?

STEP 1 Decide which measure to calculate and which units to use.

The problem asks for the distance around the box, a measure of length. Find its perimeter (inches).

STEP 2 Draw a diagram and calculate the length of the ribbon going around the box.

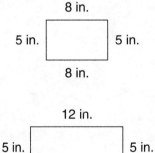

Vertical direction:
$5 + 8 + 5 + 8 = 26$ in.

Horizontal direction:
$5 + 12 + 5 + 12 = 34$ in.

STEP 3 Add the lengths: 26 in. + 34 in. = 60 in. or 5 ft
Therefore, 60 inches (or 5 feet) of ribbon will go around the box.

EXERCISE 13

(m)
milli = $\frac{1}{1000}$. 001

(c)
Centi = $\frac{1}{100}$ = .01

Directions: Solve each problem below.

1. The Eichenbergers live on a corner lot that measures 120 feet by 80 feet. They must add sidewalks along the edge of their lot next to the street. New sidewalks cost $12 per foot. How much will their new sidewalks cost?

2. Sidewalks are 5 feet wide. They are divided into sections that are 5 feet long. How many sections will there be in a sidewalk that is 120 feet long?

3. The Eichenbergers' new sidewalk will be 200 feet long and 5 feet wide. How much area will the new sidewalk cover?

4. Sidewalks are 4 inches deep. One section of sidewalk is 5 feet long and 5 feet wide. How much concrete (ft³) will be used for one section?

5. Beth is decorating her bedroom. The floor measures 12 feet by 15 feet. How much carpet (yd²) does she need to cover the floor of her bedroom?

6. Beth will add trim along the edge of her room and around the door frame. The room measures 12 feet by 15 feet. The door measures 2 feet 6 inches by 6 feet 8 inches. How much trim does she need?

7. An ice cube tray makes 12 ice cubes. Each ice cube is 3 centimeters wide, 4 centimeters long, and 3 centimeters high. Will one liter of water fill two ice cube trays?
   (**Hint:** 1 cm³ = 1 mL)

8. A college basketball court is 94 feet long and 50 feet wide. A high school basketball court is 84 feet long and 50 feet wide. How much more floor space does the college court have?

9. A 10-inch pizza costs $8, while a 12-inch pizza costs $10.50. Which size pizza is the better buy?

10. Annika's favorite part of a pizza is its crust around the edge. How much more crust does a 12-inch pizza have than a 10-inch pizza?

11. Which unit is appropriate for a perimeter measurement?
    (1) square yards
    (2) in.^{3}
    (3) cm
    (4) liter

12. Which unit is *not* appropriate for a volume measurement?
    (1) cubic centimeter
    (2) in.^{2}
    (3) m^3
    (4) cup

Answers are on page 297.

Measurement and Geometry Review

Directions: In questions 1–15, solve each problem. Show your work to the right.

1. Write the length of segment *AB*.

2. How many cups are in one gallon?

3. Find the perimeter of a rectangle with length 15 meters and width 10 meters.

4. What type of lines never intersect?

5. Change 2.5 kilograms to grams.

6. Find the diameter of a circle with radius 8 feet.

7. What figure is made up of the set of points all the same distance from a center point?

8. Change 80 ounces to pounds.

9. Find the volume of a cube whose side measures 7 meters.

10. Find the circumference of a circle with a diameter of 6 inches.

11. Change 300 centimeters to meters.

12. The perimeter of a square is 20 inches. Find the length of each side.

13. Draw and label a right angle formed by rays *PT* and *PR*.

14. Find the area of a circle that has a radius of 4 centimeters.

15. Change 64 inches to feet and inches.

Directions: Choose the correct answer to each problem. Remember the problem-solving skills you have learned.

16. Mia's quiz scores are 90, 82, 88, 89, and 74. Find the average, using the following grading scale.

A   90–100
B   80–89
C   70–79
D   60–69
F   0–59

(1) A
(2) B
(3) C
(4) D
(5) F

17. Which of the following is a set of equivalent numbers?

(1) $140\frac{1}{3}$, 47, $\frac{141}{3}$
(2) 0.04, $\frac{4}{10}$, $\frac{2}{5}$
(3) $\frac{1}{8}$, 1.25, $\frac{3}{16}$
(4) 12.5, $12\frac{1}{2}$, $\frac{24}{2}$
(5) 6.2, $6\frac{1}{5}$, $6\frac{2}{10}$

18. The regulation home plate for a baseball field has dimensions shown. How many inches of tape would you need to go around the home plate?

12 in.   12 in.

$8\frac{1}{2}$ in. $8\frac{1}{2}$ in.

17 in.

(1)   58
(2)   144.5
(3)   98
(4)   75
(5)   41

19. In her purse, Susan has two five-dollar bills, five quarters, two dimes, and four pennies. In her purse, Patty has eight dollar bills, two quarters, eight dimes, and ten nickels. Which of the following statements is true?

(1) Susan and Patty have the same number of coins.
(2) Susan has more money in her purse than Patty.
(3) Patty and Susan each have under $10 in her purse.
(4) Patty has more money in her purse than Susan.
(5) The difference in the amount of money in their purses is less than a dollar.

20. Which of the following is 18% of 300?

(1) .18
(2) 18
(3) 54
(4) 540
(5) 54,000

21. A weekday long-distance telephone call from Bozeman to Billings costs $0.41 for the first minute and $0.29 for each additional minute. At this rate, how much will a 15-minute phone call cost?

(1) $4.76
(2) $5.25
(3) $6.03
(4) $4.47
(5) Not enough information is given.

22. Which is the best buy for 1 can of beans?

(1) 2 for 79¢
(2) 45¢ each
(3) 6 for $2.69
(4) 3 for $1.39
(5) 4 for $2

23. Which equation does *not* have 5 as a solution?

   (1) $x - 1 = 4$
   (2) $x + 2 = 9$
   (3) $3 \cdot x = 15$
   (4) $x + 3 = 8$
   (5) $6 + x = 11$

24. The diagram below shows a bowling lane. How many inches wide is the lane, including the two gutters?

Gutter, $9\frac{5}{16}$ in. wide

Foul line

60 ft

62 ft 10$\frac{3}{16}$ in.

$41\frac{1}{2}$ in.

Pit

Gutter, $9\frac{5}{16}$ in. wide

   (1) $41\frac{1}{2}$
   (2) $50\frac{13}{16}$
   (3) $18\frac{5}{8}$
   (4) $59\frac{11}{16}$
   (5) $60\frac{1}{8}$

25. Use the diagram of the bowling lane above. What is the distance from the first pin to the pit?

   (1) 60 ft
   (2) $10\frac{3}{16}$ in.
   (3) 2 ft $10\frac{13}{16}$ in.
   (4) 2 ft $10\frac{3}{16}$ in.
   (5) Not enough information is given.

26. Which decimal number is rounded to the nearest thousandth?

   (1) 6.8945 rounded to 6.895
   (2) 3.61249 rounded to 3.6125
   (3) 19.1406 rounded to 19.14
   (4) 2,100 rounded to 2,000
   (5) 48,000 rounded to 50,000

27. Tsung-Chi and Juanita are going on a 1,200-mile trip. If Juanita drives about $\frac{1}{4}$ of the distance, how many miles will Tsung-Chi drive?

   (1) 300
   (2) 900
   (3) 240
   (4) 960
   (5) 4,800

Directions: Use your calculator to solve each problem.

28. What is the volume of a cube with a side of 6 inches?

29. What is the circumference of a circle with a diameter of 3 feet?

30. What is the perimeter of a rectangle with a length of 16.42 meters and a width of 8.39 meters?

Directions: Solve each problem and write the answer on the number grid.

31. Find the area of the rectangle shown. Write your answer on the number grid.

9 m

12 m   12 m

9 m

32. Find the area of triangle *ABC*. Write your answer on the number grid.

A

25 cm   15 cm

B   20 cm   C

33. Find the volume of the rectangular solid shown. Write your answer on the number grid.

3 ft

2 ft

6 ft

34. What is the total price of 16 candy bars purchased for 49¢ each?

Answers are on page 297.

Mathematics

This Posttest consists of 60 problems. It should give you a good idea of how well you learned the mathematics and problem-solving skills you studied in this book. You should take the Posttest only after you have completed all the chapters.

Record your multiple-choice answers on this page and your number grid answers on

pages 254 and 255. Check your answers with the Answer Key on pages 256–258.

Using the Evaluation Chart on page 259, circle the number of each problem that you missed to determine which skills you might need to review before you move on to Contemporary's *GED Mathematics*.

Posttest Answer Grid

#						#						#					
1	① ② ③ ④ ⑤					20	① ② ③ ④ ⑤					39	① ② ③ ④ ⑤				
2	① ② ③ ④ ⑤					21	① ② ③ ④ ⑤					40	① ② ③ ④ ⑤				
3	① ② ③ ④ ⑤					22	① ② ③ ④ ⑤					41	① ② ③ ④ ⑤				
4	① ② ③ ④ ⑤					23	① ② ③ ④ ⑤					42	① ② ③ ④ ⑤				
5	① ② ③ ④ ⑤					24	① ② ③ ④ ⑤					43	① ② ③ ④ ⑤				
6	① ② ③ ④ ⑤					25	① ② ③ ④ ⑤					44	① ② ③ ④ ⑤				
7	① ② ③ ④ ⑤					26	① ② ③ ④ ⑤					45	① ② ③ ④ ⑤				
8	① ② ③ ④ ⑤					27	① ② ③ ④ ⑤					46	① ② ③ ④ ⑤				
9	① ② ③ ④ ⑤					28	① ② ③ ④ ⑤					47	① ② ③ ④ ⑤				
10	① ② ③ ④ ⑤					29	① ② ③ ④ ⑤					48	① ② ③ ④ ⑤				
11	① ② ③ ④ ⑤					30	① ② ③ ④ ⑤					49	① ② ③ ④ ⑤				
12	① ② ③ ④ ⑤					31	① ② ③ ④ ⑤					50	① ② ③ ④ ⑤				
13	① ② ③ ④ ⑤					32	① ② ③ ④ ⑤					51	① ② ③ ④ ⑤				
14	① ② ③ ④ ⑤					33	① ② ③ ④ ⑤					52	① ② ③ ④ ⑤				
15	① ② ③ ④ ⑤					34	① ② ③ ④ ⑤					53	① ② ③ ④ ⑤				
16	① ② ③ ④ ⑤					35	① ② ③ ④ ⑤					54	① ② ③ ④ ⑤				
17	① ② ③ ④ ⑤					36	① ② ③ ④ ⑤					55	① ② ③ ④ ⑤				
18	① ② ③ ④ ⑤					37	① ② ③ ④ ⑤											
19	① ② ③ ④ ⑤					38	① ② ③ ④ ⑤											

POSTTEST

Directions: Solve each problem.

1. The cost of mailing a first-class letter is 34¢ for the first ounce and 23¢ for each additional ounce, up to 14 ounces. At this rate, how much does it cost to mail a first-class letter that weighs 4 ounces?

   (1) $0.57
   (2) $1.03
   (3) $1.26
   (4) $1.36
   (5) $4.34

2. Which three statements are true?

   Opposite sides of a rectangle
   A are perpendicular
   B are parallel
   C are the same length
   D are usually not the same length
   E intersect
   F never intersect

   (1) A, C, and F
   (2) A, D, and E
   (3) B, C, and F
   (4) B, C, and E
   (5) A, C, and E

3. Anita lives in Wyoming, which has a general state sales tax on purchases made. If Anita buys a car for $18,000, how much money will she pay in sales tax?

   (1) $ 900
   (2) $ 180
   (3) $1,800
   (4) $1,080
   (5) Not enough information is given.

4. Between which two consecutive whole numbers does $\sqrt{51}$ lie?

   (1) $\sqrt{50}$ and $\sqrt{52}$
   (2) 5 and 11
   (3) 5 and 6
   (4) 7 and 8
   (5) 25 and 26

5. A stick of butter is the same as 8 tablespoons, or $\frac{1}{2}$ cup. A cookie recipe calls for $\frac{3}{4}$ cup butter. How much butter is this?

   (1) $\frac{3}{8}$ stick
   (2) $1\frac{1}{2}$ sticks
   (3) 12 tablespoons
   (4) Both (1) and (3) are correct.
   (5) Both (2) and (3) are correct.

6. Which of the following whole numbers is the greatest?

   (1) sixty-eight thousand sixty-eight
   (2) sixty-eight thousand eighty-six
   (3) eighty-six thousand eight
   (4) eighty-six thousand sixty
   (5) eighty-six thousand six

7. Which of the following arithmetic expressions will solve the proportion $\frac{5}{9} = \frac{40}{?}$?

   (1) $5 \times 9 \div 40$
   (2) $5 \times 40 \div 9$
   (3) $9 \times 40 \div 5$
   (4) $9 \times 5 \div 40$
   (5) $40 \times 5 \div 9$

8. Which of the following lists the lengths from least to greatest?

   A 840 centimeters
   B 6 meters
   C 2,842 millimeters
   D 0.005 kilometers

   (1) C, A, B, D
   (2) C, D, B, A
   (3) D, C, B, A
   (4) B, C, A, D
   (5) A, B, D, C

9. There are five children in the Peregrino family. Two of the children have curly hair. What percent of the children in the Peregrino family do *not* have curly hair?

(1) 60%
(2) 40%
(3) 6%
(4) 4%
(5) Not enough information is given.

10. Holly paid 6% sales tax on her new refrigerator. If the refrigerator cost $580, how much sales tax did she pay?

(1) $ 6.00
(2) $ 34.80
(3) $ 348
(4) $ 580
(5) $3,480

11. The volume of a cube is 216 cubic inches. Find the length of one side.

(1) about 15 inches
(2) 6 inches
(3) about 6 inches
(4) 72 inches
(5) Not enough information is given.

12. What is the probability that a family with three children has three girls? (Assume that "boy" and "girl" are equally likely.)

(1) $\frac{1}{3}$
(2) $\frac{1}{9}$
(3) $\frac{1}{6}$
(4) $\frac{1}{27}$
(5) $\frac{1}{8}$

13. One week, Raoul worked from 7:00 P.M. to 11:00 P.M., Monday through Friday. His hourly wage is $7.50. On Saturday, he worked from 8:00 A.M. to 2:00 P.M., earning one-and-a-half times his hourly wage. He did not work on Sunday. How much money did Raoul earn that week?

(1) $217.50
(2) $172.50
(3) $236.25
(4) $204
(5) $159

Refer to the table below for problems 14–16.

Height (inches)	Desirable Weight (pounds)	
	Men	Women
58		102
60		107
62	123	113
64	130	120
66	136	128
68	145	136
70	154	144
72	162	152
74	171	
76	181	

14. What is the desirable weight for a male who is 6 feet 2 inches tall?

(1) 123 pounds
(2) 113 pounds
(3) 171 pounds
(4) 162 pounds
(5) none of the above

POSTTEST

15. According to the table, which statement is true?

(1) For a given height, a woman's desirable weight is usually 10 pounds less than a man's desirable weight.
(2) For women at least 64 inches tall, a gain of an inch in height allows a gain of about 4 pounds in weight.
(3) The desirable weight for a male who is 5 feet 5 inches is about 133 pounds.
(4) The desirable weight for a female who is 74 inches tall is about 160 pounds.
(5) All of the statements are true.

16. If a woman weighs 136 pounds, and her weight is considered desirable for her height, how tall is she?

(1) 5 feet 6 inches
(2) 5 feet 8 inches
(3) 66 inches
(4) Both (1) and (3) are correct.
(5) Both (2) and (3) are correct.

17. Which of the following lists four fractions in order from least to greatest?

(1) $\frac{7}{12}, \frac{7}{13}, \frac{7}{14}, \frac{7}{15}$
(2) $\frac{10}{3}, \frac{9}{3}, \frac{8}{3}, \frac{7}{3}$
(3) $\frac{1}{10}, \frac{1}{9}, \frac{1}{8}, \frac{1}{7}$
(4) $\frac{4}{5}, \frac{3}{5}, \frac{2}{5}, \frac{1}{5}$
(5) $\frac{1}{2}, \frac{1}{3}, \frac{1}{4}, \frac{1}{5}$

18. Which of the following amounts of money has the greatest value?

(1) eighteen quarters
(2) fifty-two dimes
(3) a five-dollar bill
(4) one hundred nine pennies
(5) sixty-four nickels

19. The perimeter of a square is 28 inches. Find the area of the square.

(1) 49 square inches
(2) 14 square inches
(3) $\sqrt{28}$ square inches
(4) 56 square inches
(5) none of the above

20. Jack and Jill expect about 100 guests at their wedding reception. How many tables should they rent, if each table seats 8 guests?

(1) 12
(2) 12.5
(3) $12\frac{1}{2}$
(4) 13
(5) 14

21. The following sign appears in front of an airport parking lot. If you park your car in the lot on Monday, January 2, at 7:00 A.M. and return on Wednesday, January 11, at 12:00 noon, how much money do you owe?

Parking Lot Rates
$1.50 per hour
Not to exceed $15 per day
Not to exceed $75 per week

(1) $150
(2) $114
(3) $154.50
(4) $112.50
(5) $120

22. The ratio of black keys to white keys on a standard piano is 9 : 13. There are 88 keys altogether. How many keys on a standard piano are black?

(1) 36
(2) 75
(3) 9
(4) 52
(5) Not enough information is given.

23. Which is least likely to happen?

   (1) Flipping a coin and getting "heads"
   (2) Drawing an ace from a standard deck of 52 cards
   (3) Drawing a face card from a standard deck of 52 cards
   (4) Rolling a number cube and getting a "4"
   (5) Rolling two number cubes and getting a sum of 5

24. If you fold a piece of notebook paper in half six times, how many rectangles of the same size are formed by the folding?

   (1) 12
   (2) 24
   (3) 32
   (4) 36
   (5) 64

25. The acreage of Yellowstone National Park is 2,219,784.68. Round this to the nearest thousand acres.

   (1) 2,000,000
   (2) 2,200,000
   (3) 2,220,000
   (4) 2,219,000
   (5) 2,219,800

26. Which equation does *not* have the solution $x = 7$?

   (1) $x - 8 = 15$
   (2) $x + 10 = 17$
   (3) $\frac{x}{7} = 1$
   (4) $9x = 63$
   (5) $\sqrt{49} = x$

27. Which of the following statements is *not* true?

   (1) The amount of surface covered by a rectangle is its area.
   (2) The distance around a triangle is its perimeter.
   (3) The distance around a circle is its circumference.
   (4) The amount of space inside a cube is its area.
   (5) The area of a circle depends on its radius or diameter.

28. The cost of a first-class stamp was increased from 32¢ to 34¢. Twenty stamps are sold in a book. Which of the following expressions describes the increased cost of a book of stamps?

   A ($.34 − $.32) × 20
   B 20 × $.34 − 20 × $.32

   (1) A
   (2) B
   (3) either A or B
   (4) neither A nor B
   (5) none of the above

29. In a survey, 45% of the people responded "yes," while the rest responded "no." How many people responded "no"?

   (1) 55
   (2) 45
   (3) more than 45
   (4) at least 55
   (5) Not enough information is given.

30. Which of the following is a set of equivalent numbers?

   (1) 5%, $\frac{1}{5}$, 0.5
   (2) 10%, $\frac{1}{10}$, 0.10
   (3) 60%, $\frac{1}{60}$, 0.6
   (4) 1%, $\frac{1}{100}$, 0.1
   (5) 32%, $\frac{32}{100}$, 32

POSTTEST

31. The median age of a set of eleven employees is 36. The employee who figured out the median age will not reveal his or her own age. The ages of the other ten employees are as follows: 32, 35, 24, 50, 29, 45, 36, 38, 25, 36. Which of the following ages is not possible for the eleventh employee?

   (1) 36
   (2) 30
   (3) 60
   (4) 48
   (5) 40

32. Eric lives in Massachusetts. He wishes to call Daniel in Hawaii. The time in Massachusetts is 5 hours later than the time in Hawaii. At what time should Eric make the call if he wishes to reach Daniel at 1:00 P.M.?

   (1) 8:00 A.M.
   (2) 9:00 A.M.
   (3) 5:00 P.M.
   (4) 6:00 P.M.
   (5) 6:00 A.M.

33. Karina is making a quilt. One quilt block is shown below. The shaded areas represent the darker fabric. Karina will sew together 12 of these quilt blocks to make the quilt. What fraction of the quilt is made of the darker fabric?

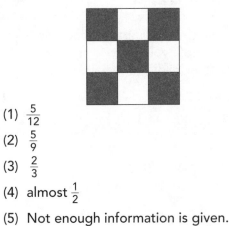

   (1) $\frac{5}{12}$
   (2) $\frac{5}{9}$
   (3) $\frac{2}{3}$
   (4) almost $\frac{1}{2}$
   (5) Not enough information is given.

34. A bag contains 15 yellow and blue marbles. The probability of randomly drawing a blue marble is $\frac{1}{3}$. How many yellow marbles are in the bag?

   (1) 10
   (2) 3
   (3) 5
   (4) 12
   (5) Not enough information is given.

35. Chang gets a paycheck biweekly (every two weeks), while Leah gets a paycheck twice each month. Which of the following statements is *not* true?

   (1) Leah and Chang get the same number of paychecks in a year.
   (2) Leah gets 24 paychecks each year.
   (3) Twice a year, Chang gets 3 paychecks in a month.
   (4) Chang gets 2 more paychecks a year than Leah gets.
   (5) Leah gets the same number of paychecks each month.

36. Which is the best buy for soda pop?

   (1) a 12-pack of 12-oz cans for $4.99
   (2) a 6-pack of 12-oz cans for $2.79
   (3) a case (24 cans) of 12-oz cans for $10
   (4) 75¢ for a 12-oz can
   (5) 79¢ for a 16-oz bottle

37. Michael makes about 60% of the free throws he attempts in basketball practice. Of the next 25 free throws he attempts in practice, how many would you expect Michael to make?

   (1) 19
   (2) 10
   (3) 20
   (4) 15
   (5) There is no way of knowing how many free throws to expect Michael to make.

38. Sonia is building a fence for a rectangular area of her yard. She wants to use all 80 feet of fencing she bought. She will place a post every 5 feet, including one at each corner. Which of the following dimensions will *not* work for the rectangular area she will fence?

(1) 5 feet by 35 feet
(2) 10 feet by 30 feet
(3) 15 feet by 25 feet
(4) 20 feet by 20 feet
(5) 40 feet by 2 feet

39. What does the expression 6^3 mean?

(1) $3 \times 3 \times 3 \times 3 \times 3 \times 3$
(2) 6×3
(3) $6 + 6 + 6$
(4) $6 \times 6 \times 6$
(5) all of the above

40. Which of the following points is (–4, 3)?

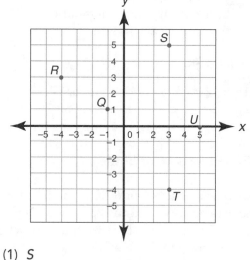

(1) S
(2) T
(3) R
(4) Q
(5) U

Refer to the following table for problems 41–43.

Human Activity	Quarts of blood pumped per minute	Number of heart beats per minute
rest	5–6	60–80
mild exercise	7–8	100–120
strenuous exercise	30	up to 200

41. How many times does an average person's heart beat while sleeping for 8 hours?

(1) 26,800
(2) 38,900
(3) 33,600
(4) 2,640
(5) 560

42. What type of activity is someone doing if the person's heart pumps between 7 and 8 gallons of blood per minute?

(1) rest
(2) mild exercise
(3) strenuous exercise
(4) an exercise level between "mild" and "strenuous"
(5) any of the above

43. How many more quarts of blood does your heart pump if you exercise strenuously, rather than mildly, for a half hour?

(1) about 2,500
(2) 80 to 100
(3) 22 to 23
(4) about 675
(5) none of the above

44. Which of the following is true of statements A and B?

A A rectangle has four right angles.
B If a square has a 2-inch side, all of its sides are 2 inches long.

(1) A is never true.
(2) A is always true.
(3) B is always true.
(4) A and B are never true.
(5) A and B are always true.

45. Which investment will earn the greatest amount of interest? (Use the formula $i = prt$.)

(1) $1,000 at 8% for 2 years
(2) $500 at 12% for 1 year
(3) $2,000 at 6% for 6 months
(4) $1,000 at 5% for 4 years
(5) $500 at 3% for 10 years

46. Thiu runs 3 miles in 25 minutes. Kai runs an 8-minute mile. Lin runs $7\frac{1}{2}$ miles per hour. Which statement is true?

(1) Thiu runs the fastest.
(2) Kai runs the fastest.
(3) Lin runs the fastest.
(4) Thiu runs faster than Kai.
(5) Lin and Kai run at the same rate.

47. A square has the same area as a rectangle that measures 4 feet by 16 feet. What is the length of a side of the square?

(1) 32 feet
(2) 8 feet
(3) $\sqrt{40}$ feet
(4) 20 feet
(5) 64 feet

48. Maria asked 100 people, "What's your favorite color—blue, red, or yellow?" The results were as follows: 44 blue, 30 red, and 26 yellow. Maria wants to draw a circle graph to display this data. What will be the measure of the central angle for the part of the circle that represents "red" as a favorite color?

(1) 108°
(2) 30°
(3) 54°
(4) 300°
(5) 150°

49. The high temperatures during a week in January in Bismarck, North Dakota, were 10°F, 15°F, 9°F, 0°F, 5°F, 21°F, and 18°F. What was the average high temperature for the week?

(1) 10°F
(2) about 10°F
(3) 11°F
(4) about 11°F
(5) 13°F

50. A circle has a circumference of 22 centimeters. Which dimension is possible for the circle? (Use the formula $C = \pi \times$ diameter, with $\pi \approx \frac{22}{7}$.)

(1) radius = 7 centimeters
(2) diameter = 7 centimeters
(3) radius = 14 centimeters
(4) diameter = 14 centimeters
(5) Both (1) and (4) are correct.

51. Which ratio will *not* form a proportion with the ratio 1 to 4?

(1) 2 to 8
(2) 4 to 1
(3) 0.5 to 2
(4) 5 to 20
(5) 10 to 40

POSTTEST

Refer to the line graphs below for problems 52–55.

ABBY'S HEIGHT CHART

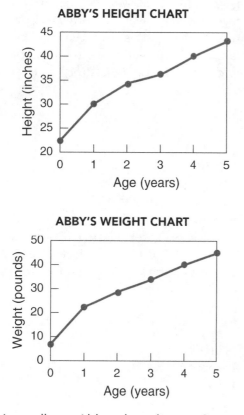

52. How tall was Abby when she was 2 years old?

(1) about 28 inches
(2) about 35 inches
(3) about 24 inches
(4) about 38 inches
(5) about 30 inches

53. How much did Abby weigh when she was about 40 inches tall?

(1) about 40 pounds
(2) about 35 pounds
(3) about 44 pounds
(4) about 30 pounds
(5) Not enough information is given.

54. In her first 5 years, how much overall weight did Abby gain?

(1) about 21 pounds
(2) about 43 pounds
(3) about 32 pounds
(4) about 44 pounds
(5) about 36 pounds

55. Which statement is true?

(1) Abby's height increased fastest during her first year.
(2) Abby's weight increased fastest during her first year.
(3) Abby's height and weight both increased fastest during her first year.
(4) Abby's height increased at a constant rate since birth.
(5) Abby's weight increased at a constant rate since birth.

Use your calculator to solve problems 56–60. Write each answer on the number grid.

56. Heather wants to make two kinds of cookies. One recipe calls for $\frac{1}{4}$ cup of brown sugar. The other recipe needs $\frac{2}{3}$ cup of brown sugar. How much brown sugar does Heather need altogether?

P O S T T E S T

57. Riley's basketball team won 70% of the games played. If there were 30 games, how many wins did Riley's team have?

58. Find the circumference of a circle that has a 6-inch diameter. (Use the formula $C = \pi d$.)

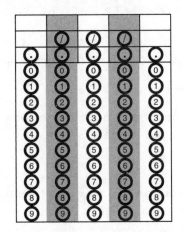

59. Find the volume of a cube with a side of 4.1 centimeters. Round your answer to the nearest whole centimeter. (Use the formula $V = s^3$.)

60. Find the value of $72 + 22 \times 5 - 38$.

Answers are on page 287.

POSTTEST

Answer Key

1. **(2)** $\$.34 + 3(\$.23) = \$.34 + \$.69 = \$1.03$

2. **(3)** Opposite sides of a rectangle are parallel, are the same length, and never intersect.

3. **(5)** You need to know the sales tax rate in order to solve the problem.

4. **(4)** $\sqrt{51}$ lies between $\sqrt{49} = 7$ and $\sqrt{64} = 8$

5. **(5)** $\frac{3}{4}$ cup $= \frac{1}{2}$ cup $+ \frac{1}{4}$ cup $= 1$ stick $+ \frac{1}{2}$ stick $= 1\frac{1}{2}$ sticks; $\frac{3}{4}$ cup $= \frac{1}{2}$ cup $+ \frac{1}{4}$ cup $=$ 8 tablespoons + 4 tablespoons = 12 tablespoons

6. **(4)** (1) 68,068; (2) 68,086; (3) 86,008; (4) 86,060; (5) 86,006

7. **(3)** $9 \times 40 \div 5 = 72$; $\frac{5}{9} = \frac{40}{72}$; $5 \times 72 = 9 \times 40$

8. **(2)** A. 840 cm = 8.4 m; B. 6 m; C. 2,842 mm = 2.8 m; D. 0.005 km = 5 m; Order: C, D, B, A

9. **(1)** 3 of the 5 children do not have curly hair; $\frac{3}{5} = 60\%$

10. **(2)** $\$580 \times .06 = \$34.80$

11. **(2)** Volume $= 6 \times 6 \times 6 = 216$; side $= 6$

12. **(5)** Let B = boy, G = girl. Eight possible outcomes: BBB, BBG, BGB, GBB, GGB, GBG, BGG, GGG. One favorable outcome: GGG. Probability $= \frac{\text{favorable outcomes}}{\text{possible outcomes}} = \frac{1}{8}$

13. **(1)** $(4 \times 5 \times \$7.50) + (6 \times \$7.50 \times 1.5) = \$150 + \$67.50 = \$217.50$

14. **(3)** 6 feet 2 inches $= (6 \times 12) + 2 = 74$ inches

15. **(5)**

16. **(2)** 68 inches $= (5 \times 12) + 8 = 5$ feet 8 inches

17. **(3)**

18. **(2)** (1) $18 \times \$.25 = \$4.50$; (2) $52 \times \$.10 = \$5.20$; (3) $\$5.00$; (4) $\$1.09$; (5) $64 \times \$.05 = \$3.20$

19. **(1)** $28 \div 4 = 7$; Area $= 7 \times 7 = 49$

20. **(4)** $100 \div 8 = 12.5$ or $12\frac{1}{2}$; rent 13

21. **(4)** from Jan. 2, 7:00 A.M. to Jan. 9, 7:00 A.M. is 1 week = \$75; from Jan. 9, 7:00 A.M. to Jan. 11, 7:00 A.M. is 2 days, and $2 \times \$15 = \$30$; Jan. 11, 7:00 A.M. to 12:00 noon is 5 hours, and $5 \times \$1.50 = \$7.50$; $\$75 + \$30 + \$7.50 = \$112.50$

22. **(1)** $\frac{\text{black}}{\text{total}} = \frac{\text{black}}{\text{black + white}} = \frac{9}{9 + 13} = \frac{9}{22}$; $\frac{9}{22} = \frac{b}{88}$; $b = \frac{88 \cdot 9}{22} = 36$

23. **(2)** (1) probability $= \frac{1}{2} = 50\%$; (2) probability $= \frac{4}{52} \approx 8\%$; (3) probability $= \frac{12}{52} \approx 23\%$; (4) probability $= \frac{1}{6} \approx 17\%$; (5) probability $= \frac{4}{36} \approx 11\%$

24. **(5)** $2^6 = 2 \times 2 \times 2 \times 2 \times 2 \times 2 = 64$

25. **(3)** $7 > 5$, so round the thousands' place up; 9 rounds up to 10, so 19 rounds up to 20.

26. **(1)** $7 - 8 \neq 15$

27. **(4)** The amount of space inside a cube is its volume, not its area.

28. **(3)**

29. **(5)** You need to know how many people responded in order to solve the problem.

30. **(2)** $10\% = \frac{10}{100} = \frac{1}{10} = 0.1 = 0.10$

31. **(2)** List the 10 ages in order from least to greatest: 24, 25, 29, 32, 35, 36, 36, 38, 45, 50; Since 36 is the median, 36 must be the 6th age when the missing age is listed. If the person was younger than 36, then the median age would be less than 36 so the missing age must be at least 36. It cannot be 30.

32. **(4)** 5 hours later than 1:00 P.M. is 6:00 P.M.

33. **(2)** 5 of the 9 squares are shaded in each quilt block, so $\frac{5}{9}$ of the quilt is made of the darker fabric.

POSTTEST

34. (1) $\frac{1}{3} = \frac{5}{15}$, so there are 5 blue marbles; 15 total − 5 blue = 10 yellow

35. (1) Leah: 12 months × 2 = 24 paychecks each year; Chang: 52 weeks ÷ 2 = 26 paychecks each year.

36. (1) (1) $4.99 ÷ 12 ≈ $.416/can; (2) $2.79 ÷ 6 ≈ $.47/can; (3) $10.00 ÷ 24 ≈ $.417/can; (4) $.75/can; (5) $.79/bottle. (1) is the best buy for a can, so compare this with (5). (1) $.42 ÷ 12 oz ≈ $.04/oz; (5) $.79 ÷ 16 oz ≈ $.05/oz; (1) is the better buy.

37. (4) 60% of 25 = 0.60 × 25 = 15

38. (5) (1) 5 + 35 + 5 + 35 = 80; (2) 10 + 30 + 10 + 30 = 80; (3) 15 + 25 + 15 + 25 = 80; (4) 20 + 20 + 20 + 20; (5) 40 + 2 + 40 + 2 = 84. By drawing diagrams, you can see that each of the first four sets of dimensions allows a post at each corner and every 5 ft.

39. (4)

40. (3)

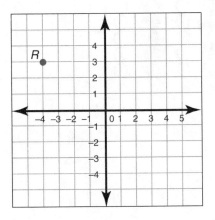

41. (3) 70 beats/minute × 60 minutes/hour × 8 hours = 33,600 beats

42. (3) 7.5 gallons × 4 = 30 quarts; strenuous

43. (4) 30 − 7.5 = 22.5; 22.5 quarts/minute × 30 minutes = 675 quarts

44. (5)

45. (4) (1) $1,000 × 0.08 × 2 = $160; (2) $500 × 0.12 × 1 = $60; (3) $2,000 × 0.06 × 0.5 = $60; (4) $1,000 × 0.05 × 4 = $200; (5) $500 × 0.03 × 10 = $150

46. (5) Thiu: 3 miles/25 minutes × 60 minutes/hour = 7.2 miles/hour; Kai: 1 mile/8 minutes × 60 minutes/hour = 7.5 miles/hour; Lin: 7.5 miles/hour

47. (2) Area of the rectangle = 4 × 16 = 64; Area of the square = 64 = 8 × 8, so side = 8.

48. (1) $\frac{30}{100} \times 360 = 108°$

49. (4) 10 + 15 + 9 + 0 + 5 + 21 + 18 = 78; 78 ÷ 7 ≈ 11

50. (2) Circumference = π × diameter; 22 cm = $\frac{22}{7}$ × diameter = $\frac{22}{7}$ × 7; diameter = 7 cm; radius = 7 ÷ 2 = 3.5 cm

51. (2) $\frac{1}{4} \neq \frac{4}{1}$

52. (2) On the top graph, find 2 years, then find the height, about 35 inches.

53. (1) On the top graph, find 40 inches, then find her age, about 4 years. Then on the bottom graph, find 4 years, then find her weight, about 40 pounds.

54. (5) Weight at age 5, about 44 pounds; weight at birth, about 8 pounds; 44 − 8 = 36

55. (3)

56. $\frac{11}{12}$ **cup** $\frac{1}{4} + \frac{2}{3} = \frac{3}{12} + \frac{8}{12} = \frac{11}{12}$

57. 21 wins $30 \times .70 = 21$

59. 69 cm³ $4.1 \times 4.1 \times 4.1 = 68.921 = 69$

58. 18.84 inches $6 \times 3.14 = 18.84$

60. 144 $72 + 110 - 38 = 144$

POSTTEST

Evaluation Chart

On the following chart, circle the number of any problem you got wrong. After each problem you will see the name of the section (or sections) where you can find the skills you need to solve the problem. When a problem involves more than one skill, the sections are separated by a slash (/).

Problem	Section	Starting Page
25	Estimation	23
6	Place Value	10
1, 13	Problem-Solving Strategies/Multiple-Step Problems	45/50
3, 14, 15, 16, 32, 35	Problem-Solving Strategies	45
20, 41, 42, 43	The Basic Operations/Problem-Solving Strategies	15/45
18	Comparing Decimals	57
21	Solving Problems Involving Decimals	62
33	The Meaning of Fractions and Mixed Numbers	78
5, 17	Comparing and Ordering Fractions	88
56	Adding Fractions and Mixed Numbers	93
2, 27, 44	Geometric Definitions	219
8	Metric Units	216
11, 58	Perimeter and Circumference	225
19	Area	229
59	Volume	233
24	Geometric Definitions/Problem-Solving Strategies	219/45
38, 47, 50	Perimeter, Circumference, Area, & Volume Problems	238
7	Solving Proportions	121
36, 46	Rates	115
22, 51	Ratios/Solving Proportions	112/121
9, 30	Common Percents, Fractions, and Decimals	129
29	Percent Problems and Proportions	136
10, 37, 57	Percent of a Number	131
23	Probability/Favorable Outcomes	173/177
31, 49	Mean, Median, Mode, and Range	144
12, 34	Probability	173
52, 53, 54, 55	Line Graphs	156
48	Drawing Circle Graphs	169
4, 39	Exponents and Square Roots	187
26	Variables and Simple Equations	196
28, 60	Arithmetic Expressions	193
40	The Coordinate Plane	204
45	Formulas and Problem Solving	200

Answer Key

Chapter 1

Exercise 1, page 11

1. 7 tens or 70
2. 9 million or 9,000,000
3. 5 ones or 5
4. 0 hundreds
5. 0 ten millions
6. 8 hundred thousands or 800,000
7. 1 thousand or 1,000
8. 6 hundred millions or 600,000,000
9. 20 thousands or 20,000
10. 5 billions or 5,000,000,000
11. 4 thousands or 4,000
12. 1 one or 1
13. 9 ten thousands or 90,000
14. 6 hundreds or 600
15. 6 tens or 60
16. 6 ones or 6

Exercise 2, pages 13–14

1. 9 tens, 7 ones
2. 8 thousands, 5 hundreds, 0 tens, 2 ones
3. 3 hundreds, 6 tens, 4 ones
4. 3 hundred thousands, 1 ten thousands, 6 thousands, 0 hundreds, 0 tens, 8 ones
5. 4 millions, 8 hundred thousands, 7 ten thousands, 0 thousands, 9 hundreds, 2 tens, 1 ones
6. 7 billions, 9 hundred millions, 1 ten millions, 5 millions, 2 hundred thousands, 4 ten thousands, 3 thousands, 6 hundreds, 0 tens, 0 ones
7. 214
8. 69,436
9. 9,190,647
10. 4,809,190,002
11. 70,933,088
12. 500,000 + 30,000 + 2,000 + 900 + 7
13. 4,000,000 + 600,000 + 5,000 + 800 + 70 + 3
14. 30,000 + 9,000 + 900 + 1

Exercise 3, pages 14–15

1.

+	1	2	3	4	5	6	7	8	9	10
1	2	3	4	5	6	7	8	9	10	11
2	3	4	5	6	7	8	9	10	11	12
3	4	5	6	7	8	9	10	11	12	13
4	5	6	7	8	9	10	11	12	13	14
5	6	7	8	9	10	11	12	13	14	15
6	7	8	9	10	11	12	13	14	15	16
7	8	9	10	11	12	13	14	15	16	17
8	9	10	11	12	13	14	15	16	17	18
9	10	11	12	13	14	15	16	17	18	19
10	11	12	13	14	15	16	17	18	19	20

2.

×	1	2	3	4	5	6	7	8	9	10
1	1	2	3	4	5	6	7	8	9	10
2	2	4	6	8	10	12	14	16	18	20
3	3	6	9	12	15	18	21	24	27	30
4	4	8	12	16	20	24	28	32	36	40
5	5	10	15	20	25	30	35	40	45	50
6	6	12	18	24	30	36	42	48	54	60
7	7	14	21	28	35	42	49	56	63	70
8	8	16	24	32	40	48	56	64	72	80
9	9	18	27	36	45	54	63	72	81	90
10	10	20	30	40	50	60	70	80	90	100

Exercise 4, page 16

1. **44**
2. **51**
3. **55**
4. **123**
5. **806**
6. **8,934**
7. **16,126**
8. **16,655**
9. **8,816**
10. **3,023**
11. **1,831 newspapers;**
    327 + 489 + 387 + 628 = 1,831
12. **6,063 T-shirts;** 2,498 + 3,565 = 6,063
13. **2,334 miles**
    456 + 482 + 449 + 479 + 468 = 2,334
14. **$2,209,780**
    $794,856 + $675,928 + $738,996 = $2,209,780

Exercise 5, page 17

1. **23**
2. **232**
3. **39**
4. **687**
5. **1,257**
6. **54,276**
7. **41,096**
8. **7,526**
9. **1,857**
10. **78,618**
11. **$387;** $525 − $138 = $387
12. **5,089 fans;** 54,067 − 48,978 = 5,089
13. **$6,850;** $8,750 − $1900 = $6,850
14. **62,358 packages**
    1,000,000 − 937,642 = 62,358

Exercise 6, page 18

1. **68**
2. **684**
3. **414**
4. **3,552**

5. **1,560**
6. **9,936**
7. **19,593**
8. **48,200**
9. **11,426**
10. **51,345**
11. **$540;** $15 × 36 = $540
12. **$1,800;** $75 × 12 × 2 = $1,800
13. **$1,748,250;** 64,750 × $27 = $1,748,250
14. **$270;** $18 × 15 = $270

Exercise 7, page 20

1. **13 r2**
2. **31**
3. **20**
4. **32**
5. **15 r8**
6. **34 r1**
7. **202 r14**
8. **109 r3**
9. **200**
10. **16 r1**
11. **$40;** $480 ÷ 12 = $40
12. **811 stamps;** 4,866 ÷ 6 = 811
13. **144 tickets;** $432 ÷ $3 = 144
14. **2,283 r19;** 47,962 ÷ 21 = 2,283 r19

Exercise 8, pages 20–21

1. **24,461**
2. **76,285**
3. **321**
4. **605,629**
5. **45,630**
6. **35**
7. **88,734**
8. **52,014**
9. **4,498**
10. **713 r4**
11. **88,632**
12. **632,479**
13. **1,367**
14. **10,335**
15. **8,176**
16. **22,419**
17. **114,780**
18. **$3.31**
19. **380,991**
20. **203,348**
21. **5,427**
22. **35,469**
23. **2,254**
24. **5,185**

Exercise 9, page 22

1. 600	16. 290
2. 900	17. 720
3. 100	18. 300
4. 600	19. 410
5. 1,300	20. 280
6. 2,500	21. 4,000
7. 3,100	22. 4,000
8. 8,700	23. 1,000
9. 3,900	24. 2,000
10. 400	25. 18,000
11. 40	26. 26,000
12. 80	27. 48,000
13. 70	28. 9,000
14. 40	29. 9,000
15. 140	30. 66,000

Exercise 10, page 23

1. $4.15; $4	5. $10.40; $10
2. $28.60; $29	6. $11.67; $12
3. $13.95; $14	7. $56.47; $56
4. $2.25; $2	

Exercise 11, pages 24–25

1. 90 + 30 = 120; rounding to tens
2. 500 − 200 = 300; rounding to hundreds
3. 200 × 400 = 800,000; rounding to hundreds and thousands
4. 130 if rounding (60 + 70) or 120 if front-end digits (50 + 70)
5. 1,200 if rounding to nearest hundred (300 + 300 + 600), 1,190 if rounding to nearest ten (280 + 320 + 590), 1,000 if front-end digits (200 + 300 + 500) or 1,200 if compatible numbers (280 + 320 + 600)
6. 5; compatible numbers (1,500 ÷ 300 = 5)
7. rounding: 6,000 (100 × 60); front-end digits: 4,500 (90 × 50); compatible numbers: 6,000 (100 × 60)
8. rounding: 5,000 (3,000 + 1,000 + 1,000 or 2,800 + 900 + 1,300); front-end digits: 3,900 (2,000 + 900 + 1,000); compatible numbers: 4,900 (2,700 + 900 + 1,300)
9. rounding: 30 (600 ÷ 20); front-end digits: 25 (500 ÷ 20); compatible numbers: 24 (600 ÷ 25) or 29 (580 ÷ 20) or 30 (600 ÷ 20)
10. rounding: 2,700 (4,900 − 2,200); front-end digits: 3,000 (5,000 − 2,000); compatible numbers: 3,000 (5,000 − 2,000)

Whole Numbers Review, page 26

1. 2 hundreds or 200
2. 6 ones or 6
3. 0 tens or 0
4. 8 ten thousands or 80,000
5. 6 thousands or 6,000
6. 4 millions or 4,000,000
7. about 400 (rounding) or 300 (front-end digits); 409
8. about 4,000 (rounding) or 3,000 (front-end digits); 3,914
9. about 1,000,000 (rounding) or 800,000 (front-end digits); 1,078,170
10. about 400 (compatible numbers or rounding); 385
11. about 920 (rounding); 933
12. about 4,000 (rounding) or 3,000 (front-end digits); 3,736
13. 1,956
14. 800,343
15. 1,403,001
16. 23,215
17. 52,126 people; 58,473 − 6,347 = 52,126
18. $72; 18 × $4 = $72
19. 200; 8,000 ÷ 40 = 200
20. 32,000; 400 × 80 = 32,000

Chapter 2

Exercise 1, pages 28–29

1. **24**
2. **63**
3. **33**
4. **428**
5. **1,533**
6. **366**
7. **11,038**
8. **4,671**
9. **128,164**
10. **337,737**
11. **50,875**
12. **117,171**
13. **103,847**
14. **99,384**
15. **10,583**
16. **361 pages;** 228 + 47 + 86 = 361
17. **27,176 pounds;** 26,700 + 476 = 27,176
18. **$962;** $350 + $275 + $150 + $87 + $49 + $51 = $962
19. **317 points;** 72 + 85 + 69 + 91 = 317
20. **136,830 fans;** 36,487 + 51,344 + 48,999 = 136,830

Exercise 2, pages 29–30

1. **6**
2. **7**
3. **13**
4. **9**
5. **323**
6. **79**
7. **3,703**
8. **377**
9. **12,382**
10. **13,525**
11. **5,744**
12. **10,176**
13. **92,675**
14. **18,867**

15. **1,123**
16. **$11;** $48 – $37 = $11
17. **3,813 tool belts;** 4,800 – 987 = 3,813
18. **9,580 fans;** 69,457 – 59,877 = 9,580
19. **$556;** $806 – $250 = $556
20. **$185,541;** $1,147,028 – $961,487 = $185,541

Exercise 3, page 31

1. **27**
2. **92**
3. **248**
4. **3,648**
5. **860**
6. **3,100**
7. **10,650**
8. **48,721**
9. **67,860**
10. **12,210**
11. **546,616**
12. **397,992**
13. **2,534,012**
14. **1,205,806**
15. **2,869,713**
16. **216 eggs;** 18 × 12 = 216
17. **$1,098;** 6 × $183 = $1,098
18. **$1,164;** $97 × 12 = $1,164
19. **$1,375,296;** $1,482 × 928 = $1,375,296
20. **$493,925;** 21,475 × $23 = $493,925

Exercise 4, page 32

1. **27**
2. **81**
3. **46**
4. **85**
5. **5**
6. **16**
7. **143**
8. **3,696**
9. **60**
10. **45**

11. 38

12. 58

13. 2,545

14. 599

15. 7,851

16. **1,990 pounds;** 7,960 ÷ 4 = 1,990

17. **$50;** $600 ÷ 12 = $50

18. **3,000 fines;** $75,000 ÷ $25 = 3,000

19. **$890;** $49,840 ÷ 56 = $890

20. **$15;** $270 ÷ 18 = $15

Calculator Review, page 33

1. 33

2. 14

3. 144

4. 24

5. 1,009

6. 19

7. 28,033

8. 300

9. 21,967

10. 882

11. 323,850

12. 945

13. 4,721

14. 5,325

15. 5,473,269

16. 385

17. **(1) 12;** 30 − 18 = 12

18. **(5) 2,460 ÷ 3;** 486 − 99 = 387; 33 × 17 = 561; 965 ÷ 5 = 193; 5,038 − 4,765 = 273; 2,460 ÷ 3 = 820

19. **(3) 20;** 10 × 36 = 360; 360 ÷ 18 = 20

20. **(2) 425 ÷ 25;** 56 × 13 = 728; 425 ÷ 25 = 17; 9 + 29 = 38; 826 − 749 = 77; 38 × 4 = 152

Chapter 3

Exercise 1, pages 36–37

1. **c.** hours of television per month; 100 hours

2. **c.** men and women finishing the class; 28 students

3. **b.** federal, state, and city taxes; $245.79

4. **c.** rent, electricity, car, and telephone expenses; $753.66

5. three and four; 7 people (3 + 4)

6. 350 and three; 1,050 napkins (350 × 3)

7. $52.49, $23.50, $15; $90.99 (52.49 + $23.50 + $15)

8. two hours, one hour, 6 P.M.; 3 P.M. (3 hours earlier than 6 P.M.)

9. underline $425 a month, rent in a year; multiplication; $425 × 12 = $5,100

10. underline twelve albums for $1.25 each; multiplication; 12 × $1.25 = $15.00

11. underline 8 cents per gallon, 26 cents per gallon, how much more; subtraction; 26¢ − 8¢ = 18¢

12. underline $70,300, risen $35,800; addition; $70,300 + $35,800 = $106,100

13. underline $525.46, 43 hours, hourly wage; division; $525.46 ÷ 43 = $12.22 per hour

14. underline over 5 million, over 11 times; multiplication; 5,000,000 × 11 = 55,000,000; over 55,000,000 female employees in 1990

Exercise 2, page 40

1. underline increasing $30, $415 now; $30 + $415 = $445

2. underline 2,975 pounds, 475 pounds, combined weight; 2,975 + 475 = 3,450 lb

3. underline Guillaume and three friends, $26.56, split equally; $26.56 ÷ 4 = $6.64

4. underline fifteen calls, twice; 15 × 2 = 30 service calls

5. underline $156 a year, monthly charge; $156 ÷ 12 = $13 per month

6. underline $1,500, pay back $985, left to pay; $1,500 − $985 = **$515**

7. underline $1.39 per gallon, 12 gallons cost; $1.39 × 12 = **$16.68**

8. underline pieces 8 inches long from a 96-inch board; 96 ÷ 8 = **12 pieces**

9. underline 64,441,087 passengers, 51,943,567 passengers, How many more; 64,441,087 − 51,943,567 = **12,497,520**

10. underline 127°F, 2°F, difference; 127 − 2 = **125°F**

Exercise 3, page 43

1. **79**	10. **32,000**
2. **190**	11. **92**
3. **5,400**	12. **4,000,000**
4. **46**	13. **240,000**
5. **700**	14. **40**
6. **152**	15. **387**
7. **116**	16. **136**
8. **71**	17. **101 adults**
9. **62**	18. **9 adults**

Exercise 4, pages 44–45

1. **about $400; rounding** (700 − 300)

2. **about 5,000 or 4,800 cans; rounding or compatible numbers** (100 × 50 or 100 × 48)

3. **about 40 miles per hour; rounding or compatible numbers** (70 − 30)

4. **about 550 or 500 feet high; rounding** (400 + 150) **or front-end digits** (400 + 100)

5. **about 300 pieces; rounding** (60 × 5)

6. **about $270; rounding** (30 × 9)

7. **about 60 miles per hour; rounding and compatible numbers** (300 ÷ 5)

8. **about $6 per hour; rounding and compatible numbers** (240 ÷ 40)

9. **about 900 calendars; rounding** (200 + 300 + 400)

10. **about $2300; rounding** (5700 − 3400)

Exercise 5, pages 48–49

1. **10 handshakes; drawing a picture**

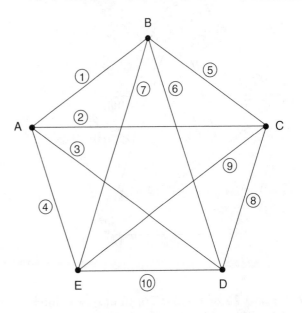

2. **1,173; guess and check; 642 + 531, 542 + 631, 632 + 541, or 641 + 532**

3. **Pittsburgh to Cleveland to St. Louis; using information from a table** (115 + 492 = 607 miles)

4. **Turtle C; drawing a picture**

5. **543 and 6; guess and check** (543 × 6 = 3,258; 643 × 5 = 3,215; 654 × 3 = 1,962)

6. **1990; using information from a table** (417,179 cars)

7. **431 × 52; guess and check** (22,412)

8. 20 times; drawing a picture

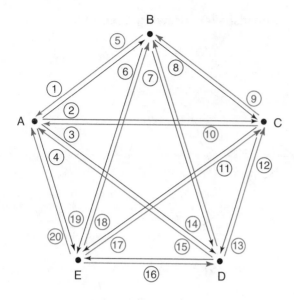

9. 86 and 75 or 85 and 76; guess and check
(86 + 75 = 161; 87 + 65 = 152)

10. 5 miles; drawing a picture

$$20 \text{ mi}$$

Day 1 $\frac{1}{2}$ of 20
       10 mi

         Day 2 $\frac{1}{2}$ of 10
              5 mi

11. a. 0   **c. –31**

     b. –31   **d. –11**

using information from a table

Exercise 6, page 51

1. **$5.10; (5 × $0.75) + (3 × $0.45) =
$3.75 + $1.35 = $5.10**

2. **$7.33; $10 – (3 × $0.89) = $10 – $2.67 =
$7.33**

3. **$131.50; (4 × $25) + (3 × $10.50) =
$100 + $31.50 = $131.50**

4. **no; $11.25 + $15.50 + $10.75 = 37.50 and
$37.50 is more than $35**

5. **no; $5.35 + $35.60 + $20 + $10 + $15 =
$85.95 and $85.95 is more than $80**

6. **$197.50; (2 × $95) + (6 × $1.25) = $190 +
$7.50 + $197.50**

7. **$25,400; $1,900 + $1,200 = $3,100;
$28,500 – $3,100 = $25,400**

8. **Kiwi; 2 × $89 = $178, and $178 is less than
$188**

9. **$10.25; $6.50 + $3.25 = $9.75;
$20 – $9.75 = $10.25**

10. **yes; $1.27 × 9 = $11.43**

Exercise 7, pages 53–54

1. **2,573**

2. **593**

3. 470

4. 47

5. 1,488

6. 13,608

7. 20

8. 2,400

Problem-Solving Review, pages 55–56

1. 8 hundreds or 800
2. 2 thousands or 2,000
3. 5 ones or 5
4. 4 hundred thousands or 400,000
5. 943
6. 18,076
7. 3,480
8. 2,437,000
9. 6,800
10. 300
11. 440
12. 23,960
13. 5,000 + 23,000 = 28,000; actual answer: 28,140
14. 3,200 × 300 = 3,500; actual answer: 3,485
15. 14,000 ÷ 40 = 350; actual answer: 329 r29
16. 22,000 − 16,000 = 6,000; actual answer: 5,775
17. 12 × 12 = $144

18. 31,000 − 23,000 = $8,000

19. 400 + 400 + 300 + 300 = 1,400

20. 400 ÷ 20 = 20

Chapter 4

Exercise 1, pages 60–61

1. 0.9	7. 0.821
2. 0.60 or 0.6	8. 0.05
3. 1.08	9. 0.007
4. 1.36	10. 6.048
5. 0.4	11. 9.81
6. 0.39	12. 23.105

13. **Four and seven hundredths**
14. **Fifteen and thirty-eight hundredths**
15. **One hundred sixty-nine thousandths**
16. **Seven and two hundred five thousandths**
17. **Nine and one tenth**
18. **Twelve and eighty-six hundredths**

19. 0.5 < 0.8	28. 3.2 < 4
20. 0.47 > 0.39	29. 0.99 > 0.954
21. 4.7 < 4.82	30. 8.09 < 8.9
22. 5.5 > 5.05	31. 6.50 < 6.57
23. .001 < .010	32. 1.33 > 1.303
24. 7.75 > .075	33. 9.08 < 9.9
25. 3.101 > 3.1	34. .03 < .25
26. 0.25 < 0.257	35. 99.9 > .999
27. 1.9 < 1.999	36. .503 > 0.5

Exercise 2, page 61

1. $9.42; $9
2. $19.75; $20
3. $43.50; $44
4. $1.41; $1
5. $20.80; $21

Exercise 3, page 63

1. 6; 5.9; 5.89	6. 29¢
2. 20; 20.5; 20.49	7. $68.54
3. 1; 1.0; 1.04	8. $0.82
4. 7; 6.7; 6.71	9. $3.74
5. $1.34	10. 54¢

11. **20 cents for 1 folder;** 100¢ ÷ 5 = 20¢
12. **9 cents for 1 pencil;** 49 ÷ 6 = 8 r1→9¢
13. **34 cents for 1 kiwi;** 100¢ ÷ 3 = $33\frac{1}{3}$¢
14. **$3.17;** 949 ÷ 3 = 316 r1→317¢ = $3.17
15. **$0.75;** 899 ÷ 12 = 74 r11→75¢ = $0.75
16. **$.21 for 1 doughnut;** $2.52 ÷ 12 = $.21

Exercise 4, page 64

1. **2.5 cm**
2. **0.38 in.; 0.4 in.**
3. **$0.34;** $3.99 ÷ 12 = $0.33 r3→$0.34
4. **$0.04; $0.40**
   139 ÷ 10 = 13 r9→14¢ = $0.14,
   99 ÷ 10 = 9 r9→10¢ = $0.10,
   $0.14 − $0.10 = 14¢ − 10¢ = 4¢ = $0.04;
   $1.39 − $0.99 = 139¢ − 99¢ = 40¢ = $0.40

Exercise 5, pages 65–66

1. $0.60	13. 9.69
2. $0.95	14. 1,023.81
3. $1.05	15. 6.3
4. $1.30	16. $2.14
5. 0.9	17. 7.6
6. $0.91	18. 32.46
7. 1.825	19. 3.978
8. 68.277	20. $7.37
9. 9.681	21. 5.502
10. 26,472	22. 8.768
11. 41.109	23. $21.28
12. 102.769	24. 362.241

Exercise 6, pages 66–67

1. **10.7 percent;** 13.1 − 2.4 = 10.7
2. **12.902 million;** 8.655 + 4.057 + 0.19 = 12.902
3. **$1.27**
4. **$21.68;** $12.93 + $2 + $6.75 = $21.68
5. **14.774**
6. **230.433**
7. **2,141.057**
8. **890.546**

9. **$629.44;** $148.26 + $286.37 + $156.82 + $37.99 = $629.44

10. **$20.64;** $50 − $29.36 = $20.64

11. **$120.77;** $39.75 + $42.31 + $11.98 + $26.73 = $120.77

12. **41.91 tons;** 428.65 − 386.74 = 41.91

Exercise 7, page 69

1. **$2.30;** 23 × $0.10 = $2.30
2. **$10.00;** 40 × $0.25 = $10.00
3. **$3.50;** 350 × $.01 = $3.50
4. **$3.75;** 75 × $.05 = $3.75
5. **$0.90;** 18 × $0.05 = $0.90
6. **$5.50;** 11 × $0.50 = $5.50
7. **$1.10;** 11 × $.10 = $1.10
8. **$4.00;** 8 × $.50 = $4.00

9. **0.15**
10. **1.68**
11. **3.15**
12. **20.4**
13. **1.35**
14. **26.16**
15. **.325**
16. **7.245**
17. **1.457**
18. **1.1814**
19. **$39.15**
20. **2.0685**
21. **19.285548**
22. **3112.61434**
23. **45.72588**

24. **$5.98;** 2.5 × $2.39 = $5.98
25. **$32.34;** 6 × $5.39 = $32.34
26. **about 34 or 35 inches; 40.8 inches** (34 × 1.2)
27. **$1.164 or $1.17** (38.8¢ × 3)

Exercise 8, page 72

1. **1.6**
2. **160**
3. **1.6**
4. **16**
5. **3**
6. **30**
7. **60**
8. **6**
9. **.09**
10. **700**
11. **4.9**
12. **4.8**
13. **23**
14. **8.1**
15. **70**
16. **160**

17. **.1959 in.;** 19.59 ÷ 100 = .1959
18. **about $.12 per ounce;**
    $1.67 ÷ 14 = $.11 r13→$.12

19. **2.1 in.; 2.14 in.**

20. **7 tapes for $5.99;**
    3 for $4.99→$4.99 ÷ 3 = $1.66 r1→$1.67;
    7 for $5.99→$5.99 ÷ 7 = $.85 r4→$.86

21. **983,403 people;**
    789,704 + 193,699 = 983,403

22. **33.1 miles;** 6.2 + 26.9 = 33.1

Exercise 9, pages 73–74

1. **35.15**

2. **56.8**

3. 8.3

4. 15.7

5. 12.6

6. 99.63

7. 250

8. 0.9

Decimals Review, pages 75–77

1. **1**
2. **0.9**
3. **$58.95**; $(5 \times \$10) + (7 \times \$1) + (6 \times \$.25) + (9 \times \$.05) = \$50 + \$7 + \$1.50 + \$.45 = \$58.95$
4. **98; 97.6; 97.64**
5. **$3.90**; $\$38.92 \div 10 = \$3.892 \rightarrow \$3.90$
6. **62.444**
7. **35.18**
8. **3.105**
9. **0.5**
10. **500**
11. **(3)**; $.382 - .328 = .054$
12. **(5)**; $\$1.75 \times 6 = \$10.50$
13. **(2)**; $23.2 \div 8 = 2.9$
14. **(4)**
15. **(5)**
16. **(4)**
17. **(4)**; $28.5 \times 17.4 = 495.9$
18. **(1)**; $.465 + .289 = .754$, $1 - .754 = .246$
19. **25.656**
20. **1,328.44**
21. **1,428.118**
22. **200**
23. **$50.25**; $\$16.49 + \$32.99 = \$49.48$; $\$50 - \$49.48 = \$50.52$
24. **$1.73**; $\$1.29 \times \$1.34 = \$1.7286$, which rounds to $1.73
25. **$1.60**; $\$19.20 \div 12 = \$1.60$

26. **$77.90**; $\$38.95 \times 2 = \$77.90$

Chapter 5

Exercise 1, pages 80–81

1. **5**	7. $9\frac{4}{9}$	13. $\frac{19}{4}$
2. $5\frac{1}{4}$	8. $12\frac{3}{8}$	14. $\frac{47}{6}$
3. $5\frac{2}{3}$	9. $9\frac{1}{3}$	15. $\frac{48}{5}$
4. $6\frac{3}{5}$	10. $\frac{29}{8}$	16. $\frac{131}{12}$
5. $6\frac{5}{6}$	11. $\frac{20}{3}$	17. $\frac{91}{10}$
6. $5\frac{3}{7}$	12. $\frac{33}{8}$	18. $\frac{88}{7}$

19. **40 slices**
20. **more**; $\frac{17}{2} = 8\frac{1}{2}$ yards
21. $2\frac{2}{3}$; $1\frac{1}{3} + 1\frac{1}{3} = 2\frac{2}{3}$
22. $3\frac{1}{7}$; $\frac{22}{7} = 3\frac{1}{7}$
23. $2\frac{2}{3}$; $8 \div 3 = 2\frac{2}{3}$
24. $1\frac{2}{3}$; $100 \div 60 = 1\frac{2}{3}$

Exercise 2, page 83

Samples are given for #1–4.

1. $\frac{6}{16}, \frac{9}{24}, \frac{12}{32}$
3. $\frac{14}{20}, \frac{21}{30}, \frac{28}{40}$

2. $\frac{2}{12}, \frac{3}{18}, \frac{4}{24}$
4. $\frac{22}{24}, \frac{33}{36}, \frac{44}{48}$

5. $3; \dfrac{3}{5}$

6. $1; \dfrac{1}{3}$

7. $7; \dfrac{7}{8}$

8. $92; \dfrac{92}{100}$

9. $27; \dfrac{27}{30}$

10. $4; \dfrac{4}{7}$

11. $48; \dfrac{48}{50}$

12. $22; \dfrac{22}{24}$

13. $9; \dfrac{9}{16}$

12. $\dfrac{50}{90}, \dfrac{27}{90}; \dfrac{5}{9} \times \dfrac{10}{10} = \dfrac{50}{90}; \dfrac{3}{10} \times \dfrac{9}{9} = \dfrac{27}{90}$

13. $\dfrac{75}{80}, \dfrac{42}{80}; \dfrac{15}{16} \times \dfrac{5}{5} = \dfrac{75}{80}; \dfrac{21}{40} \times \dfrac{2}{2} = \dfrac{42}{80}$

14. $\dfrac{117}{180}, \dfrac{76}{180}; \dfrac{13}{20} \times \dfrac{9}{9} = \dfrac{117}{180}; \dfrac{19}{45} \times \dfrac{4}{4} = \dfrac{76}{180}$

15. $\dfrac{136}{200}, \dfrac{125}{200}; \dfrac{17}{25} \times \dfrac{8}{8} = \dfrac{136}{200}; \dfrac{5}{8} \times \dfrac{25}{25} = \dfrac{125}{200}$

16. $\dfrac{4}{60}, \dfrac{3}{60}; \dfrac{1}{15} \times \dfrac{4}{4} = \dfrac{4}{60}; \dfrac{1}{20} \times \dfrac{3}{3} = \dfrac{3}{60}$

Exercise 3, page 85

1. .25
2. .875
3. 2.75
4. .75

5. .66
6. .125
7. .125
8. .425

9. .375
10. .7272 or .73
11. .467 or .47
12. .8

Exercise 4, page 86

1. $\dfrac{7}{20}$
2. $\dfrac{17}{250}$
3. $\dfrac{3}{4}$
4. $2\dfrac{2}{5}$

5. $6\dfrac{13}{25}$
6. $5\dfrac{47}{100}$
7. $1\dfrac{39}{50}$
8. $9\dfrac{9}{200}$

9. $1\dfrac{37}{40}$
10. $7\dfrac{1}{80}$
11. $4\dfrac{23}{25}$
12. $8\dfrac{1}{2}$

Exercise 5, page 87

1. 6: 6, 12, 18, 24, 30, 36, 42, 48, 54, 60;
   5: 5, 10, 15, 20, 25, 30, 35, 40, 45, 50, 55, 60; common multiples: 30, 60

2. 8: 8, 16, 24, 32, 40, 48, 56;
   12: 12, 24, 36, 48; common multiples: 24, 48

3. 9: 9, 18, 27, 36, 45, 54, 63, 72;
   36: 36, 72; common multiples: 36, 72

4. 7: 7, 14, 21, 28, 35, 42
   21: 21, 42; common multiples: 21, 42

5. 4, 3; $\dfrac{1}{2} \times \dfrac{4}{4} = \dfrac{4}{8}; \dfrac{3}{8} = \dfrac{3}{8}$

6. 12, 5; $\dfrac{4}{5} \times \dfrac{3}{3} = \dfrac{12}{15}; \dfrac{1}{3} \times \dfrac{5}{5} = \dfrac{5}{15}$

7. 28, 9; $\dfrac{7}{9} \times \dfrac{4}{4} = \dfrac{28}{36}; \dfrac{3}{12} \times \dfrac{3}{3} = \dfrac{9}{36}$

8. 3, 4; $\dfrac{1}{2} \times \dfrac{3}{3} = \dfrac{3}{6}; \dfrac{2}{3} \times \dfrac{2}{2} = \dfrac{4}{6}$

9. $\dfrac{25}{30}, \dfrac{11}{30}; \dfrac{5}{6} \times \dfrac{5}{5} = \dfrac{25}{30}; \dfrac{11}{30} = \dfrac{11}{30}$

10. $\dfrac{63}{90}, \dfrac{38}{90}; \dfrac{7}{10} \times \dfrac{9}{9} = \dfrac{63}{90}; \dfrac{19}{45} \times \dfrac{2}{2} = \dfrac{38}{90}$

11. $\dfrac{48}{90}, \dfrac{65}{90}; \dfrac{8}{15} \times \dfrac{6}{6} = \dfrac{48}{90}; \dfrac{13}{18} \times \dfrac{5}{5} = \dfrac{65}{90}$

Exercise 6, pages 89–90

1. $\dfrac{1}{4} > \dfrac{3}{16}; \dfrac{1}{4} \times \dfrac{4}{4} = \dfrac{4}{16}$ and $\dfrac{4}{16} > \dfrac{3}{16}$

2. $\dfrac{5}{8} < \dfrac{11}{16}; \dfrac{5}{8} \times \dfrac{2}{2} = \dfrac{10}{16}$ and $\dfrac{10}{16} < \dfrac{11}{16}$

3. $\dfrac{3}{4} < \dfrac{13}{16}; \dfrac{3}{4} \times \dfrac{4}{4} = \dfrac{12}{16}$ and $\dfrac{12}{16} < \dfrac{13}{16}$

4. $1\dfrac{1}{4} > 1\dfrac{1}{8}; 1\dfrac{1}{4} = 1\dfrac{2}{8}$ and $1\dfrac{2}{8} > 1\dfrac{1}{8}$

5. $1\dfrac{4}{5} > \dfrac{8}{5}; 1\dfrac{4}{5} = \dfrac{9}{5}$ and $\dfrac{9}{5} > \dfrac{8}{5}$

6. $\dfrac{16}{10} > \dfrac{6}{5}; \dfrac{6}{5} \times \dfrac{2}{2} = \dfrac{12}{10}$ and $\dfrac{16}{10} > \dfrac{12}{10}$

7. $\dfrac{3}{8} < \dfrac{3}{5}; \dfrac{3}{8} \times \dfrac{5}{5} = \dfrac{15}{40}$ and $\dfrac{3}{5} \times \dfrac{8}{8} = \dfrac{24}{40}; \dfrac{15}{40} < \dfrac{24}{40}$

8. $\dfrac{1}{4} > \dfrac{1}{6}; \dfrac{1}{4} \times \dfrac{3}{3} = \dfrac{3}{12}$ and $\dfrac{1}{6} \times \dfrac{2}{2} = \dfrac{2}{12}; \dfrac{3}{12} > \dfrac{2}{12}$

9. $\dfrac{5}{12} > \dfrac{1}{3}; \dfrac{1}{3} \times \dfrac{4}{4} = \dfrac{4}{12}$ and $\dfrac{5}{12} > \dfrac{4}{12}$

10. $\dfrac{13}{16} < \dfrac{7}{8}; \dfrac{7}{8} \times \dfrac{2}{2} = \dfrac{14}{16}$ and $\dfrac{13}{16} < \dfrac{14}{16}$

11. $\dfrac{7}{10} < \dfrac{7}{9}; \dfrac{7}{10} \times \dfrac{9}{9} = \dfrac{63}{90}$ and $\dfrac{7}{9} \times \dfrac{10}{10} = \dfrac{70}{90}; \dfrac{63}{90} < \dfrac{70}{90}$

12. $\dfrac{9}{10} < \dfrac{11}{12}; \dfrac{9}{10} \times \dfrac{6}{6} = \dfrac{54}{60}$ and $\dfrac{11}{12} \times \dfrac{5}{5} = \dfrac{55}{60}; \dfrac{54}{60} < \dfrac{55}{60}$

Exercise 7, page 92

1. $\dfrac{2}{6} + \dfrac{3}{6}; \dfrac{5}{6}; \dfrac{2}{6} + \dfrac{3}{6} = \dfrac{5}{6}$

2. $\dfrac{5}{8} - \dfrac{1}{8}; \dfrac{1}{2}; \dfrac{5}{8} - \dfrac{1}{8} = \dfrac{4}{8} = \dfrac{1}{2}$

3. $\dfrac{4}{5} + \dfrac{3}{5}; 1\dfrac{2}{5}; \dfrac{4}{5} + \dfrac{3}{5} = \dfrac{7}{5} = 1\dfrac{2}{5}$

4. $\dfrac{11}{12} - \dfrac{2}{11}; \dfrac{3}{4}; \dfrac{11}{12} - \dfrac{2}{12} = \dfrac{9}{12} = \dfrac{3}{4}$

5. $\dfrac{9}{10} + \dfrac{3}{10}; 1\dfrac{1}{5}; \dfrac{9}{10} + \dfrac{3}{10} = \dfrac{12}{10} = \dfrac{6}{5} = 1\dfrac{1}{5}$

6. $\dfrac{13}{16} - \dfrac{5}{16}; \dfrac{1}{2}; \dfrac{13}{16} - \dfrac{5}{16} = \dfrac{8}{16} = \dfrac{1}{2}$

7. $\frac{2}{3}$; $\frac{5}{12} + \frac{3}{12} = \frac{8}{12} = \frac{2}{3}$

8. $\frac{3}{4}$; $\frac{7}{8} - \frac{1}{8} = \frac{6}{8} = \frac{3}{4}$

9. $\frac{3}{8}$; $\frac{9}{16} - \frac{3}{16} = \frac{6}{16} = \frac{3}{8}$

10. $\frac{3}{5}$; $\frac{9}{10} - \frac{3}{10} = \frac{6}{10} = \frac{3}{5}$

11. $\frac{5}{8}$; $\frac{7}{16} + \frac{3}{16} = \frac{10}{16} = \frac{5}{8}$

12. $\frac{1}{3}$; $\frac{7}{18} - \frac{1}{18} = \frac{6}{18} = \frac{1}{3}$

13. $1\frac{1}{2}$; $\frac{5}{8} + \frac{7}{8} = \frac{12}{8} = \frac{3}{2} = 1\frac{1}{2}$

14. 1; $\frac{11}{20} + \frac{9}{20} = \frac{20}{20} = 1$

15. $\frac{1}{5}$; $\frac{14}{15} - \frac{11}{15} = \frac{3}{15} = \frac{1}{5}$

16. $1\frac{1}{3}$; $\frac{11}{12} + \frac{5}{12} = \frac{16}{12} = \frac{4}{3} = 1\frac{1}{3}$

17. $\frac{1}{5}$; $\frac{23}{25} - \frac{18}{25} = \frac{5}{25} = \frac{1}{5}$

18. $\frac{3}{10}$; $\frac{33}{50} - \frac{18}{50} = \frac{15}{50} = \frac{3}{10}$

19. $1\frac{2}{3}$; $\frac{8}{9} + \frac{7}{9} = \frac{15}{9} = \frac{5}{3} = 1\frac{2}{3}$

20. $\frac{13}{18}$; $\frac{31}{36} - \frac{5}{36} = \frac{26}{36} = \frac{13}{18}$

21. $1\frac{3}{10}$; $\frac{43}{100} + \frac{87}{100} = \frac{130}{100} = \frac{13}{10} = 1\frac{3}{10}$

Exercise 8, page 95

1. $\frac{5}{6} - \frac{1}{2}$; $\frac{1}{3}$ $\frac{5}{6} - \frac{1}{2} = \frac{5}{6} - \frac{3}{6} = \frac{2}{6} = \frac{1}{3}$

2. $\frac{3}{4} + \frac{7}{8}$; $1\frac{5}{8}$ $\frac{3}{4} + \frac{7}{8} = \frac{6}{8} + \frac{7}{8} = \frac{13}{8} = 1\frac{5}{8}$

3. $\frac{7}{10} + \frac{1}{4}$; $\frac{19}{20}$ $\frac{7}{10} + \frac{1}{4} = \frac{14}{20} + \frac{5}{20} = \frac{19}{20}$

4. $\frac{3}{4} - \frac{1}{3}$; $\frac{5}{12}$ $\frac{3}{4} - \frac{1}{3} = \frac{9}{12} - \frac{4}{12} = \frac{5}{12}$

5. 3; $\frac{7}{15}$

$$\frac{2}{3} = \frac{10}{15}$$
$$-\frac{1}{5} = \frac{3}{15}$$
$$\frac{7}{15}$$

6. 2; 6; $\frac{2}{3}$

$$\frac{1}{6} = \frac{2}{12}$$
$$+\frac{1}{2} = \frac{6}{12}$$
$$\frac{8}{12} = \frac{2}{3}$$

7. 3; 16; $\frac{19}{24}$

$$\frac{1}{8} = \frac{3}{24}$$
$$+\frac{2}{3} = \frac{16}{24}$$
$$\frac{19}{24}$$

8. 21; 12; $\frac{9}{28}$

$$\frac{3}{4} = \frac{21}{28}$$
$$-\frac{3}{7} = \frac{12}{28}$$
$$\frac{9}{28}$$

9. 9; 5; $\frac{2}{15}$

$$\frac{3}{10} = \frac{9}{30}$$
$$-\frac{1}{6} = \frac{5}{30}$$
$$\frac{4}{30} = \frac{2}{15}$$

10. 55, 16; $\frac{13}{20}$

$$\frac{11}{12} = \frac{55}{60}$$
$$-\frac{4}{15} = \frac{16}{60}$$
$$\frac{39}{60} = \frac{13}{20}$$

11. 8; 4; $\frac{15}{16}$

$$\frac{3}{16} = \frac{3}{16}$$
$$\frac{1}{2} = \frac{8}{16}$$
$$+\frac{1}{4} = \frac{4}{16}$$
$$\frac{15}{16}$$

12. 5, 3; $\frac{4}{5}$

$$\frac{4}{15} = \frac{4}{15}$$
$$\frac{1}{3} = \frac{5}{15}$$
$$+\frac{1}{5} = \frac{3}{15}$$
$$\overline{\quad\frac{12}{15} = \frac{4}{5}}$$

13. $\frac{7}{8}$

$$\frac{3}{8} = \frac{3}{8}$$
$$+\frac{1}{2} = \frac{4}{8}$$
$$\overline{\quad\frac{7}{8}}$$

14. $\frac{21}{32}$

$$\frac{13}{16} = \frac{26}{32}$$
$$-\frac{5}{32} = \frac{5}{32}$$
$$\overline{\quad\frac{21}{32}}$$

15. $1\frac{1}{10}$

$$\frac{4}{5} = \frac{8}{10}$$
$$+\frac{3}{10} = \frac{3}{10}$$
$$\overline{\quad\frac{11}{10} = 1\frac{1}{10}}$$

16. $1\frac{3}{20}$

$$\frac{3}{4} = \frac{15}{20}$$
$$+\frac{2}{5} = \frac{8}{20}$$
$$\overline{\quad\frac{23}{20} = 1\frac{3}{20}}$$

17. $\frac{11}{24}$

$$\frac{5}{8} = \frac{15}{24}$$
$$-\frac{1}{6} = \frac{4}{24}$$
$$\overline{\quad\frac{11}{24}}$$

18. $\frac{1}{6}$

$$\frac{11}{12} = \frac{11}{12}$$
$$-\frac{3}{4} = \frac{9}{12}$$
$$\overline{\quad\frac{2}{12} = \frac{1}{6}}$$

19. $1\frac{13}{30}$

$$\frac{3}{5} = \frac{18}{30}$$
$$+\frac{5}{6} = \frac{25}{30}$$
$$\overline{\quad\frac{43}{30} = 1\frac{13}{30}}$$

20. $\frac{5}{36}$

$$\frac{8}{9} = \frac{32}{36}$$
$$-\frac{3}{4} = \frac{27}{36}$$
$$\overline{\quad\frac{5}{36}}$$

21. $\frac{7}{12}$

$$\frac{1}{3} = \frac{4}{12}$$
$$+\frac{1}{4} = \frac{3}{12}$$
$$\overline{\quad\frac{7}{12}}$$

Exercise 9, page 96

1. $\frac{47}{8}$ 　　　　2. $5\frac{2}{5}$

3. sample answer:

$$\frac{10}{12}, \frac{15}{18}, \frac{20}{24}$$

4. **.42**; $5 \div 12 = .4166\ldots$

5. $\frac{9}{125}$

6. $\frac{7}{10} = \frac{28}{40}$; $\frac{5}{8} = \frac{25}{40}$

7. $\frac{4}{5} > \frac{3}{4}$; $\frac{4}{5} = \frac{16}{20}$ and $\frac{3}{4} = \frac{15}{20}$; $\frac{16}{20} > \frac{15}{20}$

8. $\frac{1}{16}$ **inch thicker** $\frac{11}{16} - \frac{5}{8} = \frac{11}{16} - \frac{10}{16} = \frac{1}{16}$

9. $1\frac{1}{2}$ **inches** $\frac{5}{8} + \frac{7}{8} = \frac{12}{8} = \frac{3}{2} = 1\frac{1}{2}$

10. **longer;** $\frac{1}{32}$ **inch** $\frac{5}{16} - \frac{9}{32} = \frac{10}{32} - \frac{9}{32} = \frac{1}{32}$

Exercise 10, page 98

1. $8\frac{8}{10} = 8\frac{4}{5}$

2. $1\frac{1}{4}$; $2\frac{2}{4}$; $3\frac{3}{4}$

3. $6\frac{10}{18}$; $8\frac{15}{18}$; $14\frac{25}{18} = 15\frac{7}{18}$

4. $7\frac{6}{9}$; $5\frac{4}{9}$; $12\frac{10}{9} = 13\frac{1}{9}$

5. $13\frac{1}{24}$; $8\frac{16}{24} + 4\frac{9}{24} = 12\frac{25}{24} = 13\frac{1}{24}$

6. $17\frac{11}{20}$; $7\frac{16}{20} + 9\frac{15}{20} = 16\frac{31}{20} = 17\frac{11}{20}$

7. $10\frac{17}{24}$; $5\frac{20}{24} + 4\frac{21}{24} = 9\frac{41}{24} = 10\frac{17}{24}$

8. $21\frac{17}{30}$; $12\frac{27}{30} + 8\frac{20}{30} = 20\frac{47}{30} = 21\frac{17}{30}$

9. $20\frac{23}{60}$; $9\frac{35}{60} + 10\frac{48}{60} = 19\frac{83}{60} = 20\frac{23}{60}$

10. $37\frac{51}{100}$; $20\frac{75}{100} + 16\frac{76}{100} = 36\frac{151}{100} = 37\frac{51}{100}$

Exercise 11, page 100

1. $5\frac{9}{10}$; $3\frac{5}{10}$; $2\frac{4}{10} = 2\frac{2}{5}$

2. $3\frac{2}{12} = 2\frac{14}{12}$; $1\frac{9}{12} = 1\frac{9}{12}$; $1\frac{5}{12}$

3. $9\frac{4}{12} = 8\frac{16}{12}$; $6\frac{5}{12} = 6\frac{5}{12}$; $2\frac{11}{12}$

4. $8\frac{9}{24} = 7\frac{33}{24}$; $4\frac{20}{24} = 4\frac{20}{24}$; $3\frac{13}{24}$

5. $4\frac{1}{20}$; $10\frac{16}{24} - 6\frac{15}{20} = 4\frac{1}{20}$

6. $5\frac{43}{60}$; $15\frac{18}{60} = 14\frac{78}{60}$; $9\frac{35}{60} = 9\frac{35}{60}$;

   $14\frac{78}{60} - 9\frac{35}{60} = 5\frac{43}{60}$

7. $5\frac{7}{25}$; $13\frac{25}{25}$; $13\frac{25}{25} - 8\frac{18}{25} = 5\frac{7}{25}$

8. $28\frac{11}{20}$; $39\frac{7}{20} = 38\frac{27}{20}$; $10\frac{16}{20}$; $38\frac{27}{20} - 10\frac{16}{20} = 28\frac{11}{20}$

9. $5\frac{7}{24}$ pounds;

   $1\frac{1}{4} + 2\frac{3}{8} + 1\frac{2}{3} = 1\frac{6}{24} + 2\frac{9}{24} + 1\frac{16}{24} = 4\frac{31}{24} = 5\frac{7}{24}$

10. **about $60; $68;** $2 \times 100 \times \$.30 = \$60$;
    $2 \times 100 \times \$.34 = \$68$

11. **Michael Stulze; 18 ft $2\frac{13}{16}$ in.;**

    71 ft $2\frac{1}{2}$ in. – 52 ft $11\frac{11}{16}$ in. =

    71 ft $2\frac{8}{16}$ in. – 52 ft $11\frac{11}{16}$ in. =

    71 ft $1\frac{24}{16}$ in. – 52 ft $11\frac{11}{16}$ in. =

    70 ft $13\frac{24}{16}$ in. – 52 ft $11\frac{11}{16}$ in. = 18 ft $2\frac{13}{16}$ in.

Exercise 12, page 102

1. $\frac{3}{40}$; $\frac{1}{5} \times \frac{3}{8} = \frac{3}{40}$

2. $\frac{7}{18}$; $\frac{7}{12} \times \frac{2}{3} = \frac{14}{36} = \frac{7}{18}$

3. $\frac{3}{4}$; $\frac{9}{10} \times \frac{5}{6} = \frac{45}{60} = \frac{3}{4}$

4. $\frac{11}{25}$; $\frac{44}{100} = \frac{11}{25}$

5. $\frac{9}{100}$; $\frac{3}{8} \times \frac{12}{50} = \frac{36}{400} = \frac{9}{100}$

6. $\frac{21}{40}$; $\frac{7}{5} \times \frac{3}{8} = \frac{21}{40}$

7. $23\frac{3}{5}$; $\frac{59}{10} \times 4 = \frac{236}{10} = \frac{236}{10} = 23\frac{3}{5}$

8. $27\frac{131}{135}$; $\frac{64}{15} \times \frac{59}{9} = \frac{3,776}{135} = 27\frac{131}{135}$

9. $35\frac{13}{54}$; $\frac{173}{18} \times \frac{11}{3} = \frac{1,903}{54} = 35\frac{13}{54}$

10. **40 degrees;** $104 - 32 = 72$; $\frac{5}{9} \times 72 = \frac{360}{9} = 40$

11. $4\frac{1}{2}$ **hours;** $3 \times 1\frac{1}{2} = 3 \times \frac{3}{2} = \frac{9}{2} = 4\frac{1}{2}$

Exercise 13, page 104

1. $\frac{12}{5}$

2. $\frac{1}{3}$

3. $\frac{10}{69}$

4. $\frac{1}{27}$

5. 12

6. 20

7. 28

8. 3

9. $10\frac{1}{2}$

10. $\frac{3}{2}$; $\frac{9}{16}$

11. $\frac{5}{6} \times \frac{17}{10} = \frac{85}{60} = 1\frac{25}{60} = 1\frac{5}{12}$

12. $\frac{7}{3} \div \frac{4}{9} = \frac{7}{3} \times \frac{9}{4} = \frac{63}{12} = 5\frac{3}{12} = 5\frac{1}{4}$

13. $\frac{63}{86}$; $\frac{7}{4} \div \frac{43}{18} = \frac{7}{4} \times \frac{18}{43} = \frac{126}{172} = \frac{63}{86}$

14. $1\frac{89}{186}$; $\frac{55}{12} \div \frac{31}{10} = \frac{55}{12} \times \frac{10}{31} = \frac{550}{372} = 1\frac{178}{372} = 1\frac{89}{186}$

15. $2\frac{32}{59}$; $6 \div \frac{59}{25} = 6 \times \frac{25}{59} = \frac{150}{59} = 2\frac{32}{59}$

16. $2\frac{23}{200}$; $\frac{423}{40} \div \frac{5}{1} = \frac{423}{40} \times \frac{1}{5} = \frac{423}{200} = 2\frac{23}{200}$

17. $3\frac{1}{2}$ **inches;** $21 \times \frac{1}{6} = \frac{21}{6} = 3\frac{3}{6} = 3\frac{1}{2}$

18. **22,000 pounds;** $33,000 \div 1\frac{1}{2} = 33,000 \div \frac{3}{2} =$

    $33,000 \times \frac{2}{3} = \frac{66,000}{3} = 22,000$

Exercise 14, pages 105–106

1. $\frac{3}{8}$

2. $\frac{1}{12}$

3. $\frac{9}{10}$

4. $\frac{2}{3}$

5. $\frac{1}{4}$

6. $\frac{5}{6}$

7. $\frac{1}{27}$

8. $\frac{8}{21}$

Exercise 15, pages 107–108

1. $\frac{1}{3}$ 9. $4\frac{11}{12}$

2. $\frac{2}{5}$ 10. $7\frac{11}{12}$

3. $\frac{1}{3}$ 11. $1\frac{5}{6}$

4. $\frac{4}{5}$ 12. $4\frac{31}{36}$

5. $\frac{3}{4}$ 13. $8\frac{1}{3}$

6. $\frac{2}{3}$ 14. $5\frac{11}{16}$

7. $\frac{1}{3}$ 15. $3\frac{3}{7}$

8. $\frac{5}{12}$ 16. $\frac{5}{7}$

17. **$4\frac{1}{4}$ pounds;** $2\frac{1}{2} + 1\frac{3}{4} = 4\frac{1}{4}$

18. **$2\frac{1}{4}$ yards;** $15 - 12\frac{3}{4} = 2\frac{1}{4}$

19. **4 cups;** $2\frac{2}{3} \times 1\frac{1}{2} = 4$

20. **$8\frac{2}{3}$ recipes;** $6\frac{1}{2} \div \frac{3}{4} = 8\frac{2}{3}$

Fractions Review, pages 109–111

1. $\frac{81}{100}$

2. $\frac{59}{10}$

3. $4\frac{1}{12}$

4. **sample answer:** $\frac{12}{46}, \frac{18}{69}, \frac{24}{92}$

5. $\frac{55}{90}$

6. **12;** $4 \div \frac{1}{3} = 4 \times 3 = 12$

7. **.68 or 0.68**

8. $4\frac{24}{25}$

9. **sample answer: 30**

10. $1\frac{7}{12} > 1\frac{9}{16}$

11. **$7\frac{1}{2}$ hours;** $3 \times 2\frac{1}{2} = 3 \times \frac{5}{2} = \frac{15}{2} = 7\frac{1}{2}$

12. **$2\frac{5}{8}$ miles;** $\frac{7}{8} + 1\frac{3}{4} = \frac{7}{8} + \frac{7}{4} = \frac{7}{8} + \frac{14}{8} = \frac{21}{8} = 2\frac{5}{8}$

13. $\frac{7}{8}$

14. $\frac{15}{16}$; $1\frac{3}{8} - \frac{7}{16} = \frac{11}{8} - \frac{7}{16} = \frac{22}{16} - \frac{7}{16} = \frac{15}{16}$

15. $\frac{12}{25}$; $\frac{9}{10} \div 1\frac{7}{8} = \frac{9}{10} \div \frac{15}{8} = \frac{9}{10} \times \frac{8}{15} = \frac{72}{150} = \frac{12}{25}$

16. **(3)**   21. **(2)**

17. **(2)**   22. **(4)**

18. **(1)**   23. **(5)**

19. **(4)**   24. **(1)**

20. **(3)**   25. **(4)**

26. $\frac{2}{3}$

27. $\frac{7}{10}$

Chapter 6

Exercise 1, pages 113–115

1. 6 : 7, $\frac{6}{7}$

2. 1 to 50, $\frac{1}{50}$

3. 7 to 3, 7 : 3

4. 10 to 19, 10 : 19

5. 13 to 1, $\frac{13}{1}$

6. 2 : 5, $\frac{2}{5}$

7. 1 to 3, 1 : 3, or $\frac{1}{3}$

8. 9 to 1, $\frac{9}{1}$, or 9:1; 2,000 − 200 = 1,800; $\frac{1,800}{200} = \frac{9}{1}$

9. 2 to 9, 2 : 9, or $\frac{2}{9}$

10. 1 to 2, $\frac{1}{2}$, or 1 : 2; 24 h − 8 h = 16 h; $\frac{8}{16} = \frac{1}{2}$

11. 4 to 1, $\frac{4}{1}$, or 4 : 1

12. 23 to 8, 23 : 8, or $\frac{23}{8}$; 31 days − 23 days = 8 days

13. 61 to 97, $\frac{61}{97}$ or 61 : 97; $\frac{366}{582} = \frac{366 ÷ 6}{582 ÷ 6} = \frac{61}{97}$

14. 4 to 7, 4 : 7, or $\frac{4}{7}$

15. 19 : 8, 19 to 8, or $\frac{19}{8}$; $\frac{76}{32} = \frac{76 ÷ 4}{32 ÷ 4} = \frac{19}{8}$

16. 2 : 25, 2 to 25, or $\frac{2}{25}$; $\frac{8}{100} = \frac{8 ÷ 4}{100 ÷ 4} = \frac{2}{25}$

17. 1 : 4, 1 to 4 or $\frac{1}{4}$; $\frac{25}{100} = \frac{25 ÷ 25}{100 ÷ 100} = \frac{1}{4}$

18. 4 : 1; 4 to 1 or $\frac{4}{1}$; $\frac{32}{8} = \frac{32 ÷ 8}{8 ÷ 8} = \frac{4}{1}$

19. 67 : 41, 67 to 41, or $\frac{67}{41}$; 76 + 100 + 25 = 201; 32 + 8 + 83 = 123; $\frac{201}{123} = \frac{201 ÷ 3}{123 ÷ 3} = \frac{67}{41}$

20. 100 to 101, 100 : 101, or $\frac{100}{101}$; 76 + 25 = 101

21. (1)

22. (5); 30 − 3 = 27; $\frac{27}{3} = \frac{9}{1}$; 9 to 1

Exercise 2, pages 116–117

1. **55 words per minute;** $825 \div 15 = 55$

2. **$6.50 per hour;** $\$130 \div 20 = \$6.5$

3. **22.5 miles per gallon;** $135 \div 6 = 22.5$

4. **60 miles per hour;** $210 \div 3.5 = 60$

5. **$.30 per pound;** $\$1.49 \div 5 = \$0.298 \approx \$0.30$

6. **$.10 per pencil;** $\$0.99 \div 10 = \$0.099 \approx \$0.10$

7. **$2.67 per roll;** $\$8 \div 3 \approx \$2.67$

8. **$.10 per egg;** $\$1.09 \div 12 = \$0.0908 \approx \$0.10$

9. **Bill's car;** Consuela's: $330 \div 12 = 27.5$ miles per gallon; Bill's: $300 \div 10 = 30$ miles per gallon

10. **about 0.24 kilometers per minute;** $10 \div 42.5 \approx 0.24$

11. **slower;** $50 \div 6 = 8\frac{1}{3}$ minutes per mile

12. **faster;** $416 \div 5 = 83.2$ words per minute

13. **no;** $\$2.79 \div 15 \approx \$.19$ per ounce; $\$1.99 \div 12 \approx \$.17$ per ounce

14. **12-pack, best; 6-pack, worst;** $\$2.19 \div 6 \approx \$.37$ per can; $\$3.99 \div 12 \approx \$.33$ per can; $\$8.49 \div 24 \approx \$.35$ per can

Exercise 3, pages 119–120

1. **yes;** $\frac{2}{3} = \frac{10}{15}$; $2 \times 15 = 30$; $3 \times 10 = 30$

2. **no;** $\frac{1}{4}$ and $\frac{2}{9}$; $1 \times 9 = 9$; $4 \times 2 = 8$; $9 \neq 8$

3. **no;** $\frac{16}{3}$ and $\frac{8}{1}$; $16 \times 1 = 16$; $3 \times 8 = 24$; $16 \neq 24$

4. **yes;** $\frac{5}{5} = \frac{3}{3}$; $5 \times 3 = 15$; $5 \times 3 = 15$

5. **no;** $\frac{3}{4}$ and $\frac{5}{8}$; $3 \times 8 = 24$; $4 \times 5 = 20$; $24 \neq 20$

6. **yes;** $\frac{50}{20} = \frac{10}{4}$; $50 \times 4 = 200$; $20 \times 10 = 200$

7. **no;** $\frac{1}{2}$ and $\frac{6}{9}$; $1 \times 9 = 9$; $2 \times 6 = 12$; $9 \neq 12$

8. **yes;** $\frac{8}{3} = \frac{24}{9}$; $8 \times 9 = 72$; $3 \times 24 = 72$

9–16. Sample answers are given.

9. $\frac{1}{9} = \frac{2}{18}$

10. $\frac{25}{20} = \frac{5}{4}$

11. $\frac{12}{13} = \frac{24}{26}$

12. $\frac{6}{3} = \frac{2}{1}$

13. $\frac{13}{1} = \frac{39}{3}$

14. $\frac{17}{3} = \frac{34}{6}$

15. $\frac{5}{11} = \frac{50}{110}$

16. $\frac{10}{3} = \frac{20}{6}$

17. **no;** $\frac{3}{5}$ and $\frac{4}{6}$; $3 \times 6 = 18$; $5 \times 4 = 20$; $18 \neq 20$

18. **no, because the ratios of blue to yellow are not the same;** $\frac{3}{1} \neq \frac{5}{2}$

19. **yes; yes, they both type at 65 words per minute;** $\frac{650}{10} = \frac{780}{12}$

20. **$2.18;** $\frac{\$1.09}{12 \text{ eggs}} = \frac{\$2.18}{24 \text{ eggs}}$

21. **(2)**

22. **(3)**

23. **(5)**

24. **(4)**

Exercise 4, page 122

1. **130;** $13 \times 10 \div 1 = 130$

2. **500;** $10 \times 150 \div 3 = 500$

3. **36;** $42 \times 6 \div 7 = 36$

4. **16.8;** $7 \times 12 \div 5 = 16.8$

5. **4;** $1 \times 16 \div 4 = 4$

6. **54;** $9 \times 12 \div 2 = 54$

7. **1;** $5 \times 5 \div 25 = 1$

8. **112.5;** $30 \times 15 \div 4 = 112.5$

9. **32.4;** $9 \times 36 \div 10 = 32.4$

10. **1.4;** $7 \times 1 \div 5 = 1.4$

11. **$125;** $\frac{\$100}{8 \text{ lawns}} = \frac{\square}{10 \text{ lawns}}$; $\$100 \times 10 \div 8 = \$125$

12. **3.2 liters;** $\frac{5 \text{ parts juice}}{2 \text{ parts ginger ale}} = \frac{8 \text{ liters juice}}{\square}$; $2 \times 8 \div 5 = 3.2$

13. **125 miles;** $\frac{1 \text{ in.}}{50 \text{ miles}} = \frac{2\frac{1}{2} \text{ in.}}{\square}$; $50 \times 2\frac{1}{2} \div 1 = 125$

14. **384 miles;** $\frac{32 \text{ miles}}{1 \text{ gallon}} = \frac{\square}{12 \text{ gallons}}$; $32 \times 12 \div 1 = 384$

15. **307 calories;** $\frac{\frac{3}{4} \text{ cup}}{230 \text{ calories}} = \frac{1 \text{ cup}}{\square}$; $230 \times 1 \div \frac{3}{4} \approx 307$

16. $6\frac{7}{8}$ **inches by 11 inches;** First try to enlarge

to $8\frac{1}{2}$ inches wide:

$\frac{1\frac{1}{4}}{2} = \frac{8\frac{1}{2}}{\square}$; $2 \times 8\frac{1}{2} \div 1\frac{1}{4} = 13.6$ inches

(too long for 11-inch paper). So, enlarge to

11 inches long instead: $\frac{1\frac{1}{4}}{2} = \frac{\square}{11}$;

$1\frac{1}{4} \times 11 \div 2 = 6\frac{7}{8}$ inches.

Ratios and Proportions Review, pages 123–124

1. **27;** $3 \times 63 \div 7 = 27$
2. **523**
3. **3,000**
4. **Sample answer:** $\frac{1}{3} = \frac{2}{6}$
5. **$.42;** $\$5 \div 12 \approx \$.42$
6. **4 to 1;** $\frac{8}{2} = 8 \div \frac{2}{2} \div 2 = \frac{4}{1}$
7. **6 to 7, 6 : 7**
8. **468**
9. **107**
10. **500 km;** $\frac{1 \text{ cm}}{100 \text{ km}} = \frac{5 \text{ cm}}{\square}$; $100 \times 5 \div 1 = 500$
11. **65 miles per hour;** $130 \div 2 = 65$
12. **11.18**
13. **3**
14. **no;** $\frac{2}{3}$ and $\frac{3}{10}$; $2 \times 10 = 20$; $5 \times 3 = 15$; $20 \neq 15$
15. **90 women;** $\frac{2}{3} = \frac{60}{\square}$; $3 \times 60 \div 2 = 90$
16. **(1)**
17. **(3)**
18. **(4)**
19. **250;** $\frac{6}{5} = \frac{300}{\square}$; $5 \times 300 \div 6 = 250$
20. $\frac{1}{10}$ **;** $\frac{2}{20} = \frac{1}{10}$

Chapter 7

Exercise 1, page 128

1. $\frac{1}{4}$ **; 0.25;** $\frac{25}{100} = \frac{25 \div 25}{100 \div 25} = \frac{1}{4}$
2. $\frac{2}{25}$ **; 0.08;** $\frac{8}{100} = \frac{8 \div 4}{100 \div 4} = \frac{2}{25}$
3. $\frac{1}{10}$ **; 0.1;** $\frac{10}{100} = \frac{10 \div 10}{100 \div 10} = \frac{1}{10}$
4. $\frac{33}{50}$ **; 0.66;** $\frac{66}{100} = \frac{66 \div 2}{100 \div 2} = \frac{33}{50}$
5. $\frac{1}{100}$ **; 0.01**
6. $\frac{9}{10}$ **; 0.9;** $\frac{90}{100} = \frac{90 \div 10}{100 \div 10} = \frac{9}{10}$
7. $\frac{37}{100}$ **; 0.37**
8. $\frac{3}{100}$ **; 0.03**
9. $\frac{1}{2}$ **; 0.5**
10. **60%;** $3 \div 5 = 0.6 = 60\%$
11. **9%**
12. **74%**
13. **10%;** $1 \div 10 = 0.1 = 10\%$
14. **75%;** $3 \div 4 = 0.75 = 75\%$
15. **70%**
16. **16%**
17. **35%;** $7 \div 20 = 0.35 = 35\%$
18. **4%;** $1 \div 25 = 0.04 = 4\%$
19. **2%**
20. **99%**
21. **37.5%;** $3 \div 8 = 0.375 = 37.5\%$
22. $\frac{1}{4}$ **;** $1 \div 4 = 0.25 = 25\% > 20\%$
23. **85%;** $4 \div 5 = 0.8 = 80\% < 85\%$
24. $\frac{1}{2}$ **;** $1 \div 2 = 0.5 = 50\% > 48\%$
25. **0.11;** $0.11 = 11\% > 10\%$
26. **100%;** $0.01 = 1\% < 100\%$
27. **22%;** $\frac{2}{10} = 20\% < 22\%$
28. **39%;** $.35 = 35\% < 39\%$
29. **.7;** $.7 = 70\% > 42\%$
30. **(3)**
31. **(1)**

Exercise 2, page 130

1. **25%; 0.25**

2. **$33\frac{1}{3}$%; 0.333 . . .**

3. **50%; 0.5**

4. **$66\frac{2}{3}$%; 0.666 . . .**

5. **75%; 0.75**

6. **$\frac{1}{2}$; 0.5**

7. **$\frac{1}{3}$; 0.333 . . .**

8. **$\frac{3}{4}$; 0.75**

9. **$\frac{1}{4}$; 0.25**

10. **$\frac{2}{3}$; 0.666 . . .**

11. **$\frac{3}{4}$; 75%**

12. **$\frac{2}{3}$; $66\frac{2}{3}$%**

13. **$\frac{1}{4}$; 25%**

14. **$\frac{1}{3}$; $33\frac{1}{3}$%**

15. **$\frac{1}{2}$; 50%**

Exercise 3, pages 133–134

1. **87;** $0.1 \times 870 = 87$
2. **12;** $\frac{3}{4} \times 16 = 12$

3. **$12;** $0.12 \times \$100 = \$12$
4. **33;** $\frac{1}{3} \times 99 = 33$

5. **851.2;** $0.8 \times 1{,}064 = 851.2$
6. **$3,000;** $0.05 \times \$60{,}000 = \$3{,}000$
7. **47;** $0.47 \times 100 = 47$
8. **$25;** $\frac{1}{2} \times \$50 = \$25$

9. **28,925;** $0.65 \times 44{,}500$
10. **$8;** $0.01 \times \$800 = \$8$
11. **120;** $\frac{2}{3} \times 180 = 120$

12. **$20.40;** $0.3 \times \$68 = \$20.40$
13. **23;** $1 \times 23 = 23$
14. **175;** $0.02 \times 8{,}750 = 175$
15. **12;** $\frac{1}{4} \times 48 = 12$

16. **$.98;** $0.98 \times \$1 = \$.98$
17. **$750;** $0.06 \times \$12{,}500 = \$750$
18. **$1.95;** $0.15 \times \$13.00 = \$1.95$
19. **$18;** $0.4 \times \$45 = \$18$
20. **$60;** $\frac{1}{4} \times \$80 = \$20$; $\$80 - \$20 = \$60$

21. **21;** $0.7 \times 30 = 21$
22. **$5,400;** $0.05 \times \$108{,}000 = \$5{,}400$
23. **16 wins, 4 losses;** $0.8 \times 20 = 16$; $20 - 16 = 4$
24. **$3,000;** $0.1 \times \$2{,}500 = \$250$;
    $\$250 \times 12 = \$3{,}000$
25. **20 defective, 980 not defective;**
    $0.02 \times 1{,}000 = 20$; $1{,}000 - 20 = 980$
26. **7%; 42;** $42\% + 51\% = 93\%$; $100\% - 93\% =$
    7%; $0.07 \times 600 = 42$

Exercise 4, page 135

1. **$4,000;** $\$10{,}000 \times 0.08 \times 5 = \$4{,}000$
2. **$200;** $\$2{,}000 \times 0.10 \times 1 = \$200$
3. **$50;** $\$2{,}500 \times 0.04 \times \frac{6}{12} = \$50$

4. **$324,000;** $\$120{,}000 \times 0.09 \times 30 = \$324{,}000$
5. **$150.68;** $\$5{,}000 \times 0.11 \times \frac{100}{365} \approx \$150.68$

6. **$33;** $\$600 \times 0.055 \times 1 = \$33$
7. **$480;** $\$4{,}000 \times 0.04 \times 3 = \$480$
8. **$180,000;** $\$75{,}000 \times 0.08 \times 30 = \$180{,}000$
9. **$1,770;** $\$1{,}500 \times 0.06 \times 3 = \$270$;
    $\$1{,}500 + \$270 = \$1{,}770$
10. **$1.48;** $\$150 \times 0.12 \times \frac{30}{365} \approx \$1.48$

11. **$7,492.50;** $\$18{,}500 \times 0.10 = \$1{,}850$ down
    payment; $\$18{,}500 - \$1{,}850 = \$16{,}650$ princi-
    pal; $\$16{,}650 \times 0.09 \times 5 = \$7{,}492.50$

Exercise 5, page 138

1. **20;** $\frac{\square}{80} = \frac{25}{100}$; $80 \times 25 \div 100 = 20$
2. **4;** $\frac{3}{\square} = \frac{75}{100}$; $3 \times 100 \div 75 = 4$
3. **25%;** $\frac{11}{44} = \frac{\square}{100}$; $11 \times 100 \div 44 = 25$
4. **1,250;** $\frac{200}{\square} = \frac{16}{100}$; $200 \times 100 \div 16 = 1{,}250$
5. **15;** $\frac{\square}{500} = \frac{3}{100}$; $500 \times 3 \div 100 = 15$

6. **50%;** $\frac{12}{24} = \frac{\square}{100}$; $12 \times 100 \div 24 = 50$

7. **75%;** $\frac{12}{16} = \frac{\square}{100}$; $12 \times 100 \div 16 = 75$

8. **900;** $\frac{\square}{1000} = \frac{90}{100}$; $1000 \times 90 \div 100 = 900$

9. **80;** $\frac{8}{\square} = \frac{10}{100}$; $8 \times 100 \div 10 = 80$

10. **24;** $\frac{6}{\square} = \frac{25}{100}$; $6 \times 100 \div 25 = 24$

11. **9%;** $\frac{9}{100} = \frac{\square}{100}$; $9 \times 100 \div 100 = 9$

12. **31;** $\frac{\square}{62} = \frac{50}{100}$; $62 \times 50 \div 100 = 31$

13. **700;** $\frac{7}{\square} = \frac{1}{100}$; $7 \times 100 \div 1 = 700$

14. **$33\frac{1}{3}$%;** $\frac{17}{57} = \frac{\square}{100}$; $17 \times 100 \div 51 = 33.333\ldots$

15. **49;** $\frac{\square}{49} = \frac{100}{100}$; $49 \times 100 \div 100 = 49$

16. **40;** $\frac{6}{\square} = \frac{15}{100}$; $6 \times 100 \div 15 = 40$

Exercise 6, pages 139–140

1. **21%;** $\frac{73 \text{ million}}{340 \text{ million}} = \frac{\square}{100}$; $73 \times 100 \div 340 \approx 21$

2. **7,440,000 households;** $\frac{\square}{93 \text{ million}} = \frac{8}{100}$;

   $93 \text{ million} \times 8 \div 100 = 7,440,000$

3. **112,011 people;** $\frac{\square}{215405} = \frac{52}{100}$;

   $215,405 \times 52 \div 100 \approx 112,011$

4. **68%;** $13,407 + 6,309 = 19,716$; $\frac{13407}{19716} = \frac{\square}{100}$;
   $13,407 \times 100 \div 19,716 \approx 68$

5. **24 grams;** $\frac{5}{\square} = \frac{21}{100}$; $5 \times 100 \div 21 \approx 24$

6. **$15.00; $3.00;** $\frac{12}{\square} = \frac{80}{100}$; $12 \times 100 \div 80 = 15$;
   $\$15 - \$12 = \$3$

7. **6 inches;** $\frac{\square}{24} = \frac{25}{100}$; $24 \times 25 \div 100 = 6$

8. **64 inches, or 5 ft 4 in.;** $\frac{32}{\square} = \frac{50}{100}$;

   $32 \times 100 \div 50 = 64$

9. **67%;** $\frac{16}{24} = \frac{\square}{100}$; $16 \times 100 \div 24 \approx 67$

10. **about 7 hours;** $\frac{\square}{24} = \frac{30}{100}$; $24 \times 30 \div 100 \approx 7$

11. **(2);** $\frac{5}{8} = \frac{\square}{100} = 5 \times 100 \div 8 = 62.5$

12. **(1);** $\frac{10}{25} = \frac{\square}{100} = 10 \times 100 \div 25 = 40$

13. **(4);** $8 \times 100 \div 25 = 32$; 25% of $80 = 20$

Percent Review, pages 141–143

1. **23%**

2. **0.7**

3. **102;** $0.85 \times 120 = 102$

4. **$66\frac{2}{3}$%;** $2 \div 3 = 0.666\ldots = 66\frac{2}{3}\%$

5. **$\frac{1}{4}$, 0.25**

6. **10%;** $\frac{6}{60} = \frac{\square}{100}$; $6 \times 100 \div 60 = 10$

7. **$\frac{1}{50}$;** $\frac{2}{100} = \frac{2 \div 2}{100 \div 2} = \frac{1}{50}$

8. **$1.05;** $0.15 \times \$7 = \$1.05$

9. **20;** $\frac{18}{\square} = \frac{90}{100}$; $18 \times 100 \div 90 = 20$

10. **20%;** $1 \div 5 = 0.2 = 20\%$

11. **$240;** $\$2,000 \times 0.06 \times 2 = \$240$

12. **12;** $\frac{\square}{40} = \frac{30}{100}$; $40 \times 30 \div 100 = 12$

13. **50%;** $\frac{35}{70} = \frac{\square}{100}$; $35 \times 100 \div 70 = 50$

14. **$3\frac{5}{8}$**

15. **36.15**

16. **151.2**

17. 169.2

18. 68.25

19. (2)
20. (4)
21. (1)
22. (2)
23. (5)
24. (2)
25. (4)

Chapter 8

Exercise 1, pages 147–148

1. 43 minutes; 42 + 41 + 45 + 40 + 46 + 42 + 44 = 300; 300 ÷ 7 ≈ 43

2. 42 minutes; 40, 41, 42, <u>42</u>, 44, 45, 46

3. 42 minutes

4. 6 minutes; 46 − 40 = 6

5. $105,000; $85,000; $95,500; $99,900; <u>$105,000</u>; $108,000; $120,000; $124,000

6. skiing

7. 18°; 10 + 12 + 30 + 38 + 22 + 6 + 2 + 0 + 0 + 18 + 22 + 25 + 16 + 33 + 40 + 38 + 32 + 35 + 10 + 8 + 5 + 5 + 9 + 12 + 15 + 21 + 30 + 19 = 513; 513 ÷ 28 ≈ 18

8. 2 siblings

9. 42 years; 64 − 22 = 42

10. $7\frac{1}{2}$**;** 5, $6\frac{1}{2}$, 7, <u>7</u>, <u>8</u>, $8\frac{1}{2}$, 9, 10; 7 + 8 = 15;

$15 ÷ 2 = 7\frac{1}{2}$

11. 84%; 75 + 72 + 88 + 90 + 85 + 100 + 77 + 86 = 673; 673 ÷ 8 ≈ 84

12. $40.49; $64.99 − $24.50 = $40.49

13. $60

14. $36,200 average salary; $24,000 median salary; the mean is higher because of the high salary $100,000; Mean: $24,000 + $15,000 + $100,000 + $30,000 + $12,000 = $181,000; $181,000 ÷ 5 = $36,200. Median: $12,000; $15,000; <u>$24,000</u>; $30,000; $100,000.

15. 15 days; 60 is the median, so half the remaining days of March had higher temperatures and half had lower temperatures; 31 − 1 = 30; 30 ÷ 2 = 15 days

16. 65, 66, 68, 69, 72; The mean is 68, so 68 × 5 = 340 is the sum of the five heights. The greatest is 72, so 72 − 7 = 65 is the lowest. Then 340 − (lowest + median + greatest) = 340 − (65 + 68 + 72) = 340 − 205 = 135. The two missing heights are 66 and 69: 66 + 69 = 135.

17. 25 years; 15 + 10 = 25

18. 87%; 80 × 5 = 400 = sum; 400 − (70 + 85 + 78 + 80) = 400 − 313 = 87

19. (3)   **21.** (2)
20. (4)   **22.** (1)

Exercise 2, pages 151–152

1. 8 species

2. seal family

3. dog/fox family

4. **horse family and pig family**

5. **21 species or about 20 species;**
   40 – 19 = 21 or 40 – 20 = 20

6. **rabbit family;** 19 × 2 = 38 ≈ 40

7. **5 times;** 8 × 5 = 40 or 40 ÷ 8 = 5

8. **2,000 species**

9. **lily family;** 1,000 + 2,500 = 3,500

10. **primrose, daffodil, buttercup and iris (tie), carnation and forget-me-not (tie), rose, lily; median is 1,900 species**

11. **(4); the rose family has about *three* times as many species as the daffodil family.**

Exercise 3, pages 154–155

1.

MEDALS WON BY U.S. IN
THE 1994 WINTER OLYMPICS

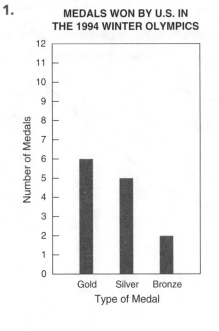

2.

GOLD MEDALS WON BY SELECTED
COUNTRIES IN THE 1994 WINTER OLYMPICS

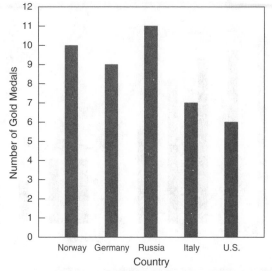

3.

MEDALS WON BY NORWAY IN
THE 1994 WINTER OLYMPICS

4.

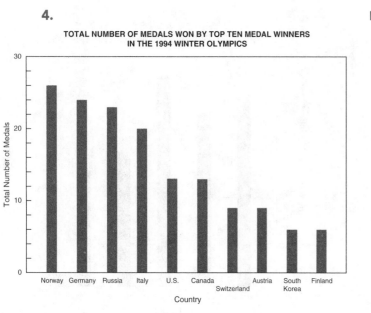

TOTAL NUMBER OF MEDALS WON BY TOP TEN MEDAL WINNERS
IN THE 1994 WINTER OLYMPICS

Exercise 5, pages 162–163

1.

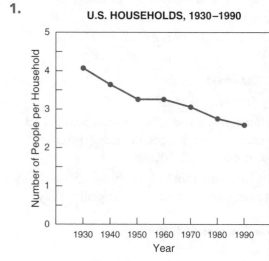

U.S. HOUSEHOLDS, 1930–1990

5. Graphs will vary.

Exercise 4, pages 158–159

1. ≈ **23°F**

2. **9:00 P.M.**

3. **2:00 P.M., 26°F**

4. **7:00 A.M., 8°F**

5. **2:00 A.M., 3:00 A.M., 5:00 P.M.,
   12:00 midnight**

6. **6:00 P.M.**

7. **6:00 A.M.**

8. **17°F;** temperatures listed in order: 8, 10, 11,
   11, 12, 13, 14, 14, 14, 15, 15, <u>16</u>, <u>18</u>, 18, 18,
   18, 19, 21, 21, 23, 24, 25, 25, 26;
   16 + 18 = 34; 34 ÷ 2 = 17

9. **18°F;** 26 − 8 = 18

10. **9:00 A.M. to 10:00 A.M., 9°F;** 19 − 10 = 9

11. **5:00 P.M. to 6:00 P.M., 7°F;** 18 − 11 = 7

12. **(3);** the temperature began to drop after 2 P.M.

13. **(5)**

2.

U.S. HOUSEHOLDS, 1930–1990

3.

U.S. CONSUMER PRICE INDEX, 1985–1993

4.

PURCHASING POWER OF THE U.S. DOLLAR, 1985–1993

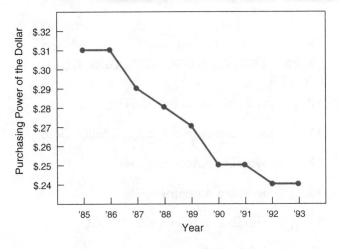

Exercise 6, pages 166–167

1. **4%**
2. **California**
3. **Alaska**
4. $\frac{1}{10}$
5. **5**
6. **17%;** California + Oregon + Washington = 11% + 4% + 2% = 17%
7. **Oregon**
8. **Alaska, 5,565 miles; California, 839 miles; Hawaii, 762 miles; Oregon, 305 miles; Washington, 152 miles;**
   $0.73 \times 7,623 \approx 5,565; 0.11 \times 7,623 \approx 839;$
   $0.10 \times 7,623 \approx 762; 0.04 \times 7,623 \approx 305;$
   $0.02 \times 7,623 \approx 152$
9. **African Americans; 92%**
10. **Whites; 58%**
11. **Females**
12. **Republicans; the graph labeled "All"**

Exercise 7, page 168

1. **(1)**
2. **(5)**
3. **(2);** $0.49 \times 10,210 \approx 5,003$
4. **(5)**
5. **(4)**
6. **(5)**

Exercise 8, pages 171–172

1.

CALIFORNIA VOTERS
PROPOSITION 187

Against 41%

For 59%

2.

POLITICS AS USUAL?

New era 32%

Not sure 5%

Politics as usual 63%

3.

HOUSE OF REPRESENTATIVES
VOTED ON IN 1994

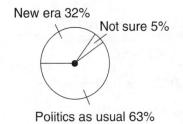

Democrat 47%

Independent
(less than 1%)

Republican 53%

4.

U.S. GULF COASTLINE

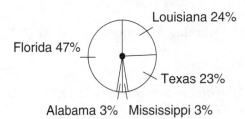

Louisiana 24%

Florida 47%

Texas 23%

Alabama 3%   Mississippi 3%

Exercise 9, pages 174–175

1. $\frac{1}{4}$, or 0.25, or 25%; $\frac{2}{8} = \frac{1}{4} = 0.25 = 25\%$

2. $\frac{1}{2}$, or 0.5, or 50%; 4 favorable outcomes: $10, $10, $50, $100; $\frac{4}{8} = \frac{1}{2} = 0.5 = 50\%$

3. **$50 and $100**

4. **$5;** 50% $= \frac{1}{2} = \frac{4}{8}$, $5 occurs 4 times

5. $\frac{1}{2}$, or 0.5, or 50%

6. 1, or 100%; $\frac{2}{2} = \frac{1}{1} = 1 = 100\%$

7. $\frac{1}{13}$, or about 0.08, or about 8%; $\frac{4}{52} = \frac{1}{13} \approx 0.08$ or 8%

8. $\frac{1}{6}$, or about 0.17, or about 17%

9. **90%;** 100% − 10% = 90%

10. $\frac{1}{10000}$, or 0.0001, or 0.01%

11. $\frac{1}{10}$, or 0.1, or 10%

12. $\frac{1}{20}$, or 0.05, or 5%; $\frac{5}{100} = \frac{1}{20} = 0.05 = 5\%$

13. $\frac{5}{9}$, or about 0.56, or about 56%; total $= 10 + 7 + 1 = 18$; $\frac{10}{18} = \frac{5}{9} \approx 0.56$ or 56%

14. **0, or 0%;** $\frac{0}{18} = 0 = 0\%$

Exercise 10, page 176

1. (2) 3. (4) 5. (5)
2. (4) 4. (1) 6. (1)

Exercise 11, pages 179–180

1. **36 possible outcomes**

2. **11 sums;** the possible sums are 2, 3, 4, 5, 6, 7, 8, 9, 10, 11, and 12.

3. **(3,1), (2,2), and (1,3);** $\frac{1}{12}$; $\frac{3}{16} = \frac{1}{12}$

4. $\frac{5}{36}$; 5 favorable outcomes: (6,2), (5,3), (4,4), (3,5), (2,6)

5. **7;** 6 favorable outcomes: (6,1), (5,2), (4,3), (3,4), (2,5), (1,6)

6. $\frac{1}{6}$; 6 favorable outcomes: (1,1), (2,2), (3,3), (4,4), (5,5), (6,6); $\frac{6}{36} = \frac{1}{6}$

7. **(5)**

8. **(4);** 11 favorable outcomes

9. **BBB, BBG, BGB, BGG, GBB, GBG, GGB, GGG**

10. $\frac{1}{8}$; 1 favorable outcome: GGG

11. $\frac{3}{8}$; 3 favorable outcomes: BGG, GBG, GGB

12. $\frac{1}{8}$; 1 favorable outcome: GGB

13. $\frac{1}{8}$; 1 favorable outcome: BBB

14. $\frac{1}{4}$; 2 favorable outcomes: BBB, GGG; $\frac{2}{8} = \frac{1}{4}$

15. **GBB, BGB, BBG**

16. $\frac{1}{8}$; 1 favorable outcome: BGB

Working with Data Review, pages 181–186

1. **36;** 28 + 37 + 19 + 51 + 40 + 31 + 22 + 40 + 63 + 40 + 25 = 396; 396 ÷ 11 = 36

2. **37;** 19, 22, 25, 28, 31, 37, 40, 40, 40, 51, 63

3. **40**

4. **44;** 63 − 19 = 44

5. **BB, BG, GB, GG**

6. $\frac{1}{18}$, or about 0.06, or about 6%; $\frac{2}{36} = \frac{1}{18} \approx 0.06$ or 6%

7. $\frac{1}{25}$, or 0.04, or 4%

8. **7 employees**

9. **Ads, Mail, and Editorial**

10.

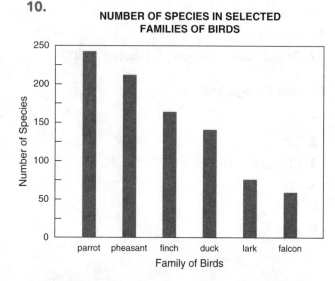

NUMBER OF SPECIES IN SELECTED FAMILIES OF BIRDS

11. about $25,000

12. about 22 years

13.

DAILY LOW TEMPERATURES
FOR ONE WEEK

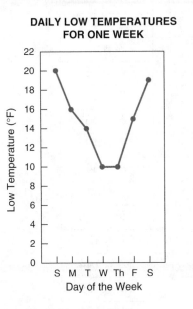

14. Food; 10% × 2 = 20%

15. $800; 0.40 × $2,000 = $800

16.

COMPONENTS
OF BLOOD

Cells 45%

Plasma 55%

17. $\frac{1}{2}$, **or 0.5, or 50%;** 3 favorable outcomes:

1, 3, 5; $\frac{3}{6} = \frac{1}{2} = 0.5 = 50\%$

18. $\frac{1}{8}$, **or 0.125, or 12.5%**

19. (4); 4 out of 5 people at the party are female

so write the proportion $\frac{4}{5} = \frac{?}{20}$ and

$4 \times 20 \div 5 = 80 \div 5 = 16$

20. (5); (1) $.69 \div 2 \approx$ \$.35; (2) \$2 \div 5 = \$.40;
(3) \$.35; (4) \$1.50 \div 4 \approx \$.38; (5) \$1 \div 3 \approx
\$.333 or \$.34

21. (4); (1) $\frac{8}{10} = .80$; 8% = .08;

(2) 0.8 = 0.80; $\frac{4}{5} = 0.80$; 8% = 0.08;

(3) 80% = 0.80; $\frac{80}{100} = 0.80$;

(4) $\frac{4}{5} = 0.80$; 80% = 0.80; 0.8 = 0.80;

(5) 8% = 0.08; $\frac{8}{100} = 0.08$; 0.8 = 0.80;

22. (2)

23. (4); $48 \times 1\frac{1}{2} = 48 \times \frac{3}{2} = 24 \times 3 = 72$ in.;
72 in. ÷ 12 = 6 ft

24. (5)

25. (3); (1) $.08 \times 2 \times p = .16p$;
(2) $.03 \times 8 \times p = .24p$; (3) $.05 \times 5 \times p = .25p$;
(4) $.12 \times 1 \times p = .12p$

26. (5); each of $\frac{3}{5}$ and $\frac{4}{7}$ is greater than one-half.

27. $\frac{1}{3}$; $\frac{4}{12} = \frac{1}{3}$

28. $375; $375 × 4 weeks = $1,500;
$1,500 ÷ 25 = $375

29. 5 bottles; $50 − $34.99 = $15.01;
$15.01 ÷ $3 = 5

Chapter 9

Exercise 1, pages 190–191

1. 2,401; $7 \times 7 \times 7 \times 7 = 2,401$

2. 1

3. 1,024; $4 \times 4 \times 4 \times 4 \times 4 = 1,024$

4. 81; $3 \times 3 \times 3 \times 3 = 81$

5. 343; $7 \times 7 \times 7 = 343$

6. 0; $0 \times 0 \times 0 \times 0 \times 0 \times 0 = 0$

7. 5; $5 \times 5 = 25$

8. 12; $12 \times 12 = 144$

9. 4; $4 \times 4 = 16$

10. 8; $8 \times 8 = 64$

11. 3; $3 \times 3 = 9$

12. 15; $15 \times 15 = 225$

13. 12,977.875

14. 16

15. 33.1776

16. 1.5

17. 110,592

18. .9

19. 156,816

20. 7.5

21.

Number	Square
1	$1^2 = 1$
2	$2^2 = 4$
3	$3^2 = 9$
4	$4^2 = 16$
5	$5^2 = 25$
6	$6^2 = 36$
7	$7^2 = 49$
8	$8^2 = 64$
9	$9^2 = 81$
10	$10^2 = 100$
11	$11^2 = 121$
12	$12^2 = 144$
13	$13^2 = 169$
14	$14^2 = 196$
15	$15^2 = 225$
20	$20^2 = 400$

22.

Number	Square Root
1	$\sqrt{1} = 1$
4	$\sqrt{4} = 2$
9	$\sqrt{9} = 3$
16	$\sqrt{16} = 4$
25	$\sqrt{25} = 5$
36	$\sqrt{36} = 6$
49	$\sqrt{49} = 7$
64	$\sqrt{64} = 8$
81	$\sqrt{81} = 9$
100	$\sqrt{100} = 10$
121	$\sqrt{121} = 11$
144	$\sqrt{144} = 12$
169	$\sqrt{169} = 13$
196	$\sqrt{196} = 14$
225	$\sqrt{225} = 15$
400	$\sqrt{400} = 20$

23. **4 and 5;** $\sqrt{16} = 4$, and $\sqrt{25} = 5$, so $\sqrt{20}$ lies between 4 and 5.

24. **12 and 13;** $\sqrt{144} = 12$, and $\sqrt{169} = 13$, so $\sqrt{150}$ lies between 12 and 13.

25. **8;** $\sqrt{60} < \sqrt{64} < \sqrt{70}$, and $\sqrt{64} = 8$

Exercise 2, page 192

1. **(2)**
2. **(3)**
3. **(5)**
4. **(1)**

5. **(3);** $1 + 2 + 3 = 6; 6^2 = 36$
6. **(2);** $\sqrt{289 - 225} = \sqrt{64} = 8$
7. **(5);** $36 - 25 = 11$
8. **(2);** $\sqrt{49} = 7; \sqrt{64} = 8; 7 + 8 = 15$

Exercise 3, page 195

1. **2;** $(12 + 4) \div (1 + 7) = 16 \div 8 = 2$
2. **21;** $3^2 + 6^2 \div 3 = 9 + 36 \div 3 = 9 + 12 = 21$
3. **19;** $\sqrt{25} + 6 \times 4 - 10 = 5 + 6 \times 4 - 10 = 5 + 24 - 10 = 29 - 10 = 19$
4. **16;** $[(30 - 8) \div 2] + 5 = [22 \div 2] + 5 = 11 + 5 = 16$
5. **4;** $24 \div (1^5 + 5) = 24 \div (1 + 5) = 24 \div 6 = 4$
6. **5;** $(2^3 + 3^3) \div 7 = (8 + 27) \div 7 = 35 \div 7 = 5$
7. **7;** $13 + 6 \times 2 \div 4 - 9 = 13 + 12 \div 4 - 9 = 13 + 3 - 9 = 16 - 9 = 7$
8. **18;** $3 \times (10 - 4) \div 9 + 4^2 = 3 \times 6 \div 9 + 42 = 3 \times 6 \div 9 + 16 = 18 \div 9 + 16 = 2 + 16 = 18$
9. **14;** $9 \times 8^0 + (6 - 1) = 9 \times 8^0 + 5 = 9 \times 1 + 5 = 9 + 5 = 14$
10. **44;** $60 - [25 - (13 - 4)] = 60 - [25 - 9] = 60 - 16 = 44$

Exercise 4, page 195

1. **(3);** (1) 35; (2) 44; (3) 80; (4) 34; (5) 44
2. **(5);** (1) 31; (2) 30; (3) 58; (4) 31; (5) 21
3. **(2);** $14 - 2^3 + 6 \times 2 = 14 - 8 + 6 \times 2 = 14 - 8 + 12 = 6 + 12 = 18$
4. **(1);** $40 + 12 \div 6 = 40 + 2 = 42$;
   (1) $6 + 4 \times 3 + 12 = 6 + 12 + 12 = 18 + 12 = 30 \neq 42$
5. **(3);** $5 \times (8 - 2) \div 4 = 5 \times 6 \div 4 = 7.5$
6. **(5)**

Exercise 5, pages 198–199

1. **yes;** $9 \times 3 = 27$
2. **no;** $10 + 3 \neq 7$
3. **yes;** $24 - 14 = 10$
4. **yes;** $4 \times 8 = 32$
5. **yes;** $\frac{22}{2} = 11$
6. **no;** $\frac{4}{5} \neq 20$
7. **$y = 7$;** $\frac{5y}{5} = \frac{35}{5}; y = 7$
8. **$n = 11$;** $n - 1 + 1 = 10 + 1; n = 11$
9. **$y = 1$;** $y + 20 - 20 = 21 - 20; y = 1$
10. **$z = 6$;** $\frac{z}{3} \times 3 = 2 \times 3; z = 6$
11. **$n = 4$;** $\frac{8n}{8} = \frac{32}{8}; n = 4$
12. **$n = 7$;** $n + 1 - 1 = 8 - 1; n = 7$
13. **$x = 36$;** $\frac{x}{4} \times 4 = 9 \times 4; x = 36$
14. **$a = 28$;** $a - 17 + 17 = 11 + 17; a = 28$
15. **$z = 9$;** $z - 4 + 4 = 5 + 4; z = 9$
16. **$a = 20$;** $\frac{10a}{10} = \frac{200}{10}; a = 20$
17. **$y = 32$;** $\frac{y}{2} \times 2 = 16 \times 2; y = 32$
18. **$x = 10$;** $x + 9 - 9 = 19 - 9; x = 10$
19. **$a = 34$;** $a + 3 - 3 = 37 - 3; a = 34$
20. **$z = 6$;** $\frac{9z}{9} = \frac{54}{9}; z = 6$
21. **$y = 14$;** $y - 8 + 8 = 6 + 8; y = 14$
22. **$a = 7$;** $\frac{a}{7} \times 7 = 1 \times 7; a = 7$
23. **$x = 18$;** $x - 15 + 15 = 3 + 15; x = 18$
24. **$x = 25$;** $\frac{2x}{2} = \frac{50}{2}; x = 25$
25. **$n = 36$;** $\frac{n}{6} \times 6 = 6 \times 6; n = 36$
26. **$z = 9$;** $z + 14 - 14 = 23 - 14; z = 9$
27. **(3);** $4 \times 3 = 12$
28. **(4);** $6 - 6 \neq 12$

Exercise 6, pages 202–203

1. **4 items;** $\$28 = n \times \$7; n = 4$
2. **\$2,000;** $\$360 = p \times 0.06 \times 3; p = \$2,000$
3. **15 hits;** $0.300 = \frac{h}{50}; h = 15$
4. **50°F;** $F = 1.8 \times 10 + 32; F = 50$

5. about 57 miles per hour; $100 = r \times 1.75$; $r \approx 57$

6. $4,000; $i = \$10,000 \times 0.08 \times 5 = \$4,000$

7. $151.96; $c = nr$; $c = 4 \times \$37.99 = \$151.96$

8. 4%; $i = prt$; $\$80 = \$1,000 \times r \times 2$; $r = 0.04 = 4\%$

9. 86°F; $F = 1.8C + 32$; $F = 1.8 \times 30 + 32 = 86$

10. 330 miles; $d = rt$; $d = 55 \times 6 = 330$

11. .300; $a = \frac{h}{n}$; $a = \frac{14}{20} = .300$

12. 5 hours; $d = rt$; $300 = 60t$; $t = 5$

13. about 2 hits; $a = \frac{h}{n}$; $0.380 = \frac{h}{5}$; $h = 1.9 \approx 2$

14. $1.245 per gallon; $c = nr$; $\$14.94 = 12r$; $r = \$1.245$

15. 3 years; $i = prt$; $\$750 = \$5,000 \times 0.05 \times t$; $t = 3$

16. 9°F; $F = 1.8C + 32$; $F = 1.8 \times 20 + 32 = 68$ $F = 1.8 \times 15 + 32 = 59$; $68 - 59 = 9$

Exercise 7, pages 206–207

1. *J*	**4.** *A*	**7.** *G*
2. *H*	**5.** *L*	**8.** *B*
3. *M*	**6.** *C*	**9.** (2, 1)

10. (−3, −2)	**14.** (5, −8)	**18.** *F, G, M, O*
11. (−8, 3)	**15.** (−7, 9)	**19.** *A, I, J, P*
12. (4, 10)	**16.** (−4, −9)	**20.** *B, E, L, N*
13. (1, −7)	**17.** *C, D, H, K*	

21–28.

29–30.

Basic Algebra Review, pages 208–211

1. 5; $5 \times 5 = 25$

2. no; $\frac{3}{8} \neq 24$

3. y = 11; $y - 7 + 7 = 4 + 7$; $y = 11$

4. 48.2°; $F = 1.8 \times 9° + 32 = 48.2°$

5. 6; $3^2 + 6 \times 2 - 15 = 9 + 12 - 15 = 6$

6. $3,750; $i = prt$; $900 = p \times 0.08 \times 3$; $p = 3,750$

7. z = 11; $\frac{3z}{3} = \frac{33}{3}$; $z = 11$

8. 32; $2 \times 2 \times 2 \times 2 \times 2 = 32$

9. 5 hours; $d = rt$; $250 = 50t$; $t = 5$

10. x = 30; $\frac{x}{2} \times 2 = 15 \times 2$; $x = 30$

11. 27; $(4 + 5) \times (6 - 3) = 9 \times 3 = 27$

12. yes; $4 \times 5 = 20$

13. 8; $8 \times 8 = 64$

14. about $.10; $c = nr$; $1.09 = 12 \times r$; $r \approx .10$

15. n = 8; $n + 19 - 19 = 27 - 19$; $n = 8$

16. 306.25

17. 62

18. (5); $\$10 \div \$1.347 \approx 7$

19. (4); $\$2,500 \times 1.5 \times .0725 = \$271.88$; $\$2,500 + \$271.88 = \$2,771.88$

20. (2); 4% of $18,000 = .04 × 18,000 = 720;
$18,000 + $720 = $18,720;
$18,720 ÷ 12 = $1,560

21. (3); 100% − 7% = 93%

22. (5); range: $115,000 − $74,000 = $41,000;
median of $74,000, $85,500, $99,900,
$109,000, and $115,000 is $99,900; mode:
none; mean: $74,000 + $85,500 + $99,900 +
$109,000 + $115,000 = $483,400;
$483,400 ÷ 5 = $96,680

23. (4); $200^1 = 200$; $5^4 = 625$; $1^{200} = 1$; $2^{10} = 1,024$;
$20^2 = 400$

24. (5); (1) $1.99 + $4.95 + 8($4.99) + 4($2.95) =
$1.99 + $4.95 + $39.92 + $11.80 = $58.66;
(2) $4.95 + $11.80 = $16.75; (4) $58.66 ÷
16 ≈ $3.67

25. (3); $20 ÷ $.05 = 400

26. $15.80; 6.37 × $2.48 = $15.7976 = $15.80

27. 88 keys; $\frac{13}{9} = \frac{?}{36}$; 13 × 36 ÷ 9 = 52 white keys;
36 black keys + 52 white keys = 88 keys
altogether

28. $686; 10% + 18% = 28%; $2,450 × .28 = $686

29. (5)

30. (4)

31. (2)

Chapter 10

Exercise 1, pages 213–214

1. pints	**5.** minutes	**9.** weeks
2. pounds	**6.** miles	**10.** yards
3. feet	**7.** days	
4. gallons	**8.** quarts	

11. 48; 12 gal × 4 = 48 qt

12. 12; 84 days ÷ 7 = 12 wk

13. 10; 30 ft ÷ 3 = 10 yd

14. 10,000; 5 T × 2,000 = 10,000 lb

15. 48; 3 lb × 16 = 48 oz

16. 5; 60 in. ÷ 12 = 5 ft

17. 4; 240 sec ÷ 60 = 4 min

18. 3; 6 c ÷ 2 = 3 pt

19. 63,360; 1 mi × 5,280 = 5,280 ft;
5,280 ft × 12 = 63,360 ft

20. 5; 300 min ÷ 60 = 5 hr

21. 108; 3 yd × 36 = 108 in.

22. 168; 1 wk × 7 = 7 days; 7 days × 24 = 168 h

23. 24; 6 qt × 2 = 12 pt; 12 pt × 2 = 24 c

24. 4; 8,000 lb ÷ 2,000 = 4 T

25. 80; 5 lb × 16 = 80 oz

26. **86,400;** 1 day × 24 = 24 h; 24 h × 60 = 1,440 min; 1,440 min × 60 = 86,400 sec

27. **3;** 15,840 ft ÷ 5,280 = 3 mi

28. **2;** 32 c ÷ 2 = 16 pt; 16 pt ÷ 2 = 8 qt; 8 qt ÷ 4 = 2 gal

29. **(3)**

30. **(2)**

Exercise 2, pages 215–216

1. **74 in.;** (6 × 12) + 2 = 72 + 2 = 74

2. **4 ft 6 in.;** 54 in.→54 ÷ 12 = 4 R6→4 ft 6 in.

3. **135 min;** (2 × 60) + 15 = 120 + 15 = 135

4. **5 h 0 min;** 300 ÷ 60 = 5

5. **2 qt 3 c;** 11 c→11 ÷ 4 = 2 R3→2 qt 3 c

6. **1 mi 4,720 ft;** 10,000 ft→10,000 ÷ 5,280 = 1 R4,720→1 mi 4,720 ft

7. **3 min 20 sec;** $3\frac{1}{3}$ = 3 min ($\frac{1}{3}$ × 60) sec = 3 min 20 sec

8. **52 wk 1 day;** 1 y = 365 days; 365 days ÷ 7 = 52R1→52 wk 1 day

9. **3 lb 2 oz;** 50 ÷ 16 = 3 R2 = 3 lb 2 oz

10. **455 sec;** 7 × 60 + 35 = 420 + 35 = 455

11. **Enrique;** Enrique: (6 × 12) + 1 = 73 in.

12. **Sue;** Ria: (8 × 60) + 45 = 525 min

13. **Can A;** Can B: 1 cup = 8 fl oz

14. **4 cups;** 20 c ÷ 2 = 10 pt; 10 pt ÷ 2 = 5 qt; 5 qt ÷ 4 = 1R1→1 gal 1 qt = 1 gal 4 c

Exercise 3, pages 217–218

1. **100**
2. **1,000**
3. **10**
4. **1,000**
5. **1,000**
6. **1,000**
7. **1,000**
8. **1,000**

9. **3.2;** 320 cm ÷ 100 = 3.2 m

10. **400;** 40 cm × 10 = 400 mm

11. **400;** 0.4 kL × 1,000 = 400 L

12. **5.5;** 5,500 g ÷ 1,000 = 5.5 kg

13. **600;** 6 m × 100 = 600 cm

14. **8.9;** 89 mm ÷ 10 = 8.9 cm

15. **6,500;** 6.5 L × 1,000 = 6,500 mL

16. **2,000;** 2 km × 1,000 = 2,000 m

17. **342;** 342,000 mg ÷ 1,000 = 342 g

18. **1,400;** 1.4 kL × 1,000 = 1,400 L

19. **10,000;** 10 kg × 1,000 = 10,000 g

20. **0.75;** 750 mL ÷ 1,000 = 0.75 L

21. **5,000;** 5 kg × 1,000 = 5,000 g

22. **6;** 600 cm ÷ 100 = 6 m

23. **7,200;** 7.2 g × 1,000 = 7,200 mg

24. **.24;** 240 m ÷ 1,000 = .24 km

25. **2;** 2,000 L ÷ 1,000 = 2 kL

26. **.512;** 512 mL ÷ 1,000 = .512 L

27. **millimeter, centimeter, meter, kilometer**

28. **kilogram, gram, milligram**

29. **500 mL;** 0.5 L × 1,000 = 500 mL

30. **2.5 L;** 250 mL × 10 = 2,500 mL; 2,500 mL ÷ 1,000 = 2.5 L

31. **70,000 g;** 70 kg × 1,000 = 70,000 g

32. **0.06 g;** 60 mg ÷ 1,000 = 0.06 g

Exercise 4, pages 219–220

1. **3 mm, or 0.3 cm**
2. **9 cm**
3. **13.5 cm**
4. **9 mm, or 0.9 cm**
5. **5.4 cm**
6. **11.7 cm**
7. **km**
8. **m**
9. **cm**
10. **cm; mm**
11. **km**
12. **cm; m**

Exercise 5, pages 220–221

Sample answers are given for 1–14.

1. **ray TQ, TS, TP, or TR**
2. **segment PT, TQ, TS, RT, PQ, or RS**
3. **line RS or PQ**
4. **right angle RTQ, RTP, PTS, or QTS**
5. **circle T**
6. **perpendicular lines RS and PQ**
7. **square CDEF**
8. **segments AF and BC, AB and DE**
9. **triangle CDE**
10. **segments AE and CF, BD and AB**
11. **angle FCE, AEC**
12. **rectangle ABDE**

13. segments AB, FC, and ED

14. angles FAB, ABC, and CDE

15. T
16. F
17. T
18. F
19. T

20. F
21. F
22. F
23. T
24. T

Exercise 6, pages 223–224

1.

2.

3.

4.

5.

6.

7.

8.

9.

10.

11.

12.

13. **90°**
14. **circle**
15. **line**
16. **right**
17. **segment**
18. **parallel**
19. **angle**
20. **perpendicular**

Exercise 7, pages 227–228

1. **24 ft;** P = s + s + s + s; 4 + 8 + 4 + 8 = 24 ft

2. **96 in.;** P = s + s + s; 32 + 32 + 32 = 96 in.

3. **62.8 m;** C = πd; ≈ 3.14 × 20 = 62.8 m

4. **40 cm;** P = s + s + s; 8 + 15 + 17 = 40 cm

5. **44 m;** C = πd; ≈ $\frac{22}{7}$ × (2 × 7) = 44 m

6. **48 mm;** P = s + s + s + s; 12 + 12 + 12 + 12 = 48 mm

7. **80 yd;** P = s + s + s + s; 30 + 10 + 30 + 10 = 80 yd

8. **50 ft;** P = s + s + s + s + s + s + s + s + s + s; 5 + 5 + 5 + 5 + 5 + 5 + 5 + 5 + 5 + 5 = 50 ft

9. **2.57 m;** C = πd; ≈ 3.14 × 1 = 3.14 m;
(3.14 ÷ 2) + 1 = 2.57 m

10. **36 in.;** P = s + s + s + s; 9 + 9 + 9 + 9 = 36 in.

11. **38 mm;** P = s + s + s + s; 8 + 11 + 8 + 11 = 38 mm

12. **45 cm;** P = s + s + s; 15 + 15 + 15 = 45 cm

13. **18.84 ft;** C = πd; ≈ 3.14 × (2 × 3) = 18.84 ft

14. **120 cm;** P = s + s + s; 30 + 40 + 50 = 120 cm

15. **132 mm;** C = πd; ≈ 3.14 × 42 ≈ 132 mm

16. **72 m;** P = s × 6; 12 × 6 = 72 m

Exercise 8, page 228

1. **4 m;** P = s + s + s + s; 16 = 4 + 4 + 4 + 4

2. **5 ft;** P = s + s + s + s; 24 = 7 + 5 + 7 + 5

3. **9 cm;** P = s + s + s; 29 = 10 + 10 + 9

4. **3.5 in.;** C = πd; 22 = $\frac{22}{7}$ × 7; d = 7;
r = 7 ÷ 2 = 3.5

5. **(1);** P = 2s + 2s; a rectangle must have 2 pairs of equal sides.

6. **(2);** C = πd; 44 = $\frac{22}{7}$ × (2 × 7)

Exercise 9, pages 231–232

1. **154 ft²;** Area = L × w; 14 × 11 = 154 ft²

2. **154 in.²;** Area = πr²; $\frac{22}{7}$ × 7 × 7 = 154 in.²

3. **81 mm²;** Area = L × w; 9 × 9 = 81 mm²

4. **900 m²;** Area = L × w; 30 × 30 = 900 m²

5. **21 yd²;** Area = L × w; 7 × 3 = 21 yd²

6. **42 ft²;** Area = $\frac{1}{2}$ b × h; $\frac{1}{2}$ × 7 × 12 = 42 ft²

7. **48 cm²;** Area = $\frac{1}{2}$ b × h; $\frac{1}{2}$ × 12 × 8 = 48 cm²

8. **486 cm²;** Area = $\frac{1}{2}$ b × h; $\frac{1}{2}$ × 36 × 27 = 486 cm²

9. **176.625 cm²;** Area = πr²; 3.14 × 7.5 × 7.5 = 176.625 cm²

10. **54 mm²;** Area = L × w; 9 × 6 = 54 mm²

11. **28.26 m²;** Area = πr²; 3.14 × 3 × 3 = 28.26 m²

12. **15 m²;** Area = $\frac{1}{2}$ bh; $\frac{1}{2}$ × 10 × 3 = 15 m²

13. **144 in.²;** Area = L × w; 12 × 12 = 144 in.²

14. **616 yd²;** Area = πr²; $\frac{22}{7}$ × 14 × 14 = 616 yd²

15. **5.2824 in.²;** Area = $\frac{1}{2}$ bh; .5 × 4.26 × 2.48 = 5.2824 in.²

16. **1,384.74 yd²;** Area = πr²; 42 ÷ 2 = 21; 3.14 × 21 × 21 = 1,384.74 yd²

Exercise 10, page 233

1. **4 m;** A = L × w; 16 = 4 × 4

2. **9 ft;** A = L × w; 36 = L × 4; L = 9

3. **10 cm;** $\frac{1}{2}$ bh; 30 = $\frac{1}{2}$ × 6 × h; = 3 × h; h = 10

4. **6 in.;** A = πr²; 120 = 3.14 × 6 × 6 = 113.04; 3.14 × 7 × 7 = 153.86

5. **(4);** A = L × w; 48 ≠ 4 × 13; 4 × 13 = 52

6. **(2);** A = $\frac{1}{2}$ bh; 12 = $\frac{1}{2}$ × 12 × 2

Exercise 11, page 235

1. **160 m³;** Volume = L × w × h; 4 × 4 × 10 = 160 m³

2. **480 ft³;** Volume = L × w × h; 12 × 5 × 8 = 480 ft³

3. **216 cm³;** Volume = L × w × h; 6 × 6 × 6 = 216 cm³

4. **1,331 in.³;** Volume = L × w × h; 11 × 11 × 11 = 1,331 in.³

5. **100 m³;** Volume = L × w × h; 20 × 5 × 1 = 100 m³

6. **2,744 in.³;** Volume = L × w × h; 14 × 14 × 14 = 2,744 in.³

7. **3 m, 3 m, 3 m;** Volume = L × w × h; 27 = 3 × 3 × 3

8. **6 ft;** Volume = L × w × h; 126 = 3 × 7 × h; 126 = 21h; h = 6; 126 = 3 × 7 × 6

9. **(3);** Volume = L × w × h; 72 = L × w × h; 9 × 8 × 0 = 0; 0 ≠ 72

10. **(1);** Volume = L × w × h; 64 = L × w × h; 4 × 4 × 4 = 64

Exercise 12, page 237

1. ***Buran*; 0.6 ft, or 7.2 in.;** 79.2 − 78.6 = 0.6 ft; 0.6 ft × 12 = 7.2 in.

2. **570,025 ft²;** Area = 755 × 755 = 570,025 ft²

3. **62 m;** 443 − 381 = 62 m

4. **144 in.³;** Volume = 12 × 12 × 1 = 144 in.³

5. **160 ft;** 53$\frac{1}{3}$ yd × 3 = $\frac{160}{3}$ yd × 3 = 160 ft

6. **square;**
Area of circle ≈ 3.14 × 1 × 1 = 3.14 in.²; Area of square = 2 × 2 = 4 in.²

2 in.

7. **$1\frac{5}{7}$ oz;** 4 weeks × 7 = 28 days; 3 pounds × 16 = 48 ounces; 48 ÷ 28 = $1\frac{5}{7}$ oz/day

8. **11 lb 1 oz;** 1-month gain: 8 lb 13 oz – 6 lb 9 oz = 2 lb 4 oz; 8 lb 13 oz + 2 lb 4 oz = 10 lb 17 oz = 11 lb 1 oz

9. **rectangular pan;** Area of 8-in. square pan: 8 × 8 = 64 in.²; Area of two 8-in. pans: 64 × 2 = 128 in.²; Area of rectangular pan: 13 × 9 = 117 in.²; because the base area is less, the brownies will be thicker.

10. **11 loaves;** 5 × 4 cups = 20 cups; 20 ÷ $1\frac{3}{4}$ = $11\frac{3}{7}$; Answer must be a whole number.

Exercise 13, pages 240–241

1. **$2,400;** $12/ft × 200 ft = $2,400

2. **24 sections;** 120 ft ÷ 5 ft = 24 sections

3. **1,000 ft²;** Area = 200 × 5 = 1,000 ft²

4. **$8\frac{1}{3}$ ft³;** Volume = 5 × 5 × $\frac{4}{12}$ = $8\frac{1}{3}$ ft³

5. **20 yd²;** 12 ft ÷ 3 = 4 yd; 15 ft ÷ 3 = 5 yd; Area = 4 × 5 = 20 yd²

6. **67 ft 4 in.;** Perimeter of room minus opening for door = 15 + 12 + 15 + 12 – 2 ft 6 in. = 51 ft 6 in.; Perimeter of door frame (3 sides) = 6 ft 8 in. + 2 ft 6 in. + 6 ft 8 in. = 14 ft 22 in. = 15 ft 10 in.; Total trim needed = 51 ft 6 in. + 15 ft 10 in. = 66 ft 16 in. = 67 ft 4 in.

7. **yes;** Volume of one ice cube = 3 cm × 4 cm × 3 cm = 36 cm³; Volume of 12 ice cubes = 12 × 36 cm³ = 432 cm³; Volume of two trays = 2 × 432 cm³ = 864 cm³ = 864 mL = 0.864 L

8. **500 ft²;** Area of college court: 94 × 50 = 4,700 ft²; Area of high school court: 84 × 50 = 4200 ft²; Difference = 4,700 – 4,200 = 500 ft²

9. **12-in. pizza;** Area of 10-in. pizza ≈ 3.14 × 5 × 5 = 78.5 in.²; 8 ÷ 78.5 ≈ $.10/in.²; Area of 12-in. pizza ≈ 3.14 × 6 × 6 = 113.04 in.²; $10.50 ÷ 113.04 ≈ $.09/in.²; the 12-in. pizza costs less per square inch.

10. **6.28 in.;** Circumference of 10-in. pizza ≈ 3.14 × 10 = 31.4 in.; Circumference of 12-in. pizza ≈ 3.14 × 12 = 37.68 in.; Difference = 37.68 – 31.4 = 6.28 in.

11. **(3)**

12. **(2)**

Measurement and Geometry Review, pages 242–245

1. **3.7 cm**

2. **16 cups;** 1 gal × 4 = 4 qt; 4 qt × 2 = 8 pt; 8 pt × 2 = 16 c

3. **50 m;** Perimeter = 15 + 10 + 15 + 10 = 50 m

4. **parallel lines**

5. **2,500 g;** 2.5 kg × 1,000 = 2,500 g

6. **16 ft;** 8 ft × 2 = 16 ft

7. **circle**

8. **5 lb;** 80 oz ÷ 16 = 5 lb

9. **343 m³;** Volume = 7 × 7 × 7 = 343 m³

10. **18.84 in.;** Circumference ≈ 3.14 × 6 = 18.84 in.

11. **3 m;** 300 cm ÷ 100 = 3 m

12. **5 in.;** 20 in. ÷ 4 sides = 5 in./side

13.

14. **50.24 cm²;** Area ≈ 3.14 × 4 × 4 = 50.24 cm²

15. **5 ft 4 in.;** 64 in. ÷ 12 = 5R4→5 ft 4 in.

16. **(2)**

17. **(5)**

18. **(1)**

19. **(2)**

20. **(3)**

21. **(4)**

22. **(1)**

23. **(2)**

24. **(5)**

25. **(4)**

26. **(1)**

27. **(2)**

28. **216 in.³**

29. **9.42 ft**

30. 49.62 m

31. 108 m²; Area = 9 × 12 = 108 m²

32. 150 cm²; Area = $\frac{1}{2}$ × 20 × 15 = 150 cm²

33. 36 ft³; Volume = 6 × 2 × 3 = 36 ft³

34. $7.84

Glossary

A

angle a figure made of two rays extending from the same point

area the amount of surface covered by the figure; measured in square units

B

bar graph a graph made up of rectangular bars that extend upward or lengthwise; the height of each bar corresponds to one number in the data set; the higher the bar, the greater the number; used to display numerical data given in categories

base a number used as a factor in a product; in the expression 2^4, *2* is called the base

C

central angle an angle formed at the center of a circle

circle a curved flat figure every point of which is the same distance from the center

circle graph a graph that shows parts of a whole; the circle is the whole, or 100%; the circle is divided into parts, and all the parts add up to 100%; often used to display data given as percents

circumference the distance around a circle

compatible numbers numbers used in mental math and estimation; they are close to the original numbers and are used instead of the numbers to make the solution easier or quicker to achieve

coordinate plane a plane formed by two number lines perpendicular to each other at 0

cross product in a proportion, the numerator of one ratio multiplied by the denominator of the other ratio

cube a rectangular solid made up of squares; the length, width, and height of a cube are equal

customary units measurement system used in the U.S.; this includes measurements such as mile, foot, pound, ounce, cup, gallon, minute, and hour

D

data information that is collected and analyzed; often, but not always, numerical

decimals numbers based on a whole being split into ten equal parts one or more times; the U.S. monetary system is based on the decimal system

denominator the aspect of a fraction that refers to the number of parts in the whole; written on the bottom of the fraction

diameter a line segment that crosses the circle through its center from one side to the other

difference the result of subtraction

digit one of the ten number symbols: 0, 1, 2, 3, 4, 5, 6, 7, 8, and 9

E

equation a statement that two amounts are equal

equivalent fractions fractions that have the same value

estimate an approximate answer

exponent a number that shows how many times the base is used as a factor in a product; in the expression 2^4, *4* is called the exponent

F

formula an equation with more than one variable; an equation that is always true

fraction a way of showing parts of a whole; made up of two numbers, the numerator and the denominator

front-end digits an estimation strategy involving the use of far-left digits, or front-end digits

H

horizontal axis on a graph, the axis running from left to right along the bottom of the graph

I

improper fraction a fraction with a numerator equal to or greater than its denominator

independent events a situation in which the outcome of one event does not depend on the outcome of the other

interest the money you earn on a savings account or pay on a loan

interest formula interest = principal × rate × time

inverse operations operations that undo each other

- The inverse of addition is subtraction.
- The inverse of subtraction is addition.
- The inverse of multiplication is division.
- The inverse of division is multiplication.

L

line a set of points continuing in opposite directions

line graph graph made up of points that are connected by line segments; often used to display data over a period of time

lowest terms describes a situation in which the numerator and denominator of a fraction cannot be divided evenly (remainder of zero) by any whole number other than 1

M

mean the average value of a data set

median the middle value of a data set listed in order

mental math strategies finding an answer without writing any numbers

metric measures measurement system used widely throughout the world; includes measurements such as meter, liter, and gram

mixed numbers values between two whole numbers, or the combination of a whole number and a fraction

mode the item that occurs most often in a data set

N

number grid grid with columns of numbers, used to display answers on the GED test

numerator the aspect of a fraction that indicates the number of parts; written on the top of the fraction

O

order of operations the set of rules agreed upon by mathematicians for finding the value of arithmetic expressions

1. Do operations within parentheses.
2. Do exponents and square roots.
3. Do multiplication and division.
4. Do addition and subtraction.

ordered pair a pair of coordinates that tell exactly where a point lies in a coordinate plane

origin the point where the x-axis and y-axis meet on a coordinate plane; its coordinates are $(0, 0)$

P

parallel lines lines that run in the same direction and that do not cross or intersect

percent a means of expressing a number as part of a whole; the word *percent* means "of 100"

period a group of three numbers set off by a pair of commas, as part of a longer number

perimeter the distance around a figure such as a triangle, rectangle, or square

perpendicular lines lines that intersect to form right angles

principal the amount of money invested or borrowed

probability the chance of something happening; a measure of how likely it is that something will happen

problem-solving strategies strategies that include drawing a picture, guessing and checking, and using information from a table

product the result of multiplication

proportion an expression made up of two equal ratios

Q

quotient the result of division

R

radius the distance from the center to any point on the curve of the circle

range the difference between the greatest and least items of a data set

rate an expression that shows a relationship between two quantities measured in different units

ratio a comparison of two numbers

ray a set of points continuing in one direction only

rectangle a four-sided figure with four right angles

rectangular solid a three-dimensional figure made up of rectangles; commonly called a box

repeating decimal a decimal number with one or more digits that repeat themselves

right angle an angle that measures 90°

rounding a common estimation strategy in which you go up or down to the nearest 0

S

segment a set of points forming the shortest path between two points

solution the value of the variable that makes the equation a true statement

square a four-sided figure with four right angles and four equal sides

square root the number that can be squared to get the original number

substitution a mental math strategy in which you change one number so it is easier to perform the operation and then change the other number by the opposite operation

sum the result of addition

T

tree diagram a diagram that shows all possible outcomes for a probability problem

triangle a three-sided figure

U

unit price the price per unit of an item

unit rate the rate for one unit of a given quantity

V

variable a letter used to represent an unknown amount

vertical axis on a graph, the axis running up and down along the left side of the graph

volume a measure of the space inside a three-dimensional figure; measured in cubic units

W

whole numbers the numbers beginning with 0, 1, 2, 3, and so on

X

x-axis the horizontal number line on a coordinate plane

x-coordinate in a coordinate plane, the point that is located on the x-axis, or horizontal axis

Y

y-axis the vertical number line on a coordinate plane

y-coordinate in a coordinate plane, the point that is located on the y-axis, or vertical axis

Index

A

addition
> on a calculator, 28
> checking, 39
> of decimals, 64
> of fractions, 91
> inverse of, 196
> of mixed numbers, 97
> of whole numbers, 15

algebra. *See also* coordinate plane; equations
> finding a square root, 189–190
> identifying bases, 187–188
> identifying exponents, 187–188
> order of operations, 193–194
> square/square root on a calculator, 189–190
> value of expressions with exponents, 188

area
> of a circle, 231
> problem solving, 236, 238–239
> of a rectangle, 229
> of a square, 229
> of a triangle, 230
> using a calculator, 230, 231

B

bar graph
> approximate locations on, 150
> composition of, 149
> drawing, 153
> horizontal axis of, 149
> reading, 150–151
> and tables, 149
> usefulness of, 149
> vertical axis of, 149

base, 187–188

C

calculator, 27–32, 107, 132, 189, 190, 226, 230, 231, 234

circle graph
> central angle in, 169–171
> composition of, 164
> drawing, 169–171
> reading, 164–165
> and tables, 164
> usefulness of, 164

circumference, 225–226
> using a calculator, 226

compatible numbers, 24, 42

compensation (substitution), 42

coordinate plane
> formation of, 204
> locating ordered pairs on, 205
> ordered pair, 204
> origin, 204
> x-axis, 204
> y-axis, 204
> x-coordinate, 204
> y-coordinate, 204

D

data. *See also* bar graph; circle graph; line graph
> center of, 144
> defined, 144
> finding the mean, 144–145
> finding the median, 145–146
> finding the mode, 146
> finding the range, 146

decimals
> adding, 64
> changing to fractions, 85
> changing to percents, 127
> common, 129
> comparing, 59
> dividing, 70–71
> expressing verbally, 58
> and the metric system, 216
> multiplying, 67–68
> and percents, 126–127
> place value chart, 58
> rounding, 62–63
> subtracting, 65
> and U.S. monetary system, 57
> writing, 57–58

denominator, 78

digits
> amount (value) of, 10–11
> combining values of, 12
> front-end, 23
> value (amount) of, 10–11

division

on a calculator, 31
of decimals, 70–71
of fractions, 102–103
inverse of, 196
of mixed numbers, 102–103
of whole numbers, 19

E

equations
    defined, 196
    and formulas, 200–202
    inverse operations in, 196
    solving, 196–198
    variables in, 196
estimation, 21, 23, 44
exponent, 187–188

F

formulas, 200–202
fractions. *See also* improper fractions
    adding, with like denominators, 90
    adding, with unlike denominators, 93–94
    changing to decimals, 84
    changing to percents, 127
    choosing common denominator, 86
    common, 129
    common multiples of, 89
    comparing (ordering), 88–89
    denominator in, 78
    dividing, 102–103
    equivalent, 82–83
    in lowest terms, 82–83
    multiplying, 101
    numerator in, 78
    and percents, 126
    renaming, 82–83
    subtracting, with like denominators, 90
    subtracting, with unlike denominators, 93–94
    using a calculator, 107

G

geometry
    area, 229–231
    base of a triangle, 229
    basic definitions in, 222–223
    basic figures in, 222–223
    circumference, 225–226
    cubic units in, 233
    diameter of a circle, 225
    height of a triangle, 229
    perimeter, 225–226
    pi, 224–225, 231
    radius of a circle, 225
    rectangular solids, 233
    solving problems in, 236, 238–239
    square units in, 229
    using a calculator, 230, 231, 234
    volume, 233–234

I

improper fractions
    changing to mixed numbers, 79
    changing to whole numbers, 79
    defined, 78
interest, 134
inverse operations, 196

L

line graph
    composition of, 156
    drawing, 160–161
    horizontal axis of, 156
    line segments on, 156
    points on, 156
    reading, 157–158
    and tables, 156
    usefulness of, 156
    vertical axis of, 156

M

mean, 144–145
median, 145–146
measurement. *See also* metric system
    customary, 212–213
    customary units of, 212
    measuring line segments, 219–220
    metric units of, 216–217
    mixed units in, 215
mental math strategies. *See also* estimation
    addition shortcuts, 23
    breaking apart numbers, 41
    defined, 41
    finding compatible numbers, 42
    multiplication shortcuts, 24
    substitution (compensation), 42

metric system
    basic units of measure in, 216–217
    basis of, 216
    changing from one unit to another, 216
    writing measurements, 219
mixed numbers
    adding, 97
    changing to improper fractions, 80
    defined, 78
    dividing, 102–103
    multiplying, 101
    renaming, 82–83
    subtracting, 99
mode, 146
multiplication
    on a calculator, 30
    of decimals, 67–68
    of fractions, 101
    inverse of, 196
    of mixed numbers, 101
    shortcuts, 24
    of whole numbers, 18

N

numbers. *See also* algebra; decimals; fractions; mixed
    numbers; whole numbers
    breaking apart, 41
    compatible, 24, 42
    estimate of, 21
    percents, 126–127, 129, 131–132
    periods of, 10
    ratios, 112
    rounding, 21
    system of, 10
number grids, 52, 73, 105
number system, 10
numerator, 78

O

operations
    clues in choosing, 38–39
    inverse, 196
    order of, 193–194
ordered pair, 204
origin, 204

P

percents

changing to decimals, 126–127
changing to fractions, 126–127
common, 129
defined, 125
of numbers, 131–132
using a calculator, 132
using proportions to find, 136–138
writing as decimals, 126–127
writing as fractions, 126–127
perimeter
    defined, 225
    finding, 225–226
    problem solving, 236, 238–239
periods of numbers, 10
pi, 224–225, 231
place value, 10–11, 57–58
probability
    calculating, 173–174
    defined, 173
    and favorable outcomes, 177–178
problems. *See also* problem solving; word problems
    checking addition, 39
    checking subtraction, 39
    choosing an operation for solving, 38–39
    with multiple steps, 50
problem solving. *See also* mental math strategies;
    problem–solving strategies
    choosing proper operations for, 34–35
    equation, 196–198
    estimating as method of, 21, 23, 44
    exponent, 187–188
    formulas in, 200–202
    geometry, 236, 238–239
    interest, 134
    mean, 144–145
    median, 145–146
    mode, 146
    order of operations in, 193–194
    percents, 125–127, 136–138
    probability, 173–174
    proportion, 121
    range, 146
    rates, 115
    ratios, 112–113
    square root, 189–190
    unit price, 200–201
    word problems, 34
problem–solving strategies
    drawing a picture, 45–46
    guess and check, 46–47

using information from a table, 47–48
proportions
    and cross products, 118
    determining existence of, 117–118
    solving, 121
    in solving percent problems, 136–138
    writing, 117–118

R

range, 146
rates, 115
ratios
    cross products in, 118
    defined, 112
    as fractions, 112
    in proportions, 117
    rates as type of, 115
    solving problems in, 112–113
    writing, 112–113
rectangular solids, 233–234
    using a calculator, 234
rounding
    decimals, 62–63
    money, 62–63
    numbers, 21

S

solution sentence, 50
square/square root on a calculator, 189–190
substitution (compensation), 42
subtraction
    on a calculator, 29
    checking, 39
    of decimals, 65
    of fractions, 91
    inverse of, 196
    of mixed numbers, 99
    of whole numbers, 17

U

unit price, 63, 115–116
unit rate, 115–116
U.S. monetary system, 57
units
    cubic, 233, 238
    customary, 212
    metric, 216
    mixed, 215
    square, 229, 238

V

volume
    of a cube, 233–234
    problem solving, 236, 238–239
    of a rectangular solid, 233–234

W

whole numbers
    described, 10
    periods of, 10, 12
    place value chart, 10
    positions of, 10, 12
    reading and writing, 12–13
word problems
    key words in, 38
    operations in, 38–39
    solving, 34–35

X

x–axis, 204
x–coordinate, 204

Y

y–axis, 204
y–coordinate, 204